Southern African Literature
An Introduction

One of King Dingane's imbongis or praise-singers, as seen by Captain Allen Gardiner in 1835.

Stephen Gray

Southern African Literature

An Introduction

BOOKS
10 East 53d St., New York 10022
(a division of Harper & Row Publishers, Inc.)

The writer wishes to acknowledge his indebtedness, for assistance given him over a long period, to Professor J.M. Leighton, and his other colleagues, in the Department of English at the Rand Afrikaans University, and to Mr Tim Couzens of the Institute for African Studies, University of the Witwatersrand; Professor André de Villiers of the Institute for the Study of English in Africa, Rhodes University; Professor Bernth Lindfors of the African and Afro-American Research Institute of the University of Texas, Austin; Professor Don Herdeck of the African Literature Department, Georgetown University.

Also to the librarians of the Rand Afrikaans University; the National English Documentation Centre and the Cory Library, Rhodes University, Grahamstown; the Gubbins Collection, University of the Witwatersrand; the Strange Collection and Africana Museum, Johannesburg; the South African Library, Cape Town, and the Special Collections of the J.W. Jagger Library, University of Cape Town; the Killie Campbell Library of the University of Natal, Durban, and the Pietermaritzburg Archives; the State Library, Pretoria; the Brenthurst Library, Johannesburg; the Royal Commonwealth Society and the British Library, London; the Humanities Research Centre, Austin, Texas, and others; and to the Human Sciences Research Council for funding research trips between them.

To the editors of the following magazines in which early drafts of some sections first appeared: *Africa Perspective, Communique, Research in African Literatures, Speak, Standpunte, Theoria* and *UNISA English Studies.*

Grateful acknowledgements are due to the following for permission to reproduce illustrations from their collections: illustrations numbered 1, 2, 3, 4, 5, 7, 9 (reproduction by courtesy of Captain Jack Stodel), 12, 13, 17, 18, Johannesburg Public Library; 8, 19, Special Collections, Jagger Library, University of Cape Town; 10, British Library; 11, South African Library; 14, 20, 21, 22, National English Documentation Centre; 15, National Film Archive; 16, Killie Campbell Africana Library; 6, Brian Astbury, for a photograph taken by him.

Published in the U.S.A. in 1979 by Harper & Row Publishers, Inc., Barnes & Noble Import Division

ISBN 0-06-492530-7
Library of Congress Catalog Card Number 79-53358

© *1979 Stephen Gray*

Printed and bound by Printpak (Cape) Ltd, Dacres Avenue, Epping, Cape, South Africa

Contents

Illustrations between pages 14–15, 92-3, 132-3, 182-3

To my mother
who taught me to hear
and my father
who taught me to watch

1 Approaches to a New Literature

THIS INTRODUCTION TO SOUTHERN AFRICAN LITERATURE comes from a divided land. Since 1961, with the proclamation of the Republic of South Africa and the entrenchment of its apartheid system, the political blueprint for the segregation of the races of the subcontinent at the tip of Africa has been thoroughly enough applied; its effects are to be felt in every facet of its literature. The spirit of the pre-republic days, which could celebrate the unity of all South African literature together with the potential unity of the land, was not to endure. The proud catalogue of the exhibition of 'The Book in South Africa' in 1960, which could feature Ezekiel Mphahlele's *Man Must Live* (1946) alongside Alan Paton's *Cry, the Beloved Country*, and William Plomer's *I Speak of Africa* (1927) alongside Sol T. Plaatje's *Mhudi* (1930),* and which marked the fiftieth anniversary of the Union of the provinces of South Africa into one nation, could not be repeated: the apartheid state would drive an author like Mphahlele abroad and ban his work at home for two decades, and would erect barriers between black and white, between English-speaker and Afrikaner, between resident writer and exile.

By the late 1960s as many as half of South Africa's English-language writers of all colours had been expelled over the borders into an international diaspora, and South African literature in English had split so irremediably and bitterly into two, with no significant subsequent interaction between the halves, that it makes sense to talk of there being two distinct literatures at present. To a student of South African letters within South Africa since the dispersal, the loss of acquaintance with works produced by those in exile has been incalculable. Although works banned or otherwise proscribed within South Africa are technically available to such a student, under certain conditions and for research purposes only, any history that quotes those works is liable to fall under the same banning. To all intents and purposes, the

*Dates refer to years of first publication. Full publication details are found in the Select Bibliography. Notes on some authors mentioned begin on p. 192.

literature of South-Africa-in-exile no longer exists in any real sense for those who stayed behind, or for those who were born after the first losses. If this introduction, when it enters upon the post-1960 crisis period, elides or omits references to the literary development of South Africa abroad, it will be not so much out of negligence, but because, no matter how much South Africans within the country might have had denied them in their literature in recent times, writers inside the country have continued to write, notwithstanding. The peculiar shape of the two-way split needs to be recorded from inside, too, until such time as the breach may be healed.

Any survey of a literature should include a statement of its extent and of its complexity. Calling a body of work a 'literature' implies that it has a distinctness, a certain completeness, so that it may be isolated from other literatures for independent scrutiny, and assumed to have certain internal cross-references which give it a unique cohesion.

But the first problem in defining South African literature is that South Africa cannot be said at present to have a very precise sense of distinctness with regard to its literature in English. One reason for this is that the literary works which derive from an English cultural world in South Africa are not, and never have been, part of a closed system. The cultural history of South Africa has always been one of a multilingual composite, within which English South African culture is merely one part of a broader historical–cultural happening; like Andrew Geddes Bain's 'Polyglot Medley', the whole story is a very mixed affair. The proper study of the English component is in relation to the totality of South African experience. However, an introduction to the works which happen to be in English would not be without some value as a preliminary exercise in defining South African literature as a whole. That whole will not be in view until the parts are assembled within a suitably all-embracing comparative theory.

The term 'South African', then, requires definition. South Africa here must be taken to mean the Southern African triangle, with Cape Town as its apex, which is merely a small part of the larger triangle of the continent of Africa. The geographic field with which this introduction is concerned consists of the territory that is currently known as the Republic of South Africa (that is, the Cape Province, the Orange Free State, Natal and the Transvaal), and includes the modern Lesotho, Botswana and Swaziland, and Rhodesia/Zimbabwe and South West Africa/Namibia, throughout which a concept of a larger English whole can be demonstrated to be operative. It is no exercise in literary colonialism to claim those independent territories bordering on South Africa proper as part of the field; such international boundaries have not held, and do not hold, for writers of Southern Africa. Because Doris Lessing, for example, might be classified as 'Rhodesian', that does not mean that in her early writing she felt no kinship with a Cape writer like Olive Schreiner. That Thomas Mofolo was brought up and educated in Lesotho (or rather the Kingdom of Basutoland) does not mean that his Sotho novels have had no impact on 'South African' writing. 'South Africa' is used here metonymically without any rigid sense of geo-political borders; it is merely a convenient umbrella term applied for interim ends.

The term 'English', for the purposes of this book, is also used in a multi-purpose sense. It includes the whole spectrum of English usage in South Africa, from what might be termed 'pure' English through to the no-man's-land type of English where it meets the other languages of the South African experience — Portuguese, Dutch-Afrikaans, French, German, and later Zulu, Sotho and other African languages — and shades into being the lingua franca of writers whose material is by no means English only. Because English has tended to prove of service in many ways within South African culture, there will be no attempt here to resist broadening the field into mutations of standard English, or even into translations into English. In South Africa, English has co-existed loosely with Dutch-Afrikaans, and with the black African languages, since about 1800. The singling out of this 175-year-old segment of the totality, then, is no attempt to assert its superiority or inferiority in relation to the other segments, but to assess its role as a literary medium in close contact with others. Maintaining a standard of English usage in South Africa based on a hypothetical British model would be doomed to exert an inhibitory influence on the emergence of what might be termed an appropriate African English. Branford's *Dictionary of South African English* (1978) would seem to indicate that there is an extensive area for linguistic research where so-called standard English has lived in symbiosis with the other languages of the subcontinent's experience. There is sufficient vocabulary, from 'aardvark' to 'Zulu', for South African English to declare its independence, and English as a lingua franca is in practice detached enough from any ruling hegemony to continue to act as a useful medium in almost all Southern African contexts, as the literature shows.

The debate about English in Africa should not, however, be thought to apply uniquely to the writing of 'black' Southern Africans; there is no watertight English (white)–African (black) distinction to be made. Any and every author who has written in English in Southern Africa has experienced some degree of language tension between what he hears around him and what his readers expect on the page. Here is an early example of a writer facing a choice between taking the way of English English or of African English, and, as far as our literary purposes are concerned, making the wrong choice.

The proofs of Thomas Pringle's 'The Bechuana Boy' were amended by S.T. Coleridge for him on the grounds that 'purity of style, and even severe propriety of words, appear to me more, the especial Duty of a Poet — who whatever political party he may favor, ought in this respect to be at once a *Radical* and *Conservative*.'[1] * Coleridge would have had the second stanza of 'The Bechuana Boy' read:

> With open (fearless?) aspect, frank yet bland,
>   And with a modest mien he stood,
> Caressing gently with his hand,
>   The Beast of gentle brood. . . .[2]

Pringle himself in an earlier draft had written:

> He came with open aspect bland,
>   And modestly before me stood,
> Caressing with a kindly hand
>   That fawn of gentle brood. . . .

By the time of its publication in *African Sketches* (1834) Pringle had settled for:

> With open aspect, frank yet bland,
>   And with a modest mien he stood,
> Caressing with a gentle hand
>   That beast of gentle brood. . . .

The moral of the story is that Pringle should have stuck to his first impulses, for, when the experience that generated the poem was closest to him, despite no end of 'purity of style', he knew that however 'impure' the thought might seem, no Tswana refugee ever regarded a springbok as a 'beast'.

The single most potent factor in the retardation of the development of South African English, and of its literature, is the fact that it has never generated its own publishing industry. As the select bibliography to this introduction shows, the overwhelming majority of English

* Notes to chapters begin on p. 183.

works by Southern Africans are to this day first published in London and/or New York, and re-imported into Southern Africa. Only a writer of true grit can avoid being pressurized into conforming to some extent to the standards of literary appropriateness prevalent in those megapolitan forums. Olive Schreiner in the 1880s kept her words like 'kopjes' in quotes; Athol Fugard takes the other option — providing his texts in their Oxford University Press editions with glossaries of Southern African English terms. Although this would be hard to assess, we must assume that writers are kept 'pure' in some way by the fear that writing local would damage their chances of publication overseas. There are many works of an extraordinary linguistic richness which remain unpublished, which would have taken their due places in the literature had Southern Africa not been so cravenly dependent on the criteria and tastes of publishers abroad.

The advent of several small publishers in South Africa like Bateleur, Ad. Donker, David Philip and Ravan Press in the 1970s has begun to reverse this trend. The poetry of a Mongane Wally Serote or a Wopko Jensma, derived as it is from an unprecedented salmagundi of linguistic impurities can now be, and is, published as its authors intended with Southern Africans as a priority audience. If a literature does not have direct access to its own language resources, it cannot grow as it should and must. A precondition to further healthy generation of Southern African literature in 'English', then, is an indigenous publishing industry conducted on editorial principles which are appropriate to it and to no other literature.

One example will suffice to illustrate. In his journal of the Second Anglo-Boer War, *Commando,* Deneys Reitz, son of F.W. Reitz, wrote:

My grandfather first went to Scotland in 1816.[3] He met Sir Walter Scott, to whom he took a lion skin which the poet Thomas Pringle had sent from Cape Town, and he became intimate with the great writer. In later days in South Africa, he loved to tell of their meetings and of the banquet at which he was present when Scott for the first time admitted that he was the author of the Waverley Novels. Both my grandfather and my father had returned to South Africa with a deep love of Scotland and Scotch literature, and at our home scarcely a night passed without a reading from Burns or Scott, so that we felt as if we were among our own people.[4]

Reitz's father, himself the son of a border storyteller, was a progenitor of Afrikaans literature with his 'verafrikaansinge' of popular English poems. The Anglo-Boer War which drove Deneys Reitz the grandson into exile was the main event of his diary, written in makeshift Dutch, the same diary which he translated into English as an act of faith that a new understanding could be reached between the two warring languages. In English the manuscript of *Commando* underwent an editorial fluency check at Faber and Faber, London, by which through many misunderstandings Reitz finally lost his lengthy battle with the British.

Many are the commentators who refer to *Commando* as a classic in English by an Afrikaner.[5] How much more of a classic it would have been for us if it had appeared as Reitz actually wrote it is the real question, for a masterpiece of South African English has been lost to us. The paragraph quoted above began, in Reitz's original:

My grandfather went to Scotland in 1816 and he knew Sir Walter Scott quite well. He took him a lion skin which the poet Thomas Pringle had entrusted him with at Capetown, and on the strength of that introduction he became intimate with the great writer and I remember how he loved to tell us of their meetings . . .[6]

One notes that Pringle personally entrusted Reitz's grandfather with transmitting a personal trophy, from one writer to another, and Reitz's editor apparently did not understand that such a fraternal spirit between writers could have existed.

In his history of all South African writing, C. Louis Leipoldt in 1936 had no doubt of the unity of the whole:

The cultural development of a country in which two people of the same race, but with different ideals and different standards of value, live side by side, necessarily presents so many points of comparison and contrast that a true estimate of its progress is difficult. Afrikanders [sic] and British are not so far removed from each other culturally as to admit of the subject being treated from opposite aspects. Their association in South Africa has been too close for that. The cultural development of each has lain along lines of its own; but the one has so markedly influenced the other that it is possible to recognize, even at the present stage, the beginnings of a national South African culture that is assimilating to itself the best and most lasting characteristics of the cultural development of each section, fashioning from them a culture . . . representative of the country . . .[7]

Leipoldt's opinion that English and Afrikaans cultures were not divergent but parallel, reinforced no doubt by his own facility at writing in both languages, has become increasingly untenable in the years since 1961. First of all, Afrikaans culture has gained its present status by stress on its own independence, often at the cost of any bonds which might link it with a developing English South African culture; and secondly, South Africa has grown increasingly away from acceptance of a belief in one common national culture representative of the whole.

Leipoldt's view of culture itself is too narrow for our purposes here. It leaves no room for any facets of a total culture that are not, in effect, Europe-inspired. African cultural activity which might be oral rather than written, for example, is excluded from his survey. Black African culture, in Leipoldt's view, should merely be assimilated into the two main streams. Nor did it occur to Leipoldt that Afrikaans writers might eventually turn round and insist, as General Piet Joubert insisted at the turn of the century, that 'we are Afrikaners, not Dutchmen. Africa is our mother country, not Europe.'[8]

We are faced with a segment of a literature which at the present time may be readily defined in terms of what it is not. Its parameters are determined by outside factors which, while giving it shape, deny it meaning. The crucial issue is whether or not South African English literature can be said to have a sense of on-going tradition, in the T.S. Eliot sense of the term: that inner motivation derived from an impetus on the writer's part to assess and revise constantly within a continuum. English writers in South Africa have at all stages of their history been at the intersection of such varied and often incompatible literary forces that their resultant focus has been formed with the South African component not infrequently being the weakest. Tradition-making, in English South Africa, has often occurred fortuitously, rather than by any planned consciousness through which the writer has fused his or her own literature's past with contemporary stimuli.

In an article called 'The South African Image', I. Pinchuk comments:

It is impossible to find a principle of unity in South African writing yet inevitable that one should seek it. To me it suggests the picture of a scrapyard where the only seeming relationship between the scattered arrangements of metal, wood, soil and grass is that they are all contained within the same area.[9]

The inevitable search that Pinchuk attempts turns out to be a frustrating one. Significantly, he chooses to describe the field in terms of someone else's scrapyard, and deduces that the clue to its wholeness is in fact to be found outside its walls. But the attempt to find a coherence within the field independent of outside factors has been a popular one, and it is on this point that most histories of Southern African literature have foundered.

In the first (and only) book-length study of the subject, Manfred Nathan's *South African Literature* (1925), the approach is that of a general survey. As Nathan states in his preface, the work is a preliminary undertaking that he hoped might herald a 'systematic treatise in English devoted to South African literature', and it was intended to 'supplement existing bibliographies and anthologies'.[10] Nathan's work is bold and comprehensive, and in some areas he relates English creative

work to developments in the burgeoning Afrikaans literature of his
time. It is more historical circumstance than any notion of exclusivity
that has him ignore the beginnings of black writing in English. His
chosen method is to work through the field chronologically, chapter
by chapter, and to subdivide by genre (travel and description, history,
biography, ethnology, poetry, drama, fiction and so on). His most
inspired gesture is not to exclude what are frequently considered the
non-literary genres. He deals with the work of some four hundred
authors, and even the humblest document is given an identificatory
sentence. Nathan assumes that all South African literature is really
English, even if English has to include other (European) languages.
His aims are remarkably modest as well; he wished to let the local
public know what they might enjoy reading.

Yet the drawback of Nathan's scheme lies in his assumption that
such genre-classifications are rigid. He allows no leeway for interconnections between history, say, and poetry, between travelogues and
the novel, and so on. It will become apparent in the course of this
work that few South African writers have felt a dedication to one
form of writing only; on the contrary, a tendency has often been a
jack-of-all-trades approach to writing about the Southern African
experience, which creates many mixed genres. Nathan's system frus-
trates the observation of fundamental and crucial links in the literature. No critic since Nathan, however, has attempted to cover the
entire catalogue again.

J.P.L. Snyman's critical study, *The South African Novel in English
(1880–1930),* opens with Schreiner's *The Story of an African Farm*
(1883) and, although he allows the ground he covers to extend into
the 1940s, closes in effect with middle Sarah Gertrude Millin (*God's
Step-children,* 1924). Like Nathan's, Snyman's is an extremely useful
reference work, for he tracked down more examples of fiction than
one might have supposed existed. Snyman's system of classification is
broadly a decade-by-decade one, though within the decades he proceeds year by year, his assumption being that literature develops by
the calendar, rather than by any more precise (yet historically hap-
hazard) internal relationships. The South African novel, detached
from its environing culture, becomes meaningless in his terms. Vladimir Klima's *South African Prose Writing in English* suffers from
similar faults — treating writers' heads like stepping stones, yet not
identifying the streams across which they lead.

Another example of starting off nobly, but on quite the wrong foot,
is Alan Lennox-Short's collection of pieces by many hands on selected

South African authors, *English and South Africa.* Its system of classification is alphabetical, but within colour lines. So-called coloured and black writers in English are, in this volume, relegated to a buffer zone between English white writers and Afrikaners in English translation, as if the race classifications of apartheid were a sound methodology for literary criticism to adopt as well.

The most acute statements of what Southern African literature is felt to be have often come about when writers have been forced to explain themselves and their fellows. Millin's article on 'The South Africa of Fiction' is one example, and Herman Charles Bosman's 'Aspects of South African Literature' is another. Guy Butler's introduction to his *A Book of South African Verse* and Jack Cope and Uys Krige's introduction to their *The Penguin Book of South African Verse,* both of which contain contributions by their editor-introducers, are others.[11] These pieces at least have the value of throwing light on how their authors determined their attitudes to the literature. Laurens van der Post likewise, in introducing the 1965 reprint of Plomer's *Turbott Wolfe,* does tend to be laying out the historical background to his own work as well. The same might in part be said for Mphahlele's introduction to Richard Rive's *Emergency.* A certain competitive partisanship, and a certain self-involvement in literary criticism, is of course a sign of engagement, not to be brushed aside. It is not, however, a substitute for an overview of a total context.

The very statement that Southern African English literature has not created a significant accompanying critical machine other than that sustained by its own authors is symptomatic of the peculiar lack of self-awareness of the literature itself. Any literature which does not carry along its own outside critical interpretations, from time to time, can be said to have no inner sense of the desirability of such literary stock-taking. As Albert Gérard states in his paper, 'Towards a History of South African Literature':

> ... the major stumbling-block is probably connected with language. Many South African intellectuals, white and non-white, are practically bilingual, fluent in English and in Afrikaans; non-white intellectuals will often have mastered one or two vernacular languages as well. But a fully informed and competent account of South African literature can only arise as the outcome of carefully allocated and organized teamwork. It is highly significant that no committee of the various departments concerned has ever been set up in any South African university for that purpose.[12]

Gérard's observation touches the core of the problem of the divided and unfocused literary scholarship of South Africa today.

Another useful collection of information is G.M. Miller and Howard Sergeant's *A Critical Survey of South African Poetry in English.* The work represents an impressive amount of detailed original research — which is, once again, helpful. Yet it is marred by a tendency to make Olympian pronouncements on the quality, or lack of quality, of the poems which, in a field such as this, tends at this stage to be a misplaced luxury if the basic foundations for value-judgements are not yet there.

Other attempts to beacon off the limits of Southern African literature in English have been of article length only. Francis Brett Young's piece, 'South African Literature', is a concise survey of strategic works that asserts more than it probes. Nevertheless, it has remained a standard view of the subject, basically unquestioned by many of his successors.[13]

Of all the attempts to classify Southern African English literature, perhaps the ones that have been least successful have been those which view it as a part of the literature of the British Commonwealth of Nations. South African writing does fall into that sphere, on paper at least, up to 1961; thereafter, while the independent black territories remain in the Commonwealth, the Republic of South Africa may be said to some extent to have separated off from the English world community. The literature of South Africa has, however, tactfully been retained within the bounds of the *Journal of Commonwealth Literature* (from 1973 onwards), and surveys like McLeod's *The Commonwealth Pen,* Walsh's *Commonwealth Literature* and New's *Among Worlds: An Introduction to Modern Commonwealth and South African Fiction* sketch South Africa's contribution to a global English-speaking and writing community that is more noted for its regional differences than its common bonds. As regards Southern African literature, these works are shallow to the point of being senseless. The days when Anthony Trollope could include South Africa in his survey of the British share of the world[14] have been lost to us for a long time, and if South Africa may be said to have bulked out the literature of Britain overseas, it does not follow that any notion of commonwealth has played a great role within South Africa. But the concept of a Southern Africa, in which the bonds between Commonwealth and adjacent extra-Commonwealth countries remain intact on a basis of day-to-day contact, does remain a reality.

The first work which can be taken with some sense of awe as a challenge in the creation of a literary–critical approach is the first edition of Mphahlele's *The African Image.* His concern is to see Southern

African English writing within the larger context of African literature and experience in general. Although he does not aim to be comprehensive, he is the first critic to pursue useful selected themes that cut through many of the boundaries established before him. By making detailed sense of particular strands, he implies that a coherent pattern is there to be found.

The same may be said of the most recent collection of critical pieces, *Aspects of South African Literature,* edited by Christopher Heywood. In his introduction, called 'The Quest for Identity', Heywood stresses the need for a modern study of this neglected branch of world literature, and undertakes to suggest some of its shape and scope. He refers to Gérard's appeal for a complete history, and his collection, although restricted to the mainly-English approach, goes a long way towards an appropriate response. For the reader in South Africa, Heywood's book, is currently banned.

The classification of South African English literature as a part of African Literature in English that Mphahlele initiated has continued, if occasionally this inclusiveness has been extended to black writers in English only.[15] The relationship is a deep and a compulsory one. As the British influence has diminished so the African has increased, and where English South African literature is studied in South Africa at all it is commonly grouped together with the African literature of today.[16]

After the problem of classification comes the matter of periodization. In the section on 'South African Literature in English' in the 1970 edition of the *Concise Cambridge History of English Literature,* George Sampson and R.C. Churchill find that their segment 'divides itself pretty easily into three periods'.[17] These are the greater part of the nineteenth century up to 1899, the period after the Second Anglo–Boer War through Union to the end of World War I, and a third period post-1920. Sampson and Churchill make no decisions as to why their two culminating dates, 1899 and 1918, should be watershed points in the long continuum, and no sense of pattern emerges from their survey as a result. Their notion of the scope of the field is thoroughly confused, too, since they include F.W. Reitz's parodies into Afrikaans, on a recommendation by Rudyard Kipling, yet fail to mention that any further Afrikaans literature developed at all. They pursue authors on the basis of passport through to an event like the Spanish Civil War (Roy Campbell), if it suits them. They imply that the one great work to emerge from the war that ended the nineteenth century and their first period is Baden-Powell's *Scouting for Boys* (1908). The Cambridge summary, in short, will not do.

The following table of periods will indicate in some tentative way what it is the intention of this introduction to establish:

1. The fabulous Stone and Iron Age oral cultures, co-existent to the present;

2. European literature from Camoens to 1800; epic origins and international travellers' tales;

3. Nineteenth-century British literature from the first British Occupation (1795) through to the end of the century; adventure-romance to realism;

4. The Second Anglo–Boer War to Union, 1899–1910; reportage and naturalism;

5. Union to the end of the Second World War, 1910–45;

6. The rise of apartheid, 1945–60;

7. The rise of African English independence, 1960—

These first and second periods fall outside the scope of the Cambridge history, but chapters 2, 3 and 7 here, dealing with the relationship between English and its predecessors on the subcontinent, will, one trusts, establish that complex bonds exist between written literature that appeared before the arrival of the British in any substantial numbers, the resident oral cultures, and the Cambridge field, which it would be foolish to ignore in the assessment of any absolute role English might have played.

The third period (covered in chapters 4 and 5 and in the early pages of chapter 6) contains an amount of literary productivity, of the extent of which Sampson and Churchill could not have had an inkling. Every aspect of Southern African literature that could possibly be taken into account had made its first rudimentary appearance by 1899, and the twentieth-century literature presents no breakthroughs that were not forecast before that watershed war. In this introduction it will hardly prove necessary to look beyond the nineteenth century in the illustration of the whole — that the modern South African writer is not aware of the fact means that he or she is doomed to repeating the nineteenth century far beyond its time. It will never prove strictly necessary to venture post-1960 into the diaspora, either, to find evidence of one or another facet of the literature which was not in evidence before.

The fourth period contains the literature of reportage that the war spawned, mostly by British visitors attracted by the news-making potential of that protracted battle which focused the entire world's attention on the subcontinent for one brief moment of exposure. It is a period for extensive name-dropping, for there were more British and other writers who did write about that holocaust than did not.[18]

The fifth period, which one might conveniently label the Smuts period, is a patternless one, lulled in the security, and lack of stimulus, of belonging to a working empire. The First World War makes no more than an incidental break in the continuity of the period, and it throws up no original talents. The real interest of the period is the development of Afrikaans literature, periodized into writers of the '20s, '30s and '40s, most adequately chronicled by scholars like Dekker and Antonissen, to whose work one refers.[19]

The sixth period, after World War Two, did produce a generation of white so-called war poets with a new consciousness of being 'strange' to Europe,[20] concerned to be African. It also threw up the black renaissance considered in chapter 7, which by 1960 had all but failed.

By the beginning of the seventh period South African English culture had begun its split into two, and the independence of South Africa's and Rhodesia's neighbours, Lesotho, Botswana and Swaziland, contributes to a spiritual change of attitudes towards black writing. This in turn brings the renewal of white writing which is in evidence in recent times. Since 1971 and the publication of Oswald Mtshali's *Sounds of a Cowhide Drum,* local publishing has perhaps learned that there is money in talking African, and has become sufficiently viable economically for a virtual golden era to be declared. It is a golden era built on insubstantial foundations, however, since it lacks its other — and necessary — half.

But Southern African literature cannot be divided into periods as above with much success. Such periods are arbitrary and open-ended, and will remain so until further research reveals the contours of the whole more clearly. Nevertheless, what is of absorbing interest at this stage is the currents which flow between the islands; the currents of language, of mode, of history and society, and of transformation. The fabulous Stone and Iron Age periods run from the background into the foreground, if necessary; Southern Africa may have discouraged, but has never actively disallowed the existence of the old with the new. The current of apartheid flows from before Sir Bartle Frere through to Dr Verwoerd; literature and politics interpenetrate uncomfortably for far longer than the term 'apartheid' has been in use. The rise of African independence as a theme could well be traced back not to the Sharpeville of 1960, but to the emancipation of the slaves in 1834, or the Mfecane of 1820, dates which the Cambridge history misses entirely, just as most South African critics do today. The very physical subcontinent, as conscious of its borders as it ever has been, has not yet jelled in literary terms into the firm landmass it should be.

But the quest for wholeness is likely to prove chimerical at the present time. In 1976, for example, the whole literature showed precisely how divided it is. During that year there were major conferences concerned with the subject in three different parts of the world: South Africa's writers in exile met in Holland; South Africa's English writers, white and black, with their vernacular associates, those not in exile, met in Johannesburg; and Afrikaans writers did the same at Broederstroom. To say that these three occasions occurred within months of one another and, according to press reports and conference papers, proceeded as if it were normal for one group to function without significant reference to the other two groups is no exaggeration.

As A.C. Partridge wrote in his introduction to *Readings in South African English Prose:*

The critic who essays to chart the *terra incognita* of S.A. English prose is, perhaps, less intrepid than foolish. In the state of our knowledge about it all he can safely do is locate the landmarks — a pleasant kloof here, a rugged eminence there, a crop of noxious sociological thorns almost everywhere . . .[21]

Partridge's metaphor is symptomatic of attitudes to the subject; he has a desert land in mind, one snarled up with natural but vicious thorns which he feels are hostile and, after all, impenetrable. But at least he knows that the territory is there to be discovered.

The guiding metaphor for this introduction is that Southern African literature is like an archipelago. The islands with their peaks protrude in set positions, even if one does not readily see the connections between them beneath the surface. Like most archipelagoes, it is related to adjacent landmasses: in this case there are three of them — most importantly, the mainland of English literature, by language and historical circumstance; diminishingly, the British Commonwealth of literature; and increasingly, the continent of Africa which gives it its actual nourishment. Although these three realms condition its location, that is not to say that it does not have an independent life of its own. This archipelago can be surveyed diachronically, as has frequently been done, but here it will prove appropriate to examine not so much what shape it has, but how it comes to have assumed some shapes peculiar to it. Its various pinnacles may have been described every so often, but what it is necessary to chart now is what tides and drifts and spins, what internal interconnections, have made them the way they are.

The continuity of Southern African literature is shown in its newspapers and reviews. James Fitzpatrick's *The Cape of Good Hope Literary Magazine* in the 1840s (cover by George French Angas) (1) followed Pringle and Fairbairn's *The South African Journal*. Campbell and Plomer's *Voorslag* gave rise to Stephen Black's *The Sjambok* and Aegidius Jean Blignaut and Herman Charles Bosman's *The Touleier* (cover by H.E. Winder) (2). In the 1960s Nat Nakasa's *The Classic* and Jack Cope's *Contrast* fed the younger writers of reviews like *IZWI*, a successor to *Wurm* (cover by H.M. Ferguson) (3), *Donga* and *New Classic*.

4 'Narina, la
Jeune Gona-
quoise' from Le
Vaillant's *Travels*.
5 Christopher
Rumford's car-
toon of Saartjie
Baartman (1810).
6 Yvonne Bryce-
land as Lena in
Athol Fugard's
production of
*Boesman and
Lena* (1969).

2 The White Man's Creation Myth of Africa

THE PURPOSE OF THIS AND THE FOLLOWING CHAPTER is to demonstrate that the 'archipelago' of Southern African literature can be surveyed, from its far-distant origins, through its intricate shoals and reefs, up to the present looming time and place, by means of two kinds of telescope, as it were, each adjusted to focus from a specific viewpoint. The point of view taken here is myth, both consciously and unconscious myth, which by its nature is given to crossing cultural and language barriers indiscriminately, when necessary, and is thus able to link areas of literature which at first sight might appear unconnected.

The consciously-created myth which is followed through the literature in this chapter is an obvious one — the myth of Adamastor. It is the white man's creation myth of Africa, ultimately derived from classical sources and applied to explain his initial experience of the black continent. Its essence is that of confrontation across a wide distance, its motivation a desire to codify and explain, if not to engage. Here we shall see how, as it is manipulated openly and knowingly by poets who are fully aware of the myth's innate properties, it develops from early epic and heroic phases into romance and irony in classic Northrop Frye terms, and in so doing awards us a sense of a certain continuing process having been operative within certain parts of Southern African literature.

In his early survey of the literature, Ian D. Colvin,[1] although he allocated considerable space to Portuguese and other travellers' records, makes no more than a passing reference to Luis de Camoens, the first European poet to record his experience of sailing around the Cape and to construct an appropriate mythic response to it. It is only with John Purves that Camoens acquires some status in South African literary criticism as the father of white poetry in South Africa. On 28 August 1909, Professor Purves delivered a lecture at the Transvaal University College on 'Camoens and the Epic of Africa', in which he issued this rousing claim: '*The Lusiads* . . . is not only the first but the

greatest of South African poems. It is our portion in the Renaissance.'[2] This opinion has held true for some South African poets,
despite the fact that Camoens's Portuguese poem remains relatively
unknown in South Africa today, doubtless on account of the prevailing notion that Portuguese is no close relative of English. Yet some
key white poets have taken an intimate knowledge of Camoens as a
precondition of their own variations on his myth. That such a clearly
defined and logical approach to interpreting some poetry in South
Africa has not been attempted since Purves's lecture might be explained by reference to Purves's own career in South Africa.

For three years, from 1910 to November 1913, he was the editor of
The South African Bookman and Quarterly Journal of the South African Home Reading Circle in Pretoria. At first *The South African Bookman* was a local version of the London *Bookman,* given over to news
and reviews of forthcoming publications by South African writers and
memorial articles on venerable South African literary figures such as
Mgr F.C. Kolbe. It also contained occasional pieces on whether or not
missing Pringle papers had been found. *The South African Bookman*
ran checklists of books in print by South Africans and admonished
bookshops to stock their own authors, even to display them alongside
the imported product. Purves had noted in his Camoens lecture that
no more than two towns in South Africa carried copies of *The Lusiads*
in their libraries, even though the work had been translated into English in its entirety no less than four times, the most recent being by
none other than Sir Richard Burton, working at it 'as an explorer for
explorers' (*The State,* p. 735). The situation has hardly changed. By
the end of No. 8 of *The South African Bookman,* Purves had resigned
as editor, noting somewhat bitterly that South African literature was
deserving of more than tea-party discussion: there was more to be discovered than that — as William Hay had reconfirmed in his 1912 edition
of Pringle's poems, Coleridge considered 'Afar in the Desert' 'among
the two or three most perfect lyric poems in the language'.

Purves intended to show that the continuum of writing in Southern
Africa was greater than the language continuity of English experience
post-1820. In his consideration of *The Lusiads,* particularly of Canto
V, which deals with the Portuguese navigators' passage around the
Cape, he footnotes much of the material for the first time from a
South African point of view. But then, instead of making the obvious
literary deductions, he falls into the trap which has regularly diverted
critics of South African literature from their true quest — he bulks out
his observations, not with empirical literary information, but with

tenuously connected biographical detail on his subject, Camoens, the luckless, one-eyed scholar of Coimbra who, after sixteen years adrift in the farthest reaches of the briefly lived Portuguese East Indian Empire, returned to his native Lisbon with a head full of actual sea-faring experience and hands full of manuscript. Like many critics in South Africa, Purves is good at wielding the biocritical method; his lecture carries conviction when it asserts that Camoens heaped into the creation of the figure of Adamastor all the scorn and detestation for the African continent that he felt when it held him, writing in his cell, in 'compulsory detention' (p. 736) from 1567 to 1569, in Mozambique, when he was trying to return home. But one might equally well deduce from such a legend that Camoens was the first white author to become a political detainee in Southern African literature, and that the poem is of interest on that account, too. The biocritical method was appropriate for a scholar of Edwardian times, but it was not given to answering major questions about the continuity of literature.

The Lusiads is not the first and greatest South African poem. Less than one-tenth of it deals with experience in South Africa's territorial waters; Vasco da Gama, the hero of its epic voyage, was not trying merely to revisit Bartholomew Diaz's Cape of Storms. His objective was India and the Spice Islands, so that rounding the bottom of Africa was no more than a matter of clearing one more obstacle on a long course to glory. *The Lusiads* is the national epic of the Lusitanian bogeymen, the sons of its eponymous hero, Lusus, and not of any very significant number of South Africans.

Nevertheless, with these qualifications clearly in mind, it is imperative to examine it by a reverse-angle shot, as it were; we look at Camoens from the vantage point of the cruel, dark and vengeful interior that he and his hero viewed as unfit for human habitation. Several of the characteristic themes of South African writing make rudimentary appearances in Canto V, and Camoens's dilemma was that of his white successors: how does a writer, at home in his own European literary environment, deal with essentially African experience?

Camoens took to precedents, and that his precedents were Homer and Virgil, particularly the latter, should not be news to us. Vasco da Gama is turned into an historical successor of Odysseus and Aeneas, the ancient sea-voyagers who extended the proscribed psyches of their audiences into new worlds. But in one sense Homer and Lucretius, and Virgil and Herodotus, let Camoens down. 'It is hard to tell you of all the dangers we experienced and the strange happenings we saw in these lonely and faraway regions . . .' says da Gama, Camoens's mouthpiece.

'Will the learned men ever explain these wonders of nature? Had the ancient philosophers seen as many things and been to as many places as I, they would have left fantastic records of true happenings in strange worlds.'[3] Vasco da Gama's aside tries to explain the difficulties he has in describing new phenomena, like water spouts and electrical tropical storms, encountered for the first time by Europeans on the way down the latitudes of the Atlantic towards the strange seas of the South Pole. In Da Gama's statement that it is 'hard to tell you of all the dangers', Camoens implies that literary precedent plays a cunning trick on a poet when the stuff of sensational poetic embellishment, good for thrills and spills, actually does occur in new experience. He has to invite suspension of disbelief in order that new realities, rather than old fantasies, enter his account.

But in his reinterpretation of what the classical Mediterranean gods stand for once they are transported across the oceans of the globe, Camoens sets up a framework of thinking that is relevant to defining the field of South African literature. The roles the gods play are modified from the roles they played in the Greek and Latin. In Camoens Mars and Venus step out of the Iberian middle ages as the patrons of all warrior-lovers. Neptune and Bacchus are now viewed as gods from the exterior, hostile and menacing, utterly foreign to the European scheme of things. This new alignment of Mars–Venus, the European controllers, against their dark, uncivilized foes in Neptune-Bacchus — what one might call the Apollonian–Dionysian dichotomy — represents the basic tension of the white–black confrontation as depicted in much of white South African literature. The colonizer dedicated to fighting for the Great White Queen against the forces of lawlessness and drunken unreason, a view that goes a long way to explaining the assumption behind a lot of later colonial literature, is prefigured in Camoens's Renaissance epic.

The Portuguese heroes advance with a truly odd selection of classical and Christian figureheads. But as they cross the equator these reassuring protectors begin to thin out in Camoens, and a statement like the following is not only an informative celestial observation but contains a certain bleakness, the anxiety of men confronted with the unexplored and therefore unnameable: 'At night the Great and Little Bear sank rapidly into the ocean' (Quintanilha, p. 2). They give way to the new stars of Fomalhaut and the Southern Cross.

Pagan (classical) mythology and Christian symbolism rub shoulders easily in *The Lusiads*. Although this point was irksome to Dryden ('Camoens . . . should be censured by all his readers, when he brings

in Bacchus and Christ into the same adventure of his fable'⁴), it does
not unduly distress us when it comes to reading Milton, as Purves
pointed out; syncretism is a necessary metaphysical skill which in
times of multiple experience becomes a means of literary enrichment.
The fact that Adamastor is derived from both those huge reservoirs of
Western experience, the Greek and Roman classics, and the Bible, at
the same time, should disturb no one today. In a multicultural situation, heterogeneity is a saving grace.

Canto V contains two episodes which are the first literary records of
European meetings with the indigenous South African population.
Here we are already entering upon Partridge's 'noxious sociological
thorns'; since the clash of colours is a predominant theme in South
African writing, it would be as well to examine these incidents in
some detail, if with caution.

Da Gama recounts their first meeting at St Helena Bay in this
manner:

> . . . the men disembarked on huge expanses of land, eager to see weird things
> where no other travellers had set foot before. . . . Suddenly I saw a black-skinned
> man, surrounded by my crew, coming towards me. He had been captured in the
> mountains while gathering honeycombs. More savage-looking than Polyphemus,
> he was also very frightened because we were unable to communicate with each
> other. I showed him gold, silver and spices, but he was not impressed. Then I
> ordered that glass beads, tinkling bells and a bright crimson cap be shown him:
> he was delighted, as we could tell from his expressions. We let him head back to
> his village that was not far off. (Quintanilha, p. 2)

Intrepid and 'eager to see weird things', the crew of the caravels
embark on the unknown. They are merely obeying orders, for, according to Boxer, Da Gama is carrying letters of credence to Prester John
from his regent, Dom Manuel I, and 'samples of spices, gold and seed-
pearls. He had orders to show these commodities to the inhabitants of
all the undiscovered places at which he might call along the African
coast, in the hope that those peoples might recognize these valuables
and indicate by signs, or through interpreters, where they might be
found.'⁵ Columbus was doing the same thing in the Caribbean at the
same time. The fact that Da Gama's first Hottentot is 'captured . . .
while gathering honeycombs' suggests an act of immediate aggression
on the part of the Portuguese. But Da Gama very truthfully admits
the pacific nature of their first victim (honeycombs and not poison
for arrows). Immediately the classical gloss is given, though not with
much conviction: however 'savage-looking', a Hottentot is not a one-
eyed giant, although the cyclops image does convey awe and an anti-

cipation of an eruption of violence. The give-away remark is that the
Hottentot was 'also very frightened'. That candid and human detail
lends the account an eye-witness quality.

Then they enact the ritual barter. Although Da Gama stresses his
generosity towards the Hottentot, one must not forget that such a
pitstop would include the Portuguese helping themselves to fresh
water and greens and meat from the Khoisan domain, a fact which is
elided here. The line: 'I showed him gold, silver and spices', also has
an uneasy ring to it. These samples were not only for purposes of
identification, but part of an invitation to the local to point the way
to the East. Not only was the Hottentot not impressed, but he could
not understand the question — it is a superbly absurd moment. The
haunting detail that Da Gama gave the Hottentot glass beads, tinkling
bells and a bright crimson cap is charming to Da Gama; such truck is,
however, of tragic significance to us, for it will in time lose the Khoisan a kingdom.

Da Gama acknowledges that a certain communication has taken
place. Camoens himself, though using a highly formal ottava rima
stanza, like Ariosto before him, is nevertheless fascinated by alternative means of communication. He has Da Gama stress that he and the
Hottentot have no language in common, yet they can read delight in
one another's expressions. In short, communication by mime, by a
sort of improvised drama, has taken place.

The following day it turns out that Fernao Veloso, the comedian of
the trip (Speedy Fernando might be the English equivalent of his
name), is also the social anthropologist of the three caravels. When
more Hottentot villagers, 'naked and black', make for the ship in the
hope of collecting more curious trinkets, Da Gama notes that:

they were so gentle and friendly that Fernao Veloso decided to go back with
them to observe their ways and customs. Bold was he, confident in his strong
arm, believing arrogantly that he had nothing to fear. He had gone from us for
a considerable time, when all of a sudden we saw him in the distance, making
for the sea in a greater hurry than when he left.
    Coelho's little boat set out to fetch him, but before it reached the shore, a
Hottentot pounced on Veloso, and then another and another. He was in great
danger, with no-one to help. While I hastened to his rescue, a whole band of
Hottentots appeared from a covering. Arrows and stones rained on us, not all in
vain, since I left with an injured leg. Yet our retaliation was such that I fear it
was not only their caps that they kept as a red souvenir of the encounter.
(Quintanilha, pp. 2–3)

At this point in his narrative, Vasco da Gama has only to indicate his wounded leg for the story to carry the evidence of experience.

Camoens has him straining for effect here, describing what after all is no more than a skirmish which, in all its thousands of pupular variations, never fails to generate excitement. One can visualize the battle — stalwart but foolhardy seamen learning their lesson at the hands of stone-throwing fiery hordes, artillery versus the inevitable arrows. The braggadocio of Da Gama's tone when he says they received more than red caps as souvenirs of the incident is forgivable, and it is a startling image of blood-letting. But the Hottentots have their baptism in blood. It does not, and cannot, enter Camoens's thinking to see the scene from the Hottentot point of view as well: a handful of pacific, diminutive honeycomb-gatherers, inadequately armed, in their turn fighting off the hostile mermen materialized out of the sea to molest them with lethally magical instruments and threatened invasion.

The meeting is archetypal to much of South African writing, as has been said, though here it appears only in an early phase. The Hottentots are, and remain, in possession of those incalculably vast landmasses; the Europeans are huddled off the coast in their vessels, not confident enough to spend even a night ashore. When Coelho, watched by the whole crew, rows for the beach to 'save' his threatened companion, the crossing is dramatized as a quick trip to the banks of hell. They were not only upside down on the globe, but so far out of gear with European normality that despite their having sailed for five months it was still a burning hot summer in the kingdom of the blacksmith, the volcano, the poisonous eruption of the hordes.

Having saved Veloso, [Da Gama continues,] we returned to our ships, only too clearly warned of the ugly malice and crude intentions of those treacherous brutes. And one presumed from their ignorance of its location that India must still be a long way off, so we hurried to sail on. (Quintanilha, p. 3)

The conclusion is over-emotive; 'ugly', 'crude' and 'treacherous' are inflated slanders, and 'their' ignorance has met its match in Da Gama's.

Frank Brownlee had no hesitation in interpreting this scene. 'One may think back to 1497 and Fernando Veloso, when blind, unreasoned fear led to the first clash between white and black in this country.'[6] At this juncture the critic is faced with not one but two ways to go to explain this fear: the first is to pursue that early meeting through the records, illustrating instances of blind, unreasoning fear at work as it dominates race relations in South Africa up to contemporary times, as Brownlee does, showing the how and the why of that fear throughout the social history of the land. But criticism with socio-political priorities has in South Africa often missed attaining the essential point of this chapter.

It is the second, the purely contextual approach to such a scene that has not been exercised sufficiently. The question to ask is not why was this preliminary skirmish fought, but how has literature shaped the artist's version of it. What sustaining myths compel it to be described the way Camoens has chosen, and what does literary technique reveal about this scene? If history and art were to be confused here, Brownlee's deduction would be reached time and again. But, in fact, not one detail of the encounter as described above is to be taken at face value, not even the implication of blind, unreasoned fear. The first scene of interracial strife in Southern African literature is not a documentary report, but a dramatized incident in an enormously complex and well-structured work of neoclassical epic which uses historical documentation for its own ends.

The context of this scene is that Da Gama, who by this stage has been speaking for two and a half cantos, is doing so at the invitation of the King of Malindi on the east coast of Africa. Although a Moslem and, as such, Da Gama's traditional enemy, he is a noble and courteous regent, as only a medieval adversary can be. Da Gama is talking to save his life, for he and his crew are afraid that their fleet will be ambushed yet again, and Da Gama needs something very practical, more practical than the mere maintenance of his honour: a reliable pilot to guide them eastwards to India on the next leg of their voyage. The king begs precisely the kind of speech that Da Gama makes when he invites him to explain himself:

Nor does the sun shine so obliquely on us here in Malindi that you should think us dull of heart and intellect beyond a proper appreciation of noble deeds. . . . The giants in their arrogance made war on Olympus, if in vain. Theseus and Pirithous were bold, in their ignorance, to assault Pluto's dark and fearsome kingdom. If history records such daring enterprises as the laying siege to both heaven and hell, to assail the fury of the ocean is another no whit less hazardous or renowned.[7]

Throughout his reply to the king, Da Gama knows that if he can present himself as a candidate for undying honour in the king's own terms, he will have saved himself and his crew. Therefore, the scene at St Helena Bay turns out to be shaped the way it is as much from first-hand observation as from the dramatic needs of a man in a tough corner. The Hottentots cannot therefore be presented in their own right; they have to be representative of 'Pluto's dark and fearsome kingdom'. The act of laying siege to heaven or hell has to be portrayed as an act of folly; hence Veloso's venture has to be dramatized as out- rageously brave, if foolish. The more inhospitable and unhelpful Da Gama makes the Hottentots, the more rhetorical sway he has gathered in formulating his appeal to the king. History is being manipulated into epic drama, and for dramatic effect an early experience has to present Africa as merciless, so that the King of Malindi will be moved to show that he is not without mercy. The rhetoric works. The king later takes them fishing.

The second encounter the king hears of, which takes place once the Cape is rounded, at Mossel Bay, is contrasted with the first, again for a good reason. It is not a dramatic incident and it is given cursory treatment. It would seem that to Camoens's mind there were only two ways of dealing with these cross-cultural meetings in terms of the precedents he had.

We landed a second time. The people of this new coast were still negroes ['Cafres'], yet more kind than those we had previously met. Dancing and cheer- ing, they came to us along the beach, bringing their wives and the fat, sleek flocks they were driving to pasture. The sultry women rode on the backs of tranquil oxen, the most valuable of their animals. They were singing pastoral songs, both in rhyme and unrhymed, accompanying themselves on rustic flutes, like Virgil's [Tityrus].

This joyful tribe treated us in a friendly manner, bringing fowls and sheep in exchange for our presents. (Quintanilha, pp. 5–6)

The complement to the heroic within the epic is the pastoral. There is a deep strain of sympathy at work here in Da Gama, and he intends the contrast between the scenes so that his meaning is clear: if you are aggressive, so are we prepared to be; if not, we are disarmed. But as the whole of *The Lusiads* is dense with pastoral details, this scene blends into Camoens's overall vision of the Tagus back home being the font of pastoral virtue and peaceful co-operation. Da Gama's mission is to trade, not to conquer. The equitable and pleasant inter- change of the Mossel Bay scene is clearly the kind of meeting he pre- fers. The sultry women riding tranquil oxen are not grotesque this time, but beautiful images of abundance and contentment. They are embodiments of Virgil's alternative to military strife and upheaval, Tityrus the shepherd as against Meliboeus the warrior. Their songs are the harmonies of peaceful order.

But once again the scene is cast in such a conventional mould that it is hard to sift out which details are derived from the African ex- perience and which from the classics. Certainly the riding of oxen was a novelty to the Portuguese. The songs were, too, and only a poet of Camoens's curiosity would insert in his poem a remark about those songs being 'rhymed and unrhymed', an observation which goes beyond building a scene into the distinctions of literary criticism. It is a fundamental moment in Southern African literature — a Western poet composing an epic poem which, if only distantly, relies on oral rhetorical formulations, pausing to take note of the techniques of other oral praise-singers who, like himself, codify and store a nation's history, its brave deeds, and its way of life in their poetry.

The celebrated Adamastor passage in *The Lusiads* is bracketed by these two encounters. It exemplifies for us how a poet facing a strange Africa went about inventing the appropriate literary symbolism, where before there had been none. The fact is that when Da Gama and his men attempted to round the Cape of Storms, it took them four grim days. The truth is also that Da Gama has to improvise, at some strategic point in his narrative, an incident which will illustrate how he has outdared even the rebellious Titans in their siege against Olympus. Assailing the fury of the oceans, the king has said, would be a suitable qualification for his respect.

Thus the Adamastor story is concocted out of all these situational dilemmas. Da Gama takes on the king down to the last detail, even in making Adamastor the last of the Titans. As Purves says of Adamastor, not quite correctly, 'the only great figure added to mythology since classical times is a South African figure' (*The State,* p. 542). He comes about not by one of what Tillyard calls Camoens's 'special interventions'[8] in the form, but as a structural necessity. Not unexpectedly, Adamastor grows to symbolize all the horrors and tribulations of Portuguese maritime history compressed into one.

I noticed, standing carefree on the prow one night [says Da Gama] that a large cloud appeared to be thickening the air. It was so fearsome that the sight of it filled us with foreboding. The turgid sea roared in the distance, as if smashing into the hollows of a reef. 'O sublime Powers!' I shouted out, 'what divine threat or secret is hidden in this terrible sea, for this is far more than an ordinary storm?'

I had hardly spoken when a muscular and powerful figure materialized in the cloud itself. It was gigantic in stature, disfigured, with a huge, sunken face and a squalid beard and sunken eyes. His expression was evil and menacing; it had a clayey pallor. His hair was matted with mud. His black mouth was filled with yellow teeth. . . . In a deep and horrifying voice, he spoke as if from the depths of underwater. (Quintanilha, p. 3)

Camoens knows how the fabulous symbols of *The Odyssey* and

The Aeneid are derived; he is on the inside of the mythopoeic process. He knows that his readers will see Table Mountain as a rocky forehead, and the caps of waves as moaning grey moustaches over hollow mouths. He knows that whirlpools will appear as sunken eyes, and that when the black maw of the sea pulls back over reefs, his audience will expect the yellow teeth. Those are the awe-inspiring details by which the tempestuous Cape is anthropomorphized into a giant.

But then the character Camoens chooses for Adamastor is not entirely the expected one. He is an old greybeard, the last of the unintelligent classical rebels. His genealogy, as he tells Da Gama, is: born of Earth and Sky. His own folly was to try and overthrow the new order of Greek gods, but by falling in love with the provocative Thetis, who betrayed his love and exiled him, he has weakened his endeavour. 'My flesh was changed into earth, my bones into rock, these limbs that you see and this face were projected over the watery spaces. My enormous body became this desolate cape, and to increase my suffering the gods encircled me with these waters of Thetis herself' (Quintanilha, p. 5). It is a delightful conceit of Camoens's to have a mythological figure actually explaining how he becomes a myth. Yet Adamastor is pathetic as well as horrific — a ham-handed oaf who, instead of fighting, tenderly gropes after a delicate, pale, erotic nymph, whose privilege makes her untouchable and whose advanced society punishes unwarranted affection with all the powers of a superior technology. His story is not unlike that of King Kong, another primal monster who reaches for an unattainable pale wraith — a contemporary version of the same myth by Edgar Wallace, who also learned about racial psychoses in Southern Africa. He is Caliban desiring Miranda, the Beast longing for Beauty.

When Da Gama himself meets Thetis towards the end of the epic, ironically enough he enjoys the consolatory copulation which Adamastor is denied. The Portuguese are a favoured race. When she leads Da Gama to the top of the mountain which is the Island of Love, she reveals to him what she thinks of Africa by means of a lecture on the globe of the world:

Here is Africa [she declares of the Titan's body] still grasping after the things of this world, uncivilized, full of savagery, with its southernmost Cape, that has always been denied you until now. Look out over the whole vast continent and see how everywhere it is the home of legions of infidels.

Observe, here is the great empire of [Mo]nomotapa with its naked blacks. . . . There is abundance of gold, the metal that men most strive after . . . and note how the Negroes live in huts without doors, as if they were nests, trusting to the

king's justice and to the protection and good faith of their neighbours. . . .
(Atkinson, p. 236)

Adamastor, then, is the home of the old heathens, the numerous
unenlightened, guardians of treasure for which their tribal communal-
ism can find no use, tragic because their aspirations towards civilization have failed. Yet Camoens is not one for gratuitous details; the
clayey features and the hair matted with mud are not only descriptive
of how the old rebel is in abeyance — this is the kind of clay and mud
out of which the new Adam will one day be born.

Adamastor's enormous grumble against the Portuguese is simply
explained; he envies them their mobility, their superior daring, their
grace. His curse is made to order: 'O, you daring race, bolder than any
other in the world . . .' (Quintanilha, p. 4). Nor is he insensitive to the
glamour of a new breed of men who in challenging destiny can break
out of the old, closed world order into the new. Camoens lets his Renaissance hero respond to Adamastor with supreme self-confidence.
Da Gama has the nerve to interrupt Adamastor's prediction of the
horrors the Portuguese will undergo and shames the giant into telling
his own ludicrous history. When Adamastor dejectedly subsides into
a brooding calm, Da Gama relates that he 'raised his hands in blessing
to the angels who had led us safely past there, praying that God might
avert the grim disasters predicted by Adamastor' (Quintanilha, p. 5).
In reply, the sun rises as they turn to face it in the East.

But the catastrophes Adamastor lays out for the Portuguese were
not to be circumvented, even if Adamastor was. Part of Camoens's
theme is that only through unendurable suffering are the final rewards
achieved. *The Lusiads* is above all a masterly illustration of the Catho-
lic belief in suffering, purgation and redemption. When D. Manuel de
Sousa de Sépulveda and D. Leonor de Sá land on the African shore
their fate is to be worse than death, as Adamastor forecasts:

They will be allowed to survive a cruel shipwreck only to suffer more grievous
wrongs. They shall see their children, the fruit of so much love and care, starve
to death. They shall see the rough, grasping Cafres strip the gorgeous lady of her
garments after a long and painful trek along the burning sands, leaving her limbs
exposed to the rigour of the elements. And their companions will witness even
worse as these two helpless lovers fall victim to the blazing, pitiless bush where
their tears, drawn out by grief, will melt the very stones. In their final embrace
they will release their souls from the prisons of their bodies with relief.
(Quintanilha, p. 4)

Trading is indeed a constant theme in *The Lusiads,* and although the

poem has commonly been read as the great European epic of mercan-
tile endeavour, such an evaluation is perhaps too simple, because the
theme of a life of pain and sacrifice (which Adamastor symbolizes and
Africa demands), and of redemption, predominates.

Da Gama himself died peacefully back in Lisbon when Camoens was
newborn, and Camoens rounded the Cape as part of Cabral's expedition of 1553, by which time Adamastor's prophecies had been enacted
to the last detail. By 1572, when *The Lusiads* was first published, the
Da Gama story had already taken on the contour of myth. By then,
however, the concept of the noble explorer, dedicated to the uphold-
ing of his honour among even, for example, the king of his enemies,
was in decay; the spiritual priorities of a Da Gama had, in Camoens's
opinion, given way to mere money-changing. His disgusted verdict was
that 'gentle blood and material wealth counted for more than learning
and literature with [his] compatriots at home and overseas' (Boxer,
p. 342). A century later Portugal's Jesuit priests would be calling their
flocks the 'Kaffirs' of Europe. Man, not money, Camoens asserted,
should be the measure of man.

Thus in the epic poetic vision, the Titan–Olympian feud, grafted
onto the feud between Crescent and Cross, becomes the mainstay of
the colonizer's vision of his mission, one which inevitably shapes his
own myth of how he needs Africa to appear. The figure of Adamastor
is at the root of all the subsequent white semiology invented to cope
with the African experience: he is menacing and inimical, and seen
across a barrier; he belongs to an older but defeated culture, and is
likely to sink the new European enlightenment if allowed within its
purlieu; although his size is gigantic, his responses are essentially
childish and they obey paternalistic directives; he is capable of love,
but only carnally, so that if he advances too presumptuously he is to
be humiliated and rendered impotent. His state is ineluctably fallen
(Camoens situates his head at the farthest remove from the Mediterranean), yet he is likely to foment rebellion once more against those
who keep cheating him of his birthright, so that his strength of arm
has to be countered with superior ingenuity. In Camoens's pseudo-
classical pagan terms, his downfall explains the creation of the landmass of Africa, yet according to Camoens's Christian beliefs he
represents heathen sin as well, still to be reclaimed by Christ. His
Titanic force, tantamount to a block mountain's, his rumbling and
earth-shaking, is not only the pent power of a vast and frighteningly
unknown continent, populated by serpents and burning stones, but a
symbol of the awe with which Africa was regarded in early experiences

of the untamed.

That these associations are continuously operative in the so-called European consciousness goes without saying. In the seventeenth and eighteenth centures, travellers' accounts of landings on the coast and journeys inland proceed in the face of Adamastor, quite frequently with references to Camoens. In the nineteenth century, Camoens's poem occasionally spurs a romance version of the myth, notably in the poetry of John Wheatley.[9] Wheatley's remarkably rich 264-line poem, 'The Cape of Storms', first published in 1830, shortly before his death at sea, proceeds with frequent references to Milton's global traders, Coleridge's images of the albatross and the doldrums, Byron's images of the libertarian spirit, and the Romantics' fervour for spectacular demonstrations of natural force.

Significantly for us here, however, Wheatley's invocation is made to the muse of Camoens:

> Spirit of Gama! round the stormy Cape,
> Bestriding the rude whirlwind as thy steed. . . .[10]

Wheatley is not antipathetic to the Adamastor myth, but in a subtle twist of the story he predicts his own death in terms of the suffering he empathizes with in the hostile monster:

> Perchance the grandest boon to be bestow'd
> By heav'n on man — the shortest, best relief
> From all his mortal sufferings, and load
> Which life entails of misery, and grief —
> The termination of his woes, might be
> As now he braves the billows of the Cape,
> To grapple with grim Death upon the sea,
> The whirlwind for its courser, and the storm its shape,
>
> So might the bark become his coffin's shell,
> The murky cloud enshroud him as his pall,
> The roar of distant thunder ring his knell,
> The lightning's flash illume his funeral!
> His winding sheet the wild white curling wave,
> The rolling billow as his bier, be lent,
> The rain his tears! the ocean for his grave,
> The Cape of Storms itself his mighty Monument!
>
> (p. 49, last two stanzas)

That the romantic poet, undergoing his own heroic struggles against the dictates of fate, should identify with the toils and resistance of the African continent itself is not very remarkable. But that Wheatley

could identify with Camoens's symbol of Africa, Table Mountain,
sufficiently to envisage it as his tombstone as well is a novel sentiment
for a poet who was, after all, merely in passage (in this case, from
India back to London). The Adamastor myth, however, is no more
than an internalized part of Wheatley's own elegy, and it is changed
no more than from the terms of externalized epic into a symbol of
personal, heroic endeavour within the romantic's extravagantly emotional world.

In one of the first avowedly Afrikaans collections of poetry, Adamastor makes his presence felt unchanged:

> Daar, vasgeplant in woeste waatre,
> Voel d'onverroerbre rots die klaatre
>   Van 'n verrestrekkende Oceaan,
> Bestrijd, gesweep door d'Orkaan
> Met vreeslik eindeloos geweld.
>
> Die wakk're seeman lang gelee
> Doorseild die onbekende see-e.
>   Hij sag die rotse-reuse-vorme
>   En noemd' dit sidd'rend *'Kaap der Storme.'*[11]

In English he is tutelary spirit of Roy Campbell's volume of poems
of 1930, named simply *Adamastor.* As Rowland Smith observes, the
central theme of the poems in this volume is 'the insight derived from
isolation and hardship',[12] and Campbell's own prophetic warnings to
his fellow colonials, as Smith remarks, are in line with Adamastor the
doomcaster's.

Campbell's poem, 'Rounding the Cape', from this volume, is a
subtle commentary on the Camoens we have discussed, and in terms
of Camoens Campbell's lyric makes good sense. Campbell himself
planted the hint in *Light on a Dark Horse:* '. . . it is only Camoe[n]s,
the greatest of all South African poets, who gives one in words a real
sense of [the Cape's] awe and the grandeur of its stormy seas in that
wonderful passage about Rounding the Cape.'[13] This thought occurred
to Campbell on his own rounding of the Cape in 1918, and the poem
is classified under 'Early Poems'. Despite the fact that Campbell
stressed his kinship with Camoens the warrior-poet ('I find a comrade
where I sought a master', 'Luiz de Camoes', 1944[14]), and underscored
the influence repeatedly, critics of Campbell's work have rigorously
avoided dealing with it in those terms. Campbell, like an island in the
stream, is there in South African poetry, and he demands consideration within his own mythographic terms of reference.

Campbell had very specific reasons for not choosing exclusively South African forebears; rightly or wrongly, he saw his own immediate English-language poetic heritage in 'The Wayzgoose' in terms of: 'A clime so prosperous both to men and kine / That which were which a sage could scarce define' (*Selected Poems*, p. 113). In 'Poets in Africa' he gave his reasons for rejecting a line of poetic activity which supposedly commenced with Pringle and 'Afar in the Desert':

> Far in the desert we have been
> Where Nature, still to poets kind,
> Admits no vegetable green
> To soften the determined mind,
>
> But with snarled gold and rumbled blue
> Must disinfect the sight
> Where once the tender maggots grew
> Of faith and beauty and delight.[15]

For all his gaudy rhapsodizing of a violent Africa and his rejection of romanticism, the one gesture of Campbell's that one can trust is his ultimate dismissal of his African experience; he chose not to reserve his admiration of the primitive for South Africa alone, but to blaze a trail back to Europe:

> I who have quaked to hear, at fifty leagues,
> The rut of Behemoths and Maelstroms roar,
> Threader of endless calms whom naught fatigues,
> Am sick for Europe's towers of ancient lore.
>
> Starred archipelagoes I've seen and islands
> Where maddening skies, to tempt the rover, flower. . . .

That is Rimbaud speaking, in Campbell's own translation ('Drunken Boat', *Selected Poems*, p. 183). But if Campbell's poetry appears in Europe about half a century behind the times, that does not mean that for South Africa it was not a rich step forward. Campbell's conception of what was South African English culture was well formulated; it is certainly in line with the general theory of this book. His eclecticism, his ability to grab whatever he needed, not from the prescribed sources, but from whatever suited him temperamentally (as Heather Jurgens notes, 'in his view there was no such thing as an original image, so that it was of slight importance that one "stole": what was important was what one did with one's loot'[16]), is the creative artist's way out of a dilemma in English South Africa in general. The fact that as a 16-year-old he chose Camoens as an ancestor, the man exiled in his youth and tossed about in the raw material of a boundless universe, longing to retire to the firm base of his spiritual homeland, suggests that Campbell, the Mithraic tauromachist and Iberian troubadour, regarded his entire South African experience as a kind of exile away from his spiritual roots. If in the end he settled for believing that he preferred obedience to 'tradition and inherited knowledge to irresponsible experiment and innovation',[17] his own genealogy was self-defined to his own convenience.

But with regard to his ideas about what constituted the South African English tradition, in an article in the *Sunday Times* of Johannesburg Campbell himself was not one to fall for a view along the lines of the 'sequence of great works' view of things — Schreiner through Plomer to Millin and Krige — and observed dryly that:

This pre-eminence [of the South African over other British colonial literatures] has been ascribed to the fact that South Africa is the one Dominion where the cheapness and abundance of coloured labour makes it possible for its European inhabitants to enjoy leisure for intellectual pursuits.[18]

Campbell's answer to that recurring chestnut, in the same piece, was immediate:

Literature is more often the result of social and racial ferment than of idleness, and most of our South African literature is the result of the clash of many creeds, races, languages, cultures and barbarisms, which sets up a more acute state of consciousness than prosperity in a homogeneous atmosphere.

Nevertheless, having celebrated that ferment, Campbell rejected it. His venture back to Europe was a consequence of the malaise he felt English South African culture suffers from — its inability to encompass the entire range of Southern African life. An Afrikaans critic like D.J. Opperman is more generous to the memory of Campbell than many English-speaking critics, and more believing in the unifying context of all South African literary experience, when he assesses the immediate influence of Campbell on the Afrikaans Dertiger poets, and adjudges the line of development of South African poetry to be translingual — from Pringle through Leipoldt to Campbell, and on to N.P. Van Wyk Louw.[19]

In hand we have a poem given scant attention by the commentators on Campbell, one which derives from Camoens, 'Rounding the Cape'. For the critic to interpret it fully, he must have recourse to the poem's own context in Southern African literature.

The low sun whitens on the flying squalls,
Against the cliffs the long grey surge is rolled
Where Adamastor from his marble halls
Threatens the sons of Lusus as of old.

Faint on the glare uptowers the dauntless form,
Into whose shade abysmal as we draw,
Down on our decks, from far above the storm,
Grin the stark ridges of his broken jaw.

Across his back, unheeded, we have broken
Whole forests: heedless of the blood we've spilled,
In thunder still his prophecies are spoken,
In silence, by the centuries, fulfilled.

Farewell, terrific shade! though I go free
Still of the powers of darkness art thou Lord:
I watch the phantom sinking in the sea
Of all that I have hated or adored.

The prow glides smoothly on through seas quiescent:
But where the last point sinks into the deep,
The land lies dark beneath the rising crescent,
And Night, the Negro, murmurs in his sleep.
                                   (*Selected Poems*, p. 17)

The poem has no real centre of its own; it achieves meaning by
allusion. One is meant to know the Camoens passage. But Campbell's
journey round the Cape is of course in the reverse direction to
Camoens's, and the gap in time makes all the difference, for it is a
period in which 'Across his back, unheeded, we have broken / Whole
forests' without engaging much of the giant's concern. There is a kind
of seriocomic chumminess between Adamastor and the poet: I know,
I know, you have prophesied disaster all this while, writhing in pain,
and we've gone on beating you into submission. It is a stark view of
the honour and glory of colonial expansionism and the white man's
civilizing mission. But if Adamastor is dormant here, he is also unsub-
dued. If Adamastor is the spirit of the wild Cape's 'flying squalls' and
towering, forbidding rocks from the seaview, by a shift of footing in
the last stanza, Campbell jettisons Adamastor as an image of terror
(plainly the Cape is no longer anything near as awe-inspiring to the
new shipbuilders) and revises the image by making 'Night, the Negro'
about to awaken.

Yet Adamastor is the figure that represents all that Campbell has
'hated or adored'; he is taking leave of all the paradoxical emotions of
the anti-romantic young poet's relationship with South Africa, land
of violence and sadism. What Campbell is bidding farewell is somewhat

sinister; the land lying dark beneath the 'rising crescent' is not only a glum image of the unenlightened home territory, but, pace Camoens again, one which is being abandoned to its true fate. The detail of that 'crescent', after Camoens, is reminiscent of the Portuguese world order of Cross versus Crescent. But just as Camoens and his Christian standards advanced against the infidel, so Campbell retreats here, allowing the infidel to rise once more, as if the civilization that rolled over Adamastor's back had not established itself at all. The political implications are irresistible; the downtrodden Adamastor, off the sweat of whose back we have lived, is ready to hold sway again. Campbell's valediction is a resigned and uneasy statement of the failure of white civilization. The storm warnings that Da Gama could bypass become in Campbell the awakening sounds of the Third World.

If Campbell chose to adopt the pose of the weary soldier-poet in this poem, a constant stance throughout his corpus, then it is that pose which results in the poem's strength. For Camoens's successor to recognize defeat in the face of Africa is a powerful manipulation of the myth. The meeting between the retreating vates and the broken-jawed Adamastor, the axe-man and the mangled slave — the one most conscientious in animating South Africa's poetic myths and the other so intractable — is a moment of supreme recognition in the literature.

There is a further reworking of Camoens in Douglas Livingstone's *The Sea my Winding Sheet*,[20] which dates from the 1950s. The Adamastor myth is singularly suited to dramatic treatment, it seems — Campbell's lyric is a dramatic monologue, and Livingstone's handling of it is a verse drama, a radio play. Worked into Livingstone's abundant references to aerial communication, appropriate to his twentieth-century maritime imagery, is, once more, Adamastor the rhetorician. When he speaks in Livingstone's drama, he retains a certain fumbling, defeated impressiveness, and Campbell's prophecy of his voice becoming the growing murmur of the sleepy negro is not fulfilled, at least not here. For Livingstone winks at Campbell when his Adamastor says, amidst the dying cadences of *Lohengrin* and of all supermen, panting and bellowing:

> To hell with the moon.
> I cannot sleep, half-dead and half-alive,
> By its mocking light.

He continues, parodying a line from Wheatley:

The sea my winding sheet;
The wind my burial Mass;
My coffin filled with rocks and strange juices.
A Man was my executioner: a Woman my jury.
Now Man jerks my resurrection
From out of the top-hat of his genius.
Adamastor is on his knees again —
Where is the Woman that will help me to my feet?
My shadow . . . I would fling my shadow . . .
Black and hulking across the bland
Pallid face of the timid World again . . .
I will walk again . . . when I can get up.
(p. 120)

Livingstone has chosen to dramatize some of Adamastor's more endearing characteristics; his habit of addressing himself in the third person, his self-deflatory articulacy by which he trips up in his own grandeur, and his reputation, in modern cartoon terms, for being a Hulk. He remains, as the narrator remarks ironically in closing the play, 'one hulking solemn mass of scrub, forest, desert and rock', collapsed, but still untamed, nevertheless. Basically, Livingstone, like his forebears, subscribes to the concept of the nobility of epic struggle, the fallen warrior wrestling with his defeat. Yet Livingstone's view is tempered with many contradictions in this piece, for, while admiring such heroic wrangles, he cannot help finding them both comical and even absurd.

The Sea my Winding Sheet is so rooted in Camoens's Canto V that it is hard to conceive of its falling into coherent patterns without the reader having done the necessary homework. Although the play has been widely presented on the air and on the stage as a piece for voices, no critic has as yet attempted to begin to elucidate it in terms of sources. The full exposition it demands would not be in place here but, in so far as the play is an illustration of the fact that there is in Southern Africa something of a central literary consciousness which can be seen to be sustained by myth, some commentary might be relevant.

Livingstone, a generation after Campbell, finds that, no matter how honourable Campbell's allegiance to the old master of South African verse might have been, the epic–heroic approach to South African subject matter can no longer be entirely valid in terms of the contemporary poet's experience. Although *The Sea my Winding Sheet* contains the largest range of classical gods since the Veldsingers at the turn of the century collectively found Pan, Daphne and Flora crouch-

ing behind every Tennysonian 'flower in the crannied wall', Livingstone does not take his task of explaining Africa in terms of the old
Greco-Latin co-ordinates too seriously. For Samson Agonistes we now
have Sweeney Agonistes; for Adamastor *'grande de membros'* like a
colossus, we now have Adamastor the perplexed buffoon. Mock-epic
is here the necessary culmination of epic. When the old forms cannot
be revived (as Campbell felt they could be), they can at least remain
with us by being turned inside out.

The tumultuous violence of the Adamastor myth, reasoned into life
by Camoens and emulated by Wheatley and Campbell, is still there in
the Livingstone version, however. In Camoens it appeared in the confrontation between formal rhetorical exclamation and the tranquil
Te Deum of the thanksgiving for having come through. In Campbell
it was there in the mixed metaphors (blood spilled over the back of
the prince of darkness), the contradictions (a phantom with sharp
ridges to his jaws), the descriptions of violence itself (the forest-
breaker's vessel being crashed down upon by the surf), and so on. In
Livingstone it is altogether subsumed into the form itself: the play is
cut together as if a very tortuous historical narrative had had a pair of
scissors taken to it and been reassembled in a new mosaic. Livingstone
works not sequentially, but by overlaying one scene upon the next, so
that bits of the stories of Thetis, Jason, Neptune, the Titans, and so
on, and for good measure modern man, talking in chorus to a collage
of dance music ranging from boogie-woogie to quella, are impacted
one on another for a common central theme to emerge. The pattern
is, as in the passage quoted, one of betrayal, burial and resurrection,
which in the final analysis is not far in spirit from Camoens's pattern-
ing of human experience.

In a cunning piece of mock-heroic, Livingstone takes up Camoens's
hesitant suggestion that Adamastor might contain the new Adam, as
the name implies. As in *The Tempest,* or as in T.S. Eliot's use of it in
The Waste Land, death by water is not an end, but a transformation;
that is the poetic thinking behind *The Sea my Winding Sheet.* It is
curious to see Camoens being reinterpreted in Eliot's way. So tongue
in cheek that it is almost as if he hardly believes it can be done, Livingstone updates Adamastor in this way:

Narrator: . . . Adamastor is, for a moment, twentieth-century Man; he is in
business somewhere; he is involved in a love affair of unusual intensity and circumstance. (*to Adamastor*) Mere time cannot save
you, Mr Astor, Tell us how it was, Adam.

Adamastor (for this piece only, adult, non-dramatic, modern):
> The empty villa stands back for the road,
> Sad-faced behind cypresses like a bloodhound
> Its nose on the paws of the drive, asleep.
>> A hermetic door folded back
>> For your touch and you entered
>> Gentle-eyed, entranced.
>
> The villa locks an arm on a courtyard
> Of still palm trees; where a stone dolphin leaps
> From the vague square of a playing-card pool,
>> Where oxygen-blue hyacinths
>> Depict a thirteen of hearts. . . .
>
> I found you just before the dawn, face down
> And drenched among the silent lily-pads. . . .
>> (pp. 114–15)

The central motif of all the poems, the collapse of a giant into form-
ing a continent with his face forward in the sea, is replayed here in
terms of a drowning in a suburban pond. Thetis's mother, Doris, comments on the implications of the great splash:

> Herakles counting corpses, near forgot,
> But searching, found and pulped the Giant's head
> As he lay dying, half-submerged by tides,
> This Giant, born with travail for his lot,
> Divided, doomed, was in confusion led.
> Around his shores my lovely Thetis rides.
> With thorn and grassy plain his form is draped.
> The continent of Africa is shaped.
>> (p. 116)

The Adamastor myth seems to have come full circle here, intact, yet
reshaped and reassembled, bit by bit. In Livingstone's view it is still a
myth of spectacular struggle and elemental, riotous action, yet dyna-
mically contained. There can be no doubt that, in redefining his predecessors over a literary continuum of some four centuries, Livingstone
is fully aware of how myth, despite surface changes, remains in essence
constant. His act of exploring the myth in his own terms, with reference to Campbell, Wheatley and Camoens before him, demonstrates
that there is indeed some coherence in the European experience of
Africa in poetry which, although at all times open to outside impulses,
remains essentially unchanged.

Such an attempt to achieve some overview of the shape of Southern
African literature must stand, then, as Table Mountain stands, jutting

brutishly out of the European's first beachhead on the subcontinent. The myth of Adamastor, which expresses the white man's anxieties about Africa, occurs in a pattern that has continuity and development from the origins to the foreground of the literature.

3 The Frontier Myth and the Hottentot Eve

JUST AS THE EUROPEAN CREATION MYTH OF AFRICA formed its Adam, so the European frontier myth within Southern Africa formed its particular Eve. A frontier myth is occasioned by a contest of cultures across a no-man's land, a barrier which shifts backwards and forwards over the same ground. The frontier myth is not complementary to the creation myth; it is consequent upon it. The creation myth serves a naming function and explains potential experience which is never embarked upon, whereas, once Camoens's beach gives way to a European foothold on African soil itself, the identificatory function of myth yields to the need to define experience, a need which the frontier myth can answer. The frontier myth has no clear beginning and no foreseeable end, that is to say, it is not narrative; for the European in Southern Africa it starts as an uneasy xenophobia, continues as a social principle, and in South Africa today could be shown to be so deeply entrenched that all of the literature is to some extent explained in terms of the pressures at work within a continuing frontier mentality.

The frontier myth itself, however, is devised not only to describe and assess a cultural gulf, but to bridge it. The history of 'Europeans' in South Africa cannot be reduced to a view of a mere private war having been continually waged from behind a border, because no matter how much the South African white enclave behind its frontier has resisted impregnation from Africa and from its indigenous peoples, the frontier myth itself, even in its most negative aspects, is an expression of interdependence, of involvement across barriers.

Therefore, for the purposes of this chapter, a peculiar form of this polymorphous myth has been selected, in order to offer us a second view across the literature from its beginnings up to recent times. One observes the myth in the respects in which it is most inclusive, whenever it coheres about its original and most reliable go-between, the Hottentot Eve. Her presence on the frontier lends the myth a quality of potential interchange, since she, as pastoral ambassadress, temptress, mediator and, ultimately, miscegenator, comes to symbolize both the attractions and the intractabilities of inland, that unknown terrain across the ever-shifting frontier.

Unlike the Adamastor myth, the myth of the Hottentot Eve is brought about by long happenstance, by continued exposure, by involving experience. The first European writers had little or no precedent in the matter of describing the Khoisan inhabitants of Africa, yet experience of these so-called Hottentots was common enough for each writer in turn to formulate his own responses to her from scratch. This time the perpetuation of the myth is not occasioned by a conscious literary continuum, for few of the writers to be discussed here are aware of the descriptions of her by their predecessors. The historical contour, rather than the content, of this myth, created largely unconsciously, and which we are tracing in a somewhat artificial way, is its meaning.

Because the Hottentot Eve is a manifestation of the white man's feelings about and interpretation of the interior, she changes her shape and her effect with the differing pressures of the Hottentots as a political factor in the course of South African history. In the sixteenth and seventeenth centuries she frequently has no name; in the eighteenth she acquires several, and achieves media-appeal so successfully that by the next century she has become a business enterprise; in the twentieth century her very identity is transformed.

The early English mariners who called in at the Cape had no Camoens aboard to give their impressions epic shape. But, as every student of English literature knows, the English Renaissance produced a brand of literature which was loosely named 'metaphysical' because, among other qualities, it was characterized by a sense of devouring inclusiveness by which medieval insularity was expanded into the geography of a new globe. When in 1577 Sir Francis Drake set off to circumnavigate the world, he was not only invalidating the medieval cosmographies, but extending the bounds of practical navigation, phasing the old faith of astrology into the new science of astronomy. As one of his crewmen recorded in that Elizabethan prose epic by many hands, Hakluyt's *The Principal Navigations, Voyages, Traffiques and Discoveries of the English Nation* (1600), the fact that he found the Cape of Storms 'a most stately thing, and the fairest cape we saw in the whole circumference of the earth'[1] need not surprise us — epic dread was giving way to a new, demystifying kind of level-headedness, a matter-of-fact confidence which could view the world as containable and controllable.

The first English traveller to land at the Cape and describe it in some detail was Sir Thomas Herbert, a relative of the poet George Herbert. He approached a peninsula which John Donne had already made familiar puns about — it was the 'hopeful promontory'[2] which Donne saw fit to compare to a whale. Herbert's escorts into the bay were, appropriately, whales:

Pengwin Isle [Robben Island] is 6 or 7 leagues from the continent, which when we got asterne we grew becalm'd, land-lockt in a sort, and were sported all the way (till we dropt anchor) by Whales, the Seas Leviathan, who after their manner thundred our welcome into *Aethiopia,* fuzzing or spouting part of the briny ocean in wantonnesse out of their oylie pipes bored by nature atop their prodigious shoulders, like so many floating Ilands concomitating us.[3]

Herbert's arrival on 1 July 1627 was as elegant as any Carolean progress and, like a true diplomat's assistant and rover, he named the first foothills he beheld, Green Point ridge and Signal Hill, King James Mount and King Charles Mount respectively. He reserved the tallest of them (Devil's Peak) for himself — it became Herbert's Mount. In surveying the measurements of Table Mountain, he multiplied its impressiveness by three — from 3 549 feet into 11 853 feet — an exaggeration entirely in line with his general tendency to overelaborate on his overseas experience.

As Norman H. Mackenzie establishes in his 'South African Travel Literature in the Seventeenth Century', Herbert was vastly more interested in style than in exact reporting. His *Some Yeares Travaile* went into four editions (1634, 1638, 1665, 1677), each an extensive revision and inflation of the notes he made on board the vessels which landed him at the Cape on his way to and from his real objective, Persia. Herbert's account of the Cape appears in Raven-Hart's *Before van Riebeeck,*[4] with the variant readings which show Herbert's keen involvement with matching the style of his travelogue to the literary fashions prevalent at each date of printing. Like Camoens, he finds himself subject to pressure as his readers back home desire the weird and wonderful to emerge from the unknown, and he has no scruples about providing thrilling exotica. One watches Drake's admirable plain-talk falling into bombast. In cataloguing the animals in which the Cape 'exuberates', Herbert makes this kind of promissory remark:

Lyons, (which usually Steele Beefe out of the water when Ships are here, fire or a lighted match only scaring them), Dromidaries, Antilopes, Apes, Baboons (venerious ones), Zebrae, Wolves, Foxes, Iackalls, Doggs, Cats, and others; and in birds in Estriches, Vultures, Cranes, and Passeflamingoes, whose feathers (equallizing the birds of Paradise) are rich crimson and pure white so amiably commixed,

that above others it inticed my pains to present it to you, which shall terminate
our curiosity touching the earth, and commence an Anatomy lecture on the most
savage (of all savage) inhabitants. . . .[5]

While his list of fauna leads into bathos, the guarantee is always apparent — there are anomalies to come. Voracious lions we can accept, but
not the 'dromidaries'. Herbert is by no means the last journalist whose
vision of Africa coincides with what he needs to see.

As Mackenzie makes clear, Herbert strives to rise above the mundane
realities of the information available to him in the ship's logs, the East
India Company reports and the commonplace books which are the
useful repositories of accumulating, dry data. His voyage is an equivalent of the young Englishman's Grand Tour, not to Rome, the
fount of culture, but to the remotest corners of the globe from which
flow substitute riches. He organizes his experience more like a ring-
master than an archivist. But since one reads Herbert neither for
natural history nor for anthropological insight — one reads him for
entertainment — his work is a crucial early example of how literary
objectives can condition receptivity. However untrustworthy Herbert
is as a source of fact, he is a reliable source of fantasy. It is particularly in his descriptions of the Hottentots, hyperbolized with each
edition, that one sees the process of documentation taking off on its
own imaginative voyage.

The Hottentot Eve's first substantial recorded appearance in the
literature takes place under these circumstances. She is one of Herbert's most savage of all savages. Commenting on her and her fellow
maidens' nudity, he writes:

. . . their bodies are naked, save that a thong or girdle of raw leather circles them,
a square peece (like the back of a Glove) is fastened to it, serving to cover their
pudenda.   (p. 16)

Anatomical details are stretched into gross libels: the Hottentot wom-
en 'give suck, the Uberous dugg stretched over her naked shoulder'
(p. 18). Sensationalism makes way for Puritan prurience when he
continues:

But I cannot commend their modesty, the women (upon receipt of anything)
returning her gratitude by discovering her shame, a curtesie taught them by
some ill-bred Boore, our men I hope have more civility.   (p. 16)

This image of the bemused Hottentot woman, smiling vertically
from between butterfly-shaped labia at the passing English Euphues,
has a companion image. Herbert adduces another bizarre 'fact': 'Most

of the men are Semi-Eunuchs, one stone being tane away by the
Nurse, either to distinguish them from ordinary men, or that Mistress
Venus allure them not from *Pallas'*(p. 16). Although these specimens
'who differ in nothing from bruit beasts save form' (p. 16) do at least
express ordinary human gratitude, Herbert solemnly informs his
readers that these 'anthropophagi' couple 'without distinction' (p. 17)
and 'as simple as they seeme, they are witty enough in craft, revenge,
and villany' (p. 19). Thus, Herbert concludes, in the Hottentot realm,
'Anarchy confounds order, no Prince of power or policie awing
them' (p. 16).

Herbert's observations may be balanced stylistically; they are not,
however, balanced scientifically. He had not heard the voice of
Othello (c. 1604) deflating such prevailing notions of the picturesque
horrors of so-called savagery. Swift's comment in the margin of his
own copy of Herbert's *Travels* is to the point:

If this book were stript of its impertinence, conceitedness, and tedious digres-
sions, it would be almost worth reading, and would then be two-thirds smaller
than it is.   1720. J. Swift.

The author published a new edition in his older days, with many additions,
upon the whole more insufferable than this.

(Mackenzie, p. 47)

When six years later Swift published *Gulliver's Travels,* he had Gulliver
cite the other Cape recorder, William Dampier, as the type of travel-
writer whose understatement and authority were to be emulated;
Swift knew well enough how to satirize a Herbert.

But Herbert's fictions are of interest here because they are at the
root of the mythopoeic process. Herbert's fantasy presents the Hottentot woman as immodest, anarchic and brutish because each of
those characteristics is schematically opposite to those which might
be called admirable in European concepts of feminine grace and
courtesy. His sense of antithesis makes him declare, for example, that
Hottentot women feel no pain in childbirth. Although Hottentot
males are not, and have never been, monorchs, and their womenfolk
are not in the habit of behaving like grovelling 'hyenas' at the appearance of a washed-up mariner's body, Herbert's contrary devices make
them so. Europe requires the Hottentot Eve and her mate to be seen
to be obscenely repellent. Subduing them is thus not only a matter of
defence, but of duty: 'We found that a dozen Musquets will chase
1000, at every discharge falling down as if thunderstruck' (*Before van
Riebeeck,* p. 121).

Similar preconceptions which control the myth of the Hottentot Eve have been responsible not only for dictating her life style, but her fate. When she first appears as a particular historical individual, she is in the household of Governor Jan van Riebeeck, founder of the Dutch East India Company station at the Cape and keeper of the journal of his settlement's first decade (1652-62), the work which John Purves called the Holinshed of South African literature.[6] Her name was Krotoa, and she 'fell under the benevolent protection of our fort'[7] before her teens. By October 1657 she was gauged to be 15 or 16 years of age, and she was 'by us called Eva, who has been in the service of the Commander's wife from the beginning and is now living here permanently and is beginning to learn to speak Dutch well' (*Journals,* vol. 2, p. 170). As Eva learned to be 'clad in clothes' (vol. 2, p. 4), she outwore her usefulness as a domestic servant. In fact, she became the company's most reliable interpreter in matters of general diplomacy to do with the adjacent Hottentot tribes. A constant theme in Van Riebeeck's *Journals* is the quest for gold and other riches that might lie across the frontier inland, and Eva is more than once charged with the company business of setting off back into the hinterland with samples of gold and seed-pearls which would surely induce larger quantities of the same to emerge from 'Monomatapa' (vol. 3, p. 281). Eva was skilful enough to persuade her own tribesmen, the Saldanhars, to whose chief she was sister-in-law, to hunt elephant in order to produce ivory at the company store (in exchange for livestock and other items, including the inevitable tobacco). Eva learned Portuguese as well, to further her entrepreneurial qualifications.

Eva the intermediary appears to have led a complex double life, for on occasion she dropped her Christian clothing for her former G-string and reverted to her old ways. Yet, as Van Riebeeck and his staff comment: 'She appears to have become already so accustomed to the Dutch diet and way of life that she will never be able to give it up completely' (vol. 3, p. 308). The Dutch way of life, in those founding days, offered her a husband in the form of the Danish explorer, Pieter van Meerhoff, to whom, as a baptized Christian, she was legally married on 5 June 1664. An early visitor to the Cape settlement like William Ten Rhyne found her *'urbana, casta, eloquens'*, that is, a 'civil, modest body, of rational discourse'.[8]

Eva's subsequent history, however, appears to exemplify much of the behaviour pattern that her 'Christian' name implies, for her fall from social acceptability and standing in early settlement society into banishment and a welter of sins committed in the acquisition of knowledge seems in accordance with the inevitable lot of all Eves. Eva van Meerhoff died at the age of approximately 22, by which time she had given birth to at least six children, of which three living and some stillborn were by her husband. Her obituary notes that:

Since [her husband's] death however at Madagascar, she had brought forth as many illegitimate ones, and for the rest, led such an irregular life, that for a long while the desire would have existed of getting rid of her, had it not been for the hope of the conversion [i.e. reconversion] of this brutal aboriginal, which was always still hovering between. Hence in order not to be accused of tolerating her adulterous and debauched life, she had at various times been relegated to Robben Island, where, though she could obtain no drink, she abandoned herself to immorality. Pretended reformation induced the Authorities many times to call her back to the Cape, but as soon as she returned, she, like the dogs, always returned to her own vomit, so that finally she quenched the fire of her sensuality by death, affording a manifest example that nature, however closely and firmly muzzled by imprinted principles, nevertheless at its own time triumphing over all precepts, again rushes back to its inborn qualities. (Schapera, p. 125)

Yet, despite her moral lapses, all the more shocking considering how many she managed to fit into her brief life, Eva was buried within the walls of the castle on the foreshore, a sinner saved.

The facets of Eva's career were observable over a lengthy period. The tenor of Van Riebeeck's relationship with her is one of give-and-take, of broad tolerance, on the grounds of her usefulness, balanced against frustration at her incomprehensible recalcitrance. Eva is at her best in the *Journals* when in open competition with the fort's other Hottentot interpreter, Doman (also called Dominee, on account of his mild appearance). Whereas Eva was merely wily, Doman possessed the opposite side of that virtue — guile, so much so that by June 1658 Van Riebeeck somewhat ruefully noted: 'We sincerely wish that he had never been to Batavia [where he learned his Dutch], or that he may be induced to go back by fair words; there he has learnt how to use fire-arms effectively, and we are now obliged to exercise great care to keep them out of his hands' (vol. 2, p. 289). Eva was at least not dangerous; she was no more than a disappointingly licentious alcoholic who left behind her not only South Africa's first officially mixed population, but a story of legendary proportions. That Eva herself has not become the source of a legend is a comment on how limiting the dominant views of South African history tend to be.

Nevertheless, Eva is indelibly part of that general myth of the Hottentot Eve, about which cling all the attractions and repulsions of attitudes to the inhabitants of the continent itself. Herbert's associations about the figure of the Hottentot Eve are basically still there: the animality, the lubricity and, in short, the very down-to-earth physicalness which, from one point of view (let us say a white point of view) is to be envied and abhorred, and, from another, perhaps, to be regarded as the carnal font of life itself. Herbert's Hottentot women may have given birth without pain, but in Eva we learn that her womanly pain earns her redemption.

As attitudes to so-called primitive people undergo a radical change, the myth of the Hottentot Eve becomes transformed. By the time a traveller like François le Vaillant encounters his version of her in the 1780s, her image has been drastically reformed in the white man's eyes. Le Vaillant, a passionate admirer of Rousseau, exemplifies best what the Hottentot woman had to put up with once the European had acquired a romantic ideology by which every primitive indigenous denizen flourishing outside the parlours of Europe had become an object lesson in true nobility. Le Vaillant treated Southern Africa as every much his personal paradise as Herbert had before him, and was likewise determined to live out *his* preconceptions for an ever more avid audience back home. Indeed, so successful was Le Vaillant's report back on his two South African adventures that it is not with Herbert or Van Riebeeck that the Hottentot enters the European consciousness with any great force; Le Vaillant's records of his two journeys into Africa were destined to become bestsellers on a scale which outdid similar works in an increasingly popular field.

Andreas Sparrman (1782), William Paterson (1789), Carl Peter Thunberg (1795)[9] and others had preceded Le Vaillant overland and were setting the trend towards encyclopedic travel-writing with their tales of the collector of all specimens great and small. Le Vaillant ventures forth with their works in hand, anxious to correlate information and to correct it, where necessary, and in this respect he is doggedly competitive. He is systematically concerned to rewrite Peter Kolbe (1719), for example, and in adopting the Hottentots as his pet cause he makes a point of demonstrating that Kolbe's sensational distortions are intolerable falsehoods. Had Le Vaillant had Herbert on hand as well, he would have been as offended by Herbert's allegations as any other romantic writer, sick with so-called civilization and in quest of a new ideal. Le Vaillant's parting shot — the last words of his five volumes of *Travels* — was that his five years of African fossicking comprised 'the only period of my life truly . . . in which the cowardice of mankind never affected me, in which I could safely defy their injustice, their benefits, and their tyrannic sway'.[10] That emphatic conclusion was reached during Le Vaillant's imprisonment during the Reign of Terror of 1793 in Paris. With the fall of Robespierre, Le Vaillant was released by the Paris Commune after a year of confinement — he had reason to prefer the 'deserts' of Africa.

Le Vaillant in turn was criticized by his successors, other travellers inland like Lady Anne Barnard (1799), John Barrow (1806) and Dr Lichtenstein (1810). But in an age that was slowly replacing preconception with patient observation, Le Vaillant stands out as the man who was not averse to talking frankly and to letting his fervent individuality be the pole of his carefully accumulated experience. As an ornithologist and botanist, Le Vaillant has taken his rightful place in South African studies only recently; but as a romantic philosopher, like the other Rousseauist in the southern hemisphere, J. Bernardin de Saint-Pierre, his contribution to our knowledge of the poetic possibilities of the interior remains unacknowledged. There is a reason: by 1800 it was English and not French culture that was colonizing the Cape, and the English overseas were too pragmatic to fall for Le Vaillant's beguiling notions — while Le Vaillant chose to live with his Eva, the English chose to live against her Doman.

One of LeVaillant's celebrated romantic rhapsodies, occasioned by a shelter near George, runs as follows:

These two apartments, naturally covered with branches and leaves impenetrably thick, afforded me a delightful and cool retreat, when harassed and covered with sweat and dust, after my hunting excursion in the morning, I retired from the heat of the day, and the scorching rays of the sun. When fatigue had sharpened my appetite, what delightful repasts! When sleep stole upon me, what voluptuous and gentle repose! Ye sumptuous grottoes of our financiers! Ye English gardens twenty times changed with the wealth of the citizen! Why do your streams, your cascades, your pretty serpentine walks, your broken bridges, your ruins, your marbles, and all your fine inventions, disgust the taste and fatigue the eye, when we know the verdant and natural bower of [Pampoen-Kraal in the Outeniquas]? [11]

When Cowper Rose, a lieutenant in the Royal Engineers, visited Le Vaillant's refuge later, he reacted as follows:

This was the spot that Le Vaillant described as so dreadful; . . . nor am I surprised that he should have lingered here, for the lover of Nature might roam far ere he could discover such varied beauty in forest, in river, and in mountain. I read his travels when a boy, and I remember then thinking it a delightful book; and even now I can sympathize in his enthusiasm for Nature; and he who has wandered in the boundless forests, beneath the grey-trunked, ancient trees, shaggy with hanging moss, or lifeless, scathed and withered branches, contrasted in their cold decay with the clusters of parasitical plants clinging around them with rich glowing colours, — who has startled the flitting, many-plumaged birds from their lone retreats, — who has felt the awe that darkens the spirit, and yet raises it, amidst the tremendous solitudes of Nature, will feel, when others smile. Thus far, then, I can follow him; but when he sentimentalizes in down-right earnest on a Hottentot girl, and minutely describes all the little palpitations of affection for a capacious-mouthed, small-eyed, snub-nosed, fuzzy-headed female, I will own that he gets beyond me. I have seen many of them — generally drunk, or, according to their own expressive phraseology, 'more drunker than sober', — but I never met with Nerina [*sic*].[12]

Rose, the second-generation English romantic, is straightforward enough about how to take Le Vaillant's brand of fervour. It was so unsuited to the English military temperament that Rose was himself unknowingly fantasizing about Narina — the 'palpitations' of Le Vaillant's courtship of her had been thoroughly watered down in all English translations of Le Vaillant up to Rose's time.

The necessary caution to make here is that we are dealing with three uses of the word 'nature': Herbert's Puritanical assumption that 'nature' is the root of all evil and to be suppressed, Rose's admission that flora and fauna are analogues of a glamorous and 'ravishing' creation from which all of its inhabitants are to be excluded, and Le Vaillant's use of the word — 'Nature' as the display of all of creation's goodness, everything and everyone included.

Le Vaillant's encounter with Narina was not merely a passing fancy; it was integral to his entire attitude to objective reality. If one accepts Le Vaillant, one has to accept his confessions about Narina too, just as one has to accept, for example, the validity of Keats's vision of the indolent Red Indian. Le Vaillant's portrait of Narina is a manifestation of an attitude rather than a sociological observation, an attitude which he was singularly well equipped to enact. There is no ranking within his thoughts; he is as enchanted collecting bugs off the carcass of a decaying whale and storing them in a bottle in the crown of his hat, as he is pacing out the measurements of Table Mountain, or protecting villagers from man-eating lions. Like Darwin, he is as absorbed in classifying finches as he is in measuring out the first giraffe specimen to be brought back to the natural history collections of Europe. His personal equipage may have been extravagant beyond belief, but his style never was. Scrupulousness acquired a quasi-religious significance for him, because it revealed both the glory and the complexity of the creation. To a man like Rose he appeared unforgiveably pleasure-loving: no other traveller could come up with a scene like the one during his second voyage, when in Namaqualand a white trash settler produced a 'sort of violin', and Le Vaillant spent three days 'scraping catgut, while the noisy crew skipped joyously around me' (vol. 2, p. 121). No other traveller's favourite musical instrument was a jew's harp. Nor was he after gold, which he called an 'inhuman metal' (vol. 2, p. 182). He despised fame, unless that fame were to be a source of pleasure to him:

These details may appear trifling to many who will read my work solely to criti-cise it; if indeed they do not criticise without reading it: but to others, perhaps, they will be more useful than those tiresome descriptions, those endless accounts which are frequently given of an insect, or a part of an insect, and the dimensions without number of an animal. To me it is pleasing to begin my journeys again; to think, to feel, and observe all that I have seen, thought, and felt in the course of them; leaving to great geniuses to contemn these trifles: and I take the greater pleasure in them, because they keep me at my own level. Such at least has ever been my plan — Plan did I say? I have none: nor could I ever discover what science there is in writing a book. Mine, however, if it is one, will always have this great advantage in my opinion, that of not being made on purpose; and this is the reason why I would not even think of it. I have so often talked over my travels, that it is not difficult for me to write them: and any one of my friends who has a good memory, and has heard me give an account of them, might easily and in the same manner write them for me. Such are the whole of my literary pretensions. (*New Travels,* vol. 2, pp. 54–5)

Although Le Vaillant's various *Travels* were written by committee, just as his illustrations were engraved by a team on his behalf, he was more concerned with the techniques of literature than he pretends. Apparent artlessness was his way of mirroring the sprawl of nature herself. Just as Bernardin de Saint-Pierre could write his Mauritian idyll, *Paul et Virginie* (1788) with such 'artless' conviction that Marie Antoinette cried over it all the way to the guillotine, so Le Vaillant could make the equivalent statement about the inherent goodness of untarnished man:

. . . the sight of these good savages, who entrusted themselves in my hands, by troops, without fear, and without the least suspicion, always restored me to my natural character, which is that of gentleness, tolerance, and the love of ease; and never were the ideas of conquest and empire, which sometimes spring from ob-stacles and resistance, so soon or so completely driven away as by the mild and frank behaviour of these sons of nature. (vol. 2, pp. 234–5)

It is in these terms that we learn of Narina, the innately genteel savage incarnate. She was a Gonaqua whom Le Vaillant spotted bath-ing on the banks of the Great Fish River, and she was as comely as 'the youngest of the Graces'.

My young savage soon grew accustomed to me [he wrote]. I plied her with endless
questions because I found her answers to be so full of charm. Nothing could equal
the pleasure that I took in watching her. . . . I asked her to stay with me, making
her all sorts of promises; but especially when I talked to her about taking her to
my country, where all the women are queens in charge of powerful hordes of
slaves, far from being tempted by my offer, she turned down that proposal outright, and gave herself up to gestures of impatience and amusement.[13]

None of the commentators on Le Vaillant included in the Library
of Parliament publication (from which the celebrated lewd plate of
the Hottentot Eve was in some printings omitted) scrutinizes this
scene in its played-down English translation, let alone in the original
text. Even a commentator like Jane Meiring[14] dismisses the Narina
affair as if it were of little consequence. But when Le Vaillant interprets it for himself, we see that he has extremely specific attitudes
towards her, attitudes that proliferate in and vitalize French romanticism generally. Baudelaire's first published poem, *A Une Dame Creole*
(1845), which recapitulates the above sentiments, is an example.

When Le Vaillant turns his Hottentot Eve into a literary concept,
he honours her in letting her at least bear a name from her own environment:

I found her name difficult to pronounce, and disagreeable to my ears, and it
meant nothing to my spirit; I baptised her and named her *Narina*, which in Hottentot means *flower;* I begged her to keep this beautiful name that suited her in
a thousand ways; she promised me to carry that name as long as she lived, as a
souvenir of my passing through her country and as evidence of her love; for she
was no stranger to such sentiments, and in her naive and touching language she
confirmed all that was impressive in my first impressions of Nature. Thus, in the
wastes of the African desert [he concludes], I had learned that one didn't have
to be daring to be happy. (p. 369)

The lesson learned from this encounter with a 'savage' belle is one
of playful modesty and, above all, reciprocal humanity. The Le Vaillant who has a reputation for elaborate postures and rodomontade
is not in evidence here — he experienced, and should be seen to have
experienced, confirmation of his conviction that the less civilized the
beings of the planet, the more virtuous they are. Le Vaillant, in his
disillusion with Europe, entered Africa to be educated afresh across
the frontier, and it was the Hottentot Eve herself who taught him a
lesson in fulfilment.

Le Vaillant's version of the myth, however, did not take root in
South African literature. There were good practical reasons why in
the nineteenth century South African white society should need a

different attitude to the frontier. Le Vaillant and all his predecessors had not come to stay. But with the arrival of a permanent white English-speaking population in the two great immigrations (of 1820, and of a generation later with the discovery of diamonds in Kimberley), the notion of the frontier itself became changed. Once a settled agrarian and increasingly industrializing culture came into day to day conflict with the nomadic culture of the Hottentot Eve, what was to Le Vaillant no more than an educational barrier, the poles of which he was delighted to reverse, became a barrier which was a matter of life and death. It is not necessary to expand on the full implications of such a new contest in the history of South Africa here, for the myth tells the essential story sufficiently well.

By 1810 the Hottentot Eve takes on a new kind of flesh and bone in the shape of Saartjie Baartman. She was bought at that date by an English dealer and exported from Caffraria to the funfairs and circuses of Europe as an exhibit, the first of many. Her fortunes were by no means as illustrious as her nickname would suggest. Billed as the 'Hottentot Venus', the diminutive Saartjie rocked the cartoonists of Britain with her steatopygous buttocks not into idle sympathy, but into gross lampoons; in Paris her anomalous figure unchained a series, not of love songs, but of musical grotesqueries *a la Hottentote*.[15] She died not of adulation, but of alcoholic poisoning, on New Year's Eve, 1816. One notes her ultimate debasement: instead of being accorded the right of burial, like an animal she was destined to take her place in the Museum of Man in the Palais du Chaillot where, to this day, her rigid skeleton and her decanted brain stare out at the Eiffel Tower, symbol of the age of steel and of progress which was to disposses her people. Saartjie Baartman is a key ikon in the history of the myth, a statement that it had reached a turning-point at which the Hottentot Eve faced extinction unless she changed her form.

Her story coincides with a turning-point in South African literature, the point at which writers about South Africa blend into becoming South African writers; that is, the point at which writers who used to raid the subcontinent and report back their findings to Europe phased into becoming those who, with a new sense of belonging, wrote for internal use as well. There is no precise watershed point; from, say, 1800 onwards every English-language writer in Southern Africa will, to some extent, begin to exhibit a dual loyalty in his work, for his focus will grow diffused over a European and a Southern African readership. The same Saartjie who was a sideshow curiosity in Europe was also a fact of everyday life on the frontier, so that once the exportable image of her was substituted for a more realistic appraisal of her, one might say that South African writing had begun to grow into its own.

The result of this split in audiences is aptly satirized by an early Cape writer like George Duff in a poem called 'The South African Exhibition':

> Walk in, walk in, we've Lions here!
> And crested Serpent shapes of fear,
> The Hartebeest and Buffalo,
> And Camel-leopard we can shew!
> The Elephant and Tiger too,
> The lordly Eland and the Gnu,
> The Wild Dog and Hyena fell,
> And more than there is room to tell!

(Spoken.) — 'Walk in, walk in, ladies and gentlemen! — the opportunity may never occur again.' 'This way mam, if you please.' 'Lawks ma! look at that horrible looking whats o' name in the glass case?' 'Oh dear! sir, pray what's that?' 'That, marm, is the vunderful pisonus and pestiferous Puff Adder, that springs twenty feet backwards at one spring, and always lights on the tip of his tail, just as you see him there!' 'Hilloa! Sammy, what's all that row about in the other room?' 'Vy, master, its only the Hottentot Wenus a singing one of her out-landish songs all about catch me caccleback!' (Aside.) — 'Sammy, she mustn't have any more gin, she gets too obstropolous!' . . . 'Oh my! well I never! and pray, mister, what is this pretty looking animal like a goat with such fine twisted horns?' 'A very unkimmon specie of animal that, sir, the first specimen ever brought to England alive, its called the Spring Buck, — they crosses the desert in large herds, sometimes a million or two on 'em together . . . only fancy vot a sight, ladies and gentlemen!' . . .[16]

A reaction to such travelling shows of South African curiosities comes from Charles Dickens:

Think of the two men and the two women who have been exhibited about England for some years. Are the majority of persons — who remember the horrid little leader of that party in his festering bundle of hides, with his filth and his antipathy to water, and his straddled legs, and his odious eyes shaded by his brutal hand, and his cry of 'Qu-u-u-u-aaa!' (Bosjesman for something desperately insulting, I have no doubt) — conscious of an affectionate yearning towards that noble savage, or is it idiosyncratic in me to abhor, detest, abominate, and abjure him? I have no reserve on this subject, and will frankly state that, setting aside that stage of the entertainment when he counterfeited the death of some creature he had shot, by laying his head on his hand and shaking his left leg — at which time I think it would have been justifiable homicide to slay him — I have never seen that group sleeping, smoking, and expectorating round their brazier, but I have sincerely desired that something might happen to the charcoal smouldering therein, which would cause the immediate suffocation of the whole of the noble strangers.[17]

Within South Africa attitudes to the Bushman and Hottentot had clearly to take a different tack. Although they were in due course indeed to be smoked out of their hiding-places, and shot down to the penultimate man, that is not to say that they could not play a role in the burgeoning cultural life of the frontier. When Andrew Geddes Bain chose his version of the myth of the Hottentot Eve, he wrote it exclusively for internal consumption. In the creation of Kaatje Kekkelbek as a character he could, like no writer before him, rely entirely on his audience comprehending every nuance of her case. Bain made a choice which, although circumstances have seen to it that it lost him the reputation he deserves as a seminal South African writer, gave him untold strength as an artist. In deciding not to write 'for export', Bain found he no longer needed to describe exteriors, nor to expatiate upon them in an explanatory manner. He had only to let his Hottentot appear and talk for herself in her own terms, terms which he knew would be incomprehensible to an audience 'back home' (and which are incomprehensible to no small number of South Africans to this day). With Bain the Hottentot Eve came home, as it were. Significantly, this new immediacy appeared in drama first. Of the three major literary genres it would seem that drama, being the most perishable of the three (within South Africa few drama scripts have been published), is also the one that demands and can accommodate the scrupulous kind of mimetic language-usage which poetry and fiction, working as they do not with live audiences but through the printed page, tend not to find useful.

In Bain's sketch of Kaatje Kekkelbek, she has so creolized English with her own regional lingo, one which Bain is happy to echo, that she is not only a source of historical linguistic delights, but of a kind of defiantly convincing mirth which is unique to her. Once she talks, our view of her must pass from airy, speculative generalities into the particularities of an authentic and complex situation.

Bain's *Kaatje Kekkelbek, or Life among the Hottentots,*[18] was first performed by the Graham's Town Amateur Company in 1838, and enjoyed great popular approval thereafter. When Kaatje made her debut on stage (playing a jew's harp), she was, as every Afrikaans-speaking pupil knows, also making an early and vital contribution to the origins of the Afrikaans language. Her contribution to South African English was no less substantial, for the linguistic bredie out of

which Bain derives his theatre was concocted with a strong strain of
mutated English as well. Bain's use of this type of mixed language
works two ways. Firstly, it shows that it is drawn from the market-
place where Dutch, English and a host of indigenous tongues interfuse
once they deal with common concerns: land, stock-theft, liquor, food
and justice. It falls well within the threshold of both the average white
settler's and the Hottentot's ken. Secondly, it is reset into a sophisti-
cated and witty English cultural context, so that its literary effect falls
outside Kaatje's ken. Thus Bain's language works with a double impact:
it carries the shock of immediate recognition, while at the same time
Kaatje's apparent slips of the tongue let loose a series of nimble inter-
lingual English and Dutch puns which, although supposedly beyond
her control, have ready meanings for an audience receptive to satirical
double-talk. 'Jan Bull' for 'John Bull', 'Extra Hole' for 'Exeter Hall'
and 'Temper Syety' for 'Temperance Society' are hilariously apt
lapses to make. Although the topical allusions in *Kaatje Kekkelbek*
are so strongly local that it is not easy to reconstruct the impact of
the sketch today, and for us it needs the footnoting it receives in
Lister's text, we may deduce that in its historical context it was a
potent work of art.

Kaatje Kekkelbek was written to be sung to the tune of 'Cawdor
Fair', or of 'How Cruel was the Captain', so that the music hall context for a maid's complaint was established. We may be sure that the
man who played her on stage let her have a 'lekker jol', for *Kaatje
Kekkelbek* is mined with alliterative plosives:

> My name is Kaatje Kekkelbek,
>   I come from Katrivier,
> Daar is van water geen gebrek,
>   But scarce of wine and beer.
>
> (Lister, p. 198)

At the end of each stanza Kaatje interrupts her song to interpolate
commentary; here Bain adapts the received music hall form of the
sketch to this new turn with perfection, as the traditional interpola-
tions serve to underline Kaatje's moniker of Kekkelbek the chatter-
box. Yet her garrulous behaviour is by no means mere babble. Where
Kaatje Kekkelbek scores so powerfully as a character on the South
African stage is in the way she uses it as her hearing-ground, as her
court of appeal. Bain builds into his sketch of her several factors
which show that he means the case about 'Life among the Hottentots'
to be heard with sympathy and in depth. Kaatje is there on the stage

in the first place because Dr John Philip has recently taken two of her fellow Kat River Settlement Hottentots to London to give evidence of their political condition before the Aborigines Committee of the House of Commons. Kaatje's point is that if Jan Tzatzoe and 'Oom Andries' can speak there on her behalf and, under Philip's supervision, at Exeter Hall, she must be allowed to speak for herself back home, and in the broadest, most graphic terms. Basically, although Bain is dealing with types, he wants to point out that politically 'staged' Hottentots are categorizeable, but that once an audience sees through the staging, they can perceive the actual individual human being behind the frum-pery. Given that context of the news from England, Kaatje comes across through all the devious techniques of the theatre as wonderfully actual — in her own voice, unprompted, uncontrollable, unmanipul-ated. Presentation matches theme here, for her whole plea is that she be allowed to keep doing her own thing, that she be allowed to *be*. If Bain has social reform or Hottentot rights in mind, those concerns are tangential to his main interest — letting Kaatje show that she has had to learn to be a great survivor, and that we can accept her predicament through laughter.

Kaatje revolts against her missionary education and the alphabet:

> Myn A B C at Ph'lipes school
>   I learnt a kleine beetje,
> But left it just as great a fool
>   As gekke Tante Meitje.
>   (p. 198)

Her lapses of language are an insult to the integrity of English instruc-tion, and the failure of its three R's in getting across to Kaatje is coun-terbalanced by her triumph at not letting her sense of folly be sup-pressed. For her to be a 'gek' is a trenchant irony, as we know we are to expect the profoundest wisdom from the English stage's most accredited fools.

> But a b, *ab,* and i n, *ine,*
>   I dagt met uncle Plaatje,
> Aint half so good as brandewyn,
>   And vette karbonatje.
>   (p. 199)

Bain was hardly to know that another Plaatje would later have the same sentiments as Kaatje's to express about the pre-settler state of the tribesmen, 'Work was of a perfunctory nature [then], for mother earth yielded her bounties and the maiden soil provided ample sustenance for man and beast.'[19] But here Bain's point is that what Kaatje has learned from her pastoral elders is that meat and drink are more important than book-learning, even though, in the collision between pastoral and agricultural cultures which Kaatje dramatizes, the 'brandewyn' is a killer, and that fat cutlet has to be stolen on the hoof.

Bain's control over the linguistic implications of Kaatje's song is remarkable; he lets Kaatje say 'vette karbonatje' rather than 'greasy chop', not only because the words have an authentic gusto to them. The word 'karbonatje' has a lengthy history in English as well as in Afrikaans. In English it has associations of hacking raw meat to bits and grilling it on coals ('carbonado' = 'braaivleis') and also of greed, as when Autolycus uses the word in connection with barbecuing toads and adders' heads (*The Winter's Tale,* IV, iii, l. 268). Herbert uses 'carbonado' to describe what the Hottentots do to the three-day-old corpse of one of his mariners they supposedly exhume (Mackenzie, p. 45). The associations of hot coals and the reek of fat meat have by this stage in the history of the appearance of the Hottentot in Western literature acquired stock proportions, and no commentator has failed to mention the Hottentot's alleged love of animal fat, preferably stinking. 'Vette karbonatje' is a phrase packed with deeply sensual undertones of gratification. That anything that is carbonized turns black and hellish goes without saying. Bain knew that 'fat chop' would not have anything near the same emotional clout.

The same is true of the wording throughout Kaatje's song. Phrases such as 'a schelm boer het ons gavang' are full of a deep playfulness, particularly since a word like 'skelm' is usually reserved by whites to describe their underlings. That Kaatje can say that a Boer is 'een moer slimme ding!' (p. 119) is an outrageous profanity, particularly when her qualification that the *'Hot'nots en Kaffers het hom slim gemaak!'* drives home the jab. Bain sees that Kaatje's 'slim' one-upmanship puts race relations into the arena of farce, where insult, the licence to indulge in irreverent rudeness, endless nigglings about the downright unfairness of fate, and getting away with the deed are delightfully pleasing. Kaatje insinuates that the reason the Boers have quit the Cape on that historical saga, the Great Trek, nowadays myth enough ('die moervreter zeg dat hy neit meer kan klaar kom met de Engelse Gorment!' (p. 199)), is that all the fun has gone out of the chaotic and immoral old frontier days. The farce expresses her commitment to disorder.

But Kaatje's boldest irreverence is reserved for the killjoy English with their policies of border control, passes and forced convict labour. Once convicted for theft, she translates for us:

'Six months hard work,' which means in Dutch,
  'Zes maanden lekker leven!'

(p. 200)

Her scorn for the sentencing judge, whose wig she compares to the mop the English 'die vloer mee schoon maak' (p. 200), cloaks a serio-comic but very real complaint. She has to deflate the Englishman's awe for all judges so that the process of law and order, with all its lengthy 'speetses', the same process which usurps her sway over the land, stands opposed.

That Kaatje is neither terror-struck nor even reformed by prison is one of those rich ironies, but the fact that she regards prison as one of the few ways left open to her to get free board and lodging is tragic. Bain sees that the old Hottentot way of life of vagrancy and free food-gathering is irrepressible, even within the walls of an English jail. But the truth is that, although Kaatje puts a bold face on her prison experiences, she emerges severely melancholic. That Kaatje could use such a word at all is profoundly moving: 'melancholy' one associates with the gravest romantic dejection, with a Coleridge or a Keats who writes his way out of it in deeply 'blue' stanzas. Kaatje's response to the 'melancholies' is to drown them in liquor, to conquer them, not in the noble metres of English romantic verse, as Pringle does in a poem like 'Afar in the Desert', but in the frenzied jingle that Bain's piece is.

Kaatje's last gesture, the one that presumably brought the house down, was to turn her notorious backside on the audience — a gross piece of buffoonery, appropriate to a bill of farcical plays. When Bain has Kaatje make this outrageous move, he means it both to elicit a belly-laugh and to express an earthy protest. Kaatje is really very disillusioned with the way she is treated by frontier society, and when she exits direct to the 'Gov'neur' she means her last exclamation: '. . . myn right wil ik hebbe!' (p. 202). The meaning she gives the word 'right' is not the same as 'regte.'

That little Kat, the personification of her dwindling people, as her name suggests, was a memorable shrew whom the English had yet to tame. Her story arises from a close-contact situation; from 1837 Bain engineered the Queen's Highway on the frontier from Fort Beaufort to Post Retief, through the 'Hottentot Arcadia' of the Kat River Settlement, where he also unearthed the rocky fossil-remains of the

Adamastor-like jaw of *Pareiasaurus serridens,* or the Blinkwater Monster, the first prehistoric creature to abandon crawling on all fours for walking upright. With Kaatje we are already a long way from Pringle's 'brown Dinah', who remains a shadowy victim off-stage, or from the same poet's Hottentot shepherd, who is seen from a distance only:

> Mild, melancholy, and sedate, he stands,
> Tending another's flock upon the fields . . . [20]

— the posing, dispossessed melancholic, no less.

If one considers Southern African English literature to be an addendum to English literature, one has to nominate Pringle as the founding father, but if one chooses to view Southern African English literature as a part of a multilingual African literature, one has to hold up Andrew Geddes Bain as a more appropriate transitional figure. In his hands Le Vaillant's Narina turns into a besotted wench before our eyes; the noble savage turns from a pensive tribal dignitary into a benighted, human problem in need of human answers.

The deeper qualities of the myth of the Hottentot Eve remain intact here: Kaatje Kekkelbek is still the personification of a kind of femininity, a kind of earthiness which supposedly is endemic to prelapsarian Africa, and her Eve-like sensuality continues to suggest a powerful fecundity that is still part of the fascination the outside observer has for her. That she should now assume a blatantly proletarian comic mask is not only an example of Bain finding his precedents within the Elizabethan dramatic tradition, but an index of the complexity of his view of Eastern Province frontier society: Kaatje wants not only Hottentot rights, but her rights as an individual woman.

Of all the characteristics which Bain assigns to her, the one that is most accusatory is her disgust at the way her spells in prison cut her off from her white lover. No sooner is she out of jail than:

> Next morn dy put me in blackhole,
> For one Rixdollar stealing,
> And knocking down a vrouw dat had
> Met myn sweet heart some dealing.
>
> (p. 201)

She claims that she has 'as much right to steal and fight' (p. 201) as anyone else, but that the greatest injustice of all (greater than merely disturbing the peace) is to lock a woman in the black hole when a 'teef' (i.e. a white bitch) has stolen her man. To Bain the Hottentot Eve is no longer a sub-human who couples indiscriminately; she is beginning to look very much like, and have the feelings of, a monogamous bourgeoise.

It is in that role that she appears in a work that studies her in terms of twentieth-century urban society, Stephen Black's *Love and the Hyphen*. The unpublished typescript of this full-length play is stored in the Johannesburg Public Library, together with much other unpublished Black material. Black called himself the father of South African drama, but he knew he had been beaten to it with an outspoken coloured leading lady by Bain. Like Bain's, his motives for animating the myth of the Hottentot Eve were anything but purely literary — he conceived of her as good entertainment.

Her name, this time, is Sophie September, and her motto is: 'I can be obstroperlous because I'm under der Junion Jack in der Metropolis of der Junion' (Act III, p. 19). Black is not over-careful about dates; the Sophie speaking here is dated 1908, the year that *Love and the Hyphen* was first produced at the vaudeville Tivoli Theatre in Cape Town. The complete Ms. of the play describes it as a 'Stage Skit on Cape Social Conditions'. In 1928 Black rewrote and revised it, with an additional 'preface', and a 'postscript' in which his characters reappear 'twenty years later'. Perhaps the fact that the play is not published is due to Black's own view of a script: it was a text to be improvised around for hundreds of performances in the hands of his own touring company (from 1908 to 1912, and again on its revival in 1928). Black the practical showman wrote for changing tastes in mobile theatre conditions, not for enduring literary glory, and South African publishing has seen to it that *Love and the Hyphen* has gone the way of all English satirical theatre — into bankruptcy and oblivion.

Love and the Hyphen was Black's first play. Like so much work after the turn of the century, it came about thanks to a kind word from Rudyard Kipling. He advised the young newspaper reporter to 'go on writing "specials" of the coloured people as you are doing. He told me the life of these folks was an undercurrent of Cape Town which I had knowledge of, a vein to be worked. Peg out your claim . . . get a hearing locally; the rest will come,' said Kipling.[21] He added, according to Black, that South African literature would 'come of itself . . . no use trying to force it. But your country is 300 years old; the time has come to begin. . . . South Africans boast so of their country; but who has described it? Not they. I want them to do so.'

Like Bain's sketch, Black's skit is of great socio-historical interest; for that reason alone it does not deserve obscurity. But it also has a claim to being a watershed point in the literature, because Black chose to go local professionally when South African English theatre had chosen to, and still chooses to, remain a diluted imitation of the international theatre scene. Black's own initial problems were those which are still operative in a culture that lives parasitically off imported models rather than from within itself. In writing about his revival of *Love and the Hyphen,* Black commented:

We scoured South Africa for people who knew something about South African characters but our few actors and actresses had been painstakingly learning to impersonate costers, lords, old English solicitors, stage Frenchmen, Irish begorrabhoys and Scottish comedians, so that none of them could give the faintest idea of a Cape boy, a Boer jong or a Dutch tante.[22]

The (white) actress who played Sophie evidently managed to construct her role successfully from kitchen sources, if one is to judge from the popular reception of the play, just as Black himself built Sophie out of raw neighbourhood experience, specifically that of the Cape Town magistrates courts.

'The original *Love and the Hyphen* was clean fun and kindly satire,' wrote the anonymous reviewer of *The Cape* (1 February 1929). 'Mr Black was out to make you laugh and he did that and no more. Now, by way perhaps of bringing it "up to date", he has interspersed the dialogue with doubtful witticisms and a broad type of humour which certainly wouldn't have been tolerated in the original Lady Mushroom's day. . . . The preface and epilogue which are new are, I regret to say, an error in judgment and good taste. In a country like this with its eternal problem of black and white, the incidents of the epilogue are a pity. To make fun before an audience of mixed races of the problem of the illicit mixing of the races is unwise and unnecessary.' So much for the stock Philistine response of a culture which prizes trivial amusement above literary engagement, and propriety above enlargement of insight.

Black takes precisely those social attitudes as his target in *Love and the Hyphen.* The hyphen in question is the 'trait d'union' of the well-to-do, the double-barrelled surname. When in Act II, Frikkie January the gardener, Sophie's coloured boyfriend, asks her what this much-prized, unionizing hypen could be, her opinion is sufficiently flattening: 'No, I don't know, but it's got three feathers like der Prince of Wales and I tink it must be a kind of volstruis' (p. 14).

The white characters who grace Cape society in Black's play derive from Sheridan by way of Oscar Wilde; the play is regular comedy of manners. Captain Hay-Whotte (the Aide-de-camp to His Excellency and a 'humbug'), Hugh Spavin-Glanders and the nubile Gwendoline are all repeats of familiar nineteenth-century drawing-room comedy roles, gone somewhat insipid in their overpoweringly lush colonial setting. Black's potshots are predictable, and delectable:

Lady Mushroom: Alice has colic or cholera or something. That's the worst of these English maids — they will get colic in the hot weather. We shall have to use salted servants as they use salted horses up-country. (p. 17)

Lynda: Have you been Home before?
Gerald van Kalabas: Well not exactly Home, but I once went with the football team to Robben Island. (also p. 17)

But Black's theme of social-climbing and snobbery is played through that underside of the colonial society, the 'non-white' servants' quarters, as well, so that their snobberies and ambitions compare and contrast with telling effect. For Black the frontier has become the class barrier between masters and their servants.

Sophie (to Frikkie): Talk proper language, you black nigger. [Our daughter's] no bastard because she was born after I married you. (p. 76)

Sophie's daughter is in fact fathered by Corporal Smith, a variation on Kipling's Tommy Atkins. Sophie has always held that: 'All the ladies is med after der regiment. I will have my corporal or kill me with poison seepdip' (p. 32). Sophie's daughter, Cornelia Violet Smith, escapes the domestic class into becoming a cashier in a tickey bazaar. And Frikkie, watching his 'daughter' try for white, is unable to complain. Van Kalabas, the 'Boer jong' of the play, has his own brand of social climbing, too; when he returns to the scene of his youthful gaucheries in the postscript of the play, now a South African diplomat in service in the United States, his delightful conclusion is: 'Marcus Garvey says "Africa for the Africans", but I say "America for the Afrikaners",' and off he goes, sold out to the Jazz Age and its flappers.

Black's theme is a Shavian one: what happens when economic necessity meets moral pretension? In Black's eyes, Sophie is only one of many who cannot afford the luxury of a moral existence. Her greatest moment of pretension is her appearance in Act III at the Elite Tea Gardens (revised into the Jazz Tea Rooms), decked out in a feather boa (borrowed from her madam) and twirling a parasol, demanding she be served tea since she has the money saved up.

Gwendoline de Gadde, trembling at the sight of a coloured on the premises, staring social ruin in the face, appeals to Sophie: 'It's me you're hurting, Sophie. You don't want to spoil my trade?' To which Sophie replies: 'I don't care what I spoil, so long as I get my own way' (p. 39).

Sophie's own way in the end is a luxury (second class) taxi which backs onto the stage in the postscript, bearing her off complete with her twenty years' accumulation of Western possessions, steam radio included. In exchange for a little whoring, a little discreet theft, and a lot of nerve, she has acquired enough material wealth and two educated 'white' kids to retire on. Frikkie's bitter curtain line to the play, as he sees his liberated woman drive into the future, is: 'You can all go to hell!'

Black's comedy is sharp and skilful. His metaphor throughout the play is that the struggle for rank and repute is like an all-round attack of 'scarlet fever'. Sophie understands scarlet fever better than anyone else on stage, and she defines it as a lust for military uniforms. Her frankness, like Kaatje's, is disarming. When Frikkie querulously challenges her on her ambitions with the observation that: 'All coloured girls is med after khakis', her reply is blatantly outspoken, although her attitude is no different from Lady Mushroom's:

Sophie: Yes, before I go to bed every night I pray God must make me a good
girl en give me er Tommie every time. (p. 14)

That God granted her desire takes us out of the bounds of literature into demography; that Eva's descendants number over a million in an official South African racial group all of their own is a matter for the census-taker. But that Black saw miscegenation symbolically as part of a larger upwardly-mobile social drive, and let his loud-mouthed wench spell it out, is not without interest in the study of Southern African literature. Black and Shaw would have agreed with one another: let the colours run, let the frontier dissolve.[23]

The comedy writer in the fluid early 1900s could afford to let his coloured heroine talk for herself. Perceval Gibbon's *Souls in Bondage* (1904) — the first published example of a 'try for white' theme in fiction in South Africa — is explicit in the same way. But for some writers after Union who chose to manipulate the myth of the social frontier, they found it so entrenched as a bulwark of law and order against chaos that they could hardly let the Hottentot Eve occupy centre stage at all, and as a result her comic function becomes diverted into the terms of the most ineluctable tragedy. By 1924 we have Sarah Gertrude Millin's *God's Step-children*, which Stephen Black might well have written his 1928 postscript specifically to refute. After Schreiner's *The Story of an African Farm*, it is the work which has enjoyed the greatest acclaim inside and outside South Africa. In the United States alone, *God's Step-children* went into ten editions. It made Sarah Gertrude Millin's name so convincingly that it was not until 1948, with Paton's *Cry, the Beloved Country*, that its hold on the South African imagination was challenged.

In *God's Step-children* Millin describes the Hottentot seductress as she embarks on a sin of our fathers, and emphasizes that her act will reverberate through anything up to a century of misery and unrelieved suffering. She is seen in terms which make Herbert's distaste seem quite acceptable. That Millin tries to build her own horror of mixed blood into tragic material is a fact; but it is also a fact that she had no tragic feeling for her characters. *God's Step-children*, as Snyman remarks with faint surprise, was, amongst other things, 'used in Germany as a racial novel in the campaign against the Jews',[24] which, considering Millin's own Jewish origins, is an irony. The reason for Millin's failure to achieve the effect of tragedy is simple: *God's Step-children* purports to be about the pain and distress caused by discrimination, but its actual content maintains that discrimination is necessary and desirable. In Millin's view of the racial mix, any man who is driven by his baser instincts to cohabit with a 'non-white' sows a curse that taints all of history. Millin cannot accept that mixing of bloods is irreversible; she stews and simmers over it, sensitizing the reader into getting to know the outward symptoms which are to be avoided — frizzy hair, brown half-moons on the toenails, humiliated eyes that may see far, but which contain no beauty, only shame. There is no barrack-room vigour here, only compounding degeneracy and disgrace.

In her fictional ancestor of the South African colour curse, the Rev. Andrew Flood in Canaan, she sees:

He was a tall, bony man, with hollow blue eyes, wistful and yet fervent, his teeth projected slightly, so that he had difficulty in closing his mouth; and his chin, strained with the effort of assisting his lips to meet, was pricked with little holes. The bones of his long face were prominent, and they seemed to move visibly when he became agitated, as happened very often. His skin was naturally pale, but it was almost always flushed with ardour ...[25]

He is motivated by a 'tremendous sermon preached about the essential equality of all human beings, whatever their colour, in the eyes of the Creator', to which Millin's retort is that: 'It was, throughout Britain, the creed of the moment' (p. 4). That it should not have been the

creed of her South Africa of 1820 to 1920, the period covered by the
novel, is Millin's purpose to demonstrate. The Rev. Andrew Flood
lapses into Hottentot arms, not because Millin can conceive of a Hottentot as being appealing to him, or a suitable mate for him, but
because he is incapable of inspiring a white woman to marry him.
Only such a debased specimen would 'sow seeds of disaster in a clean
land', as Snyman puts it (p. 59). Again, when Flood's grand-daughter
marries a man who 'snapped his fingers at the sanctities of race'
(p. 189), Millin means that we must watch for another wave of woe.
She, Elmira, has a painful time at her convent school, but gets away
with it for a while as being 'Spanish'. Her dilemma is expressed as
follows by one of Elmira's schoolmates:

. . . whatever they are, they aren't pure, [my father] says. I heard him tell mother
that he couldn't stand mongrels. He says they've got the bad of both sides. What
would you do if you found out you had coloured blood in you, Elmira, with that
dark skin and all? I'd drown myself or something, wouldn't you? (p. 123)

The view that a so-called coloured automatically inherits the worst of
both progenitors, a view to which Millin and her faithful commentator,
Snyman, both subscribe, was a sufficiently commonly held prejudice
for it to go untested. But when Elmira is asked not to return to the
convent (together with three Jewish girls), Millin does not have her
suicide; she has her live on to face a fate worse than death. 'And life
goes on' is Millin's favourite and ominous refrain.

But what is truly distorted in Millin's vision, something that assumes
tragic proportions when it comes to the matter of making a national
literature, is that her dogma of separateness can allow no insight beyond the frontier that encloses its own white viewpoint. When she
does depict the Hottentot bastard view of things in this novel, it is
from a distance only and it is done, not with understanding or with
irony, but with contempt. Here we have Flood's daughter, Deborah,
cradling the baby Elmira:

And as she sang the little tune she saw again the river at Canaan — they called it
the Vaal now; and she saw her father, the Rev. Andrew Flood, wandering around
like an ejected spirit, with his lost-looking blue eyes and his lips which would not
close over his big teeth . . . and she saw the Hottentots of Canaan dancing under
the naked moon. . . . She herself had not participated in their lunar festivals, but
she had gone with the other Hottentot children dancing down to the river to the
sounds of their singing, a line of little girls with vessels on their heads for water,
swaying their hips to the rhythm of the song they were making — some little
tune or other endlessly repeated — their voices ringing out loud and wild on the

high notes. . . .

But these things were past for her and hers. How different life was these days;
how one tried to be just like the white people . . . how one was *getting* white.
(pp. 108–9)

What Millin means to convey here is a half-Hottentot's regret at the
loss of the pastoral days, and we must grant that she wants also to
convey the woman's own contempt for her own past and the details
which would give away the ancestral origins of the new grandchild.
Millin shows Deborah gripped in the process of consciously trading
her heredity for whiteness, her step-relationship for being a true
child of God. It is a moot point as to whether the contempt here is
functional within the novel or imposed by Millin's own views on the
issue: it would be possible for Deborah to come to think of Hottentot
song as endlessly monotonous, and full of shrieks, but we also know
from earlier in the novel that Millin herself has no time for undressed
'lunar festivals'. Yet Millin writes better than she knows; that a coloured could be taught that white perceptions are exclusive and unattainable, but that she ought to aspire to them nevertheless, is an
historical truth (see Adam Small's *Kanna Hy Kô Hystoe*). But that a
coloured should not be allowed to have her own perceptions of her
own father (Flood is seen identically by Millin and by his daughter)
is another matter. Millin's fiction is so in the grip of her own limiting
imagination, from which it gathers its obsessive repetitions and driving
rhetoric, that, for all its persuasive power, it ends up merely as an
illustration of separatist doctrine.

Millin's patron, Field-Marshal the Right Honourable J.C. Smuts,
shows that she was by no means alone in her responses to the coloured
(as opposed to colour) problem. In his foreword to *King of the Bastards*,[26] another Millin saga, this time about the first white Transvaler,
Coenraad Buys, he typifies what one might call the British policy view
of the subject that held sway roughly from Union in 1910 to 1948.
According to Smuts, we can see in *King of the Bastards* 'the formative
forces which have shaped this history of ours. The tragedy of colour
which in South Africa stands revealed for all to see it [*sic*], in wonder
and awe, but not in despair' (p. v). The story of Buys 'and his harem
of native women [is a] South African horror'. Smuts's description of
the pre-Trek days of the Mfecane as presented by Millin is:

The powerful black chiefs pass with their tribes and their armies and their crimes
through these pages in a vast panorama of human suffering and destruction. . . .
Millions of natives — men, women and children — lost their lives in that time of

trouble in which central and eastern South Africa were largely reduced to a wilderness before the White rule imposed order on the scene. (p. iv)

To categorize characters like Buys who 'bestrode the stage', Smuts has a theory of tragedy derived from A.C. Bradley: 'What he might have been and achieved, under a better star! But there was a twist in him, as there sometimes is in great men. And so in the end all went wrong in irretrievable disaster, and this great personal force was wasted and lost in the frustration and desolation through which he moved. . . . His story reads like Shakespearian tragedy moving towards inevitable doom' (p. vii).

Smuts does not say it outright, but he means that Buys's 'tragic flaw' is his taste for black flesh. Literary interpretation along these lines is as unfair to Bradley and Shakespeare as it would be to assume that Desdemona had to die merely because she married a black man. Millin and Smuts see destiny in terms of the colour frontier, while the real problem lies in quite another direction — it is racism. By the time Millin holds sway, Bain and Black are suppressed, or at least forgotten, which amounts to the same thing; the myth of the colour frontier has so displaced the Hottentot Eve that she has passed beyond white consideration. Only the curlicues of her crissy hair (which she wears 'after the *African* mode', as Herbert noted [*Before van Riebeeck*, p. 119]) and the parings of her horny toenails are on exhibition. She is denied all her functions as the literature moves into accepting white exclusivity and apartheid beliefs.

But our lady of the interior does make one further convincing appearance in the literature, and her return performance makes additional sense in the light of all the above. Her last role to date is as the heroine of Athol Fugard's play, *Boesman and Lena.* The work was premiered in Kaatje Kekkelbek's old stamping ground, Grahamstown, in July 1969, during a conference at Rhodes University on 'South African Writing in English'. Although Fugard's plays of the 'sixties, of which *Boesman and Lena* is the third of the Port Elizabeth trilogy, have almost always been in production in South Africa (though not always to the unsegregated audiences Black enjoyed) and Fugard's band of actors has received a general following, his work has spurred little detailed criticism. With the exception of some of the record-breaking black township dramas of the 'sixties and 'seventies, *Boesman and Lena* on stage and on film has been seen by more South African audiences than any other South African play. It has travelled extensively outside South Africa as well, which is to some extent surprising if one considers Fugard's uncompromising way of writing a South African drama.

The language of *Boesman and Lena* is intensely regional, slangy, abrupt and even obscenely 'Hotnot' at times, designed to have visceral rather than intellectual impact. As stage language, however, it transcends the merely regional; whatever is italicized in the various printed texts of *Boesman and Lena* on grounds of its 'foreignness' to standard English is not italicized in the mouths of actors and actresses. Fugard's new language is the vocabulary of outcasts making themselves heard and felt from beyond the pale. The language experience is as shocking and as powerful in its effect as Kaatje's must have been one hundred and thirty years before.

Yet, although Kaatje and Lena share striking areas of common ground, *Boesman and Lena* is not an ephemeral variety turn; it is part of a consistent dramatist's lengthy process of finding the theatrical language appropriate to his on-going theme: man in isolation, man in dread. Lena the coloured woman is a variation on a very characteristic Fugard figure: the woman in search of inner fulfilment.

In mounting coloured characters on the stage in familiar European theatrical terms, Fugard is implicitly saying that 'the problem' is not unique to South Africa, nor can it be shrugged aside as some mighty tragic error, as Smuts would do in the passages quoted. Through the theatricality Fugard makes the audience watch the 'colour problem' talking, and his play stresses that Boesman and Lena's problems, although they are induced by specifically South African official brutalities, are — to say the very least of them — once again well within the frontiers of an audience's understanding. His coloured characters are as full of comprehensible pain and suffering, and anguish — his dominant theme — as any of his white characters. As an artist, Fugard's imagination knows no reason why they should be different. Thus, the feeling that his play conveys, through actors and actresses (generally) in blackface, through literary allusion to well-known sources, through a stripped, low-key intensity, is in South Africa one of the profoundest statements of his time.

To isolate, then, aspects of *Boesman and Lena* that are characteristically 'Hotnot' is to do the play a disservice, if the 'Hotnots' are really working as representatives of universal models. Nevertheless, since the precedents are so obvious, and since the purpose here is to determine whether or not a myth-tracking critical approach can assist in achieving a sense of the shape of Southern African literature, it might be worth examining Fugard's Lena, out of the context of the play, in

terms of this supposedly coherent frontier myth of the Hottentot
Eve. The crucial test here is one of coincidence against some greater
apprehensible pattern. From internal evidence it is safe to assume
that Fugard does not know *God's Step-children,* just as Millin did not
know Black's Sophie; and if Black knew his Bain, the chain of influences does not follow on backwards all the way to our original source,
Herbert, for it is an alarming characteristic of the criticism of Southern
African literature that every work is invariably hailed as a 'first' even
if it is, in fact, a case of old hat with new feathers. If the changing
attitudes to the Hottentot Eve indeed form a pattern, it is also safe to
assume that no writer mentioned here has been consciously aware of
his part in its formation. The myth has functioned in spite of, not
because of, writers.

So we have Lena's story. In the play she is the more vocal than her
man: all the writers here reach consensus on this point; Eva earned
her living with her tongue (interpreter); Le Vaillant enjoyed Narina's
mellifluous naivety; Kaatje Kekkelbek was an inveterate cackler;
Sophie had more verbal staying-power than anyone else in the Imperial high noon; Elmira, although she was not given room to talk in the
novel, is conceived of as part of a society of chronic chanters and
dancers; and Lena is — well, shrill. She is a figure who must be heard
(rather than watched or felt). What she says is always brazen, or
earthy, or robust, or seductive, certainly outspoken; Lena's consistent
demand of Boesman is that he come out with it, that he *say it.* She is
acquisitive: Le Vaillant's only scruple about Narina was that she
helped herself to every trinket he had, and here Lena is the one who
could have been placated by saving the junk of their flattened pondok:
'Might be whiteman's rubbish, but I can still use it'[27] is her attitude.
She is invariably grasping after white man's throw-aways, subdued
with valueless objects which have useful functions for her, not ex-
cluding beautification. She also has social ambitions which her counterpart rejects; her aggression is caused by not being able to join the
company of the invaders, whereas her mate remains hostile and intractable (the Eva–Doman, Sophie–Frikkie contrast). Lena's impulse
towards achieving a place within the master's society is so strong that
on the outset of their trek she is tempted to drop out in favour of
settling for domestic service, and when Boesman imposes the isolation
of their mudflats existence on her, she opts for the Outa's company,
which is lower than a 'brak's' company, rather than be a lone outsider.

Yet the Hottentot Eve yearns for her former unfallen condition, as
Lena yearns for her days of lunar dancing at Coegakop and the days

when she could cradle Boesman in song. Her presence is associated with narcotics: she drinks wildly and smokes tobacco, two habits which at various times have placed her beyond the realm of acceptable white society; she'll trade in her natural dagga-smoking habits for liquor that stupefies her all the quicker. Brandy and syphilis and cross-culturation will get her in the end, and her man will die like the animal he is thought to be. Lena forgoes her share of Boesman's 'dop' on this evening as she knows it is a fatal weakness in her that conquers her willpower and forces an easy submission. The self-assertion of the Hottentot Eve in the writer's imagination can be forestalled temporarily, but never gainsaid.

The common characteristics of the Hottentot Eve throughout the gallery are overwhelmingly in favour of our having to see her as an archetype that recurs through the centuries, one which, despite superficial variations conditioned by the writer's point of view within his own period, continues intact. Above all, her leading characteristic — that of seductress or love goddess, rather than mere household woman — is the one which remains dominant, perplexing and alluring, to be confronted and to be overwhelmed. She is not a case of Eve the innocent, but of Eve always about to fall.

In Fugard's reworking of the myth what is truly remarkable is his not being aware of the historical process behind his play. He is hardly interested in Lena's being a Hotnot-white offshoot at all. The only physical labelling she is given is that she wears 'one of those sad dresses that reduce the body to an angular, gaunt cipher of poverty' (p. 167). There is a reference in the stage directions to the straightness of her neck when carrying a burden on her head. She acquires 'brown' attributes, associated as she is with the brown mud between her toes and the burnt-out veld landscape around her, to be sure. But Boesman is the one who has trouble classifying himself racially, who is worried about rating himself above a cave-dweller (Herbert's Troglodite) and above the intruding 'kaffer' in status. In his quest for freedom he desires to be able to stand upright, and it is his failure to discover how to achieve this which generates his violent aggression. Yet Fugard does not see Lena's predicament in racial terms at all: her dilemma is, as has been said, a social rather than a political one. Her 'brownness' is incidental to her quandary; the play is ultimately more about the strains of the marriage bond between her and her husband than the colour problem which aggravates it.

Lena's one moment of absolute truth happens to be one that we would readily associate with the past versions of the Hottentot Eve.

It comes with Lena's outburst which is beyond speech and beyond 'white' means of expression. It is worked out in the second act as an affirmation of faith in the power to keep existing. In her monologue to the dummy Outa, she says:

It's a hard mother to us. So we dance hard. Let it feel us. Clap with me.
   (Lena is now on her legs. Still clapping she starts to dance. In the course of it Boesman's head appears in the opening to the shelter. He watches her.)
   (Speaking as she makes the first heavy steps.)
   So for Korsten. *So* for the walk. *So* for Swartkops. *This* time. *Next* time. *Last* time.
   (Singing.)

> Korsten had its empties
> Swartkops got its bait
> Lena's got her bruises
> Cause Lena's a *Hotnot meid.*
>
> Kleinskool got prickly pears
> Missionvale's got salt
> Lena's got a Boesman
> So it's always Lena's fault.
>
> Coegakop is far away
> Redhouse up the river
> Lena's in the mud again
> *Outa's* sitting with her.

(p. 208)

This is her moment of release, her ritual dance which transcends her earthly imprisonment, a moment out of time. One slips back into remembering the account written by Alvaro Velho of Da Gama's Saturday afternoon bash with the coastal dwellers of Mossel Bay, already considered in Camoens's version:

... there arrived about two hundred blacks, large and small, bringing with them about twelve cattle, oxen and cows, and four or five sheep; and when we saw them we went ashore at once. And they at once began to play on four or five flutes, and some of them played high and others played low, harmonising together very well for blacks from whom music is not to be expected; and they danced like blacks. The Commander ordered the trumpets to be played, and we in the boats danced, and so did the Commander when he again came to us. When this festivity was ended we went ashore where we had been before, and there we bartered a black ox for three bracelets ... (*Before van Riebeeck*, pp. 5-6)

— the first account in the literature of Dionysus overtaking Apollo. Lena's lyric acquires rhythm from her own bodily movements, and the form of her song generates itself as she impels it along. Her im-

provisation falling into metre, with its satisfying locking into place
with rhyme, is half nonsense poem, half sly innuendo. But during this
performance of hers the absolutely open joy that bursts through speaks
as an affirmation of her own inner resistance, her small, powerless but
inextinguishable being in a hostile universe.

Significantly, it precipitates Boesman's break-through into self-
knowledge. As she completes her routine, the stage direction is: *She
stops, breathing heavily, then wipes her forehead with her hand and
licks one of her fingers.* Then she says:

Sweat! You see, *Outa*, sweat. Sit close now, I'm warm. You feel me? (p. 209)

And her glow of inner life transfuses her, for a while. Her pain becomes bearable, her burden tolerable. She has shown us how she
liberates herself orgiastically.

But part of the strength of Fugard's portrait of Lena the beach-
comber is in the way he creates her *against* the drift of our preconceptions about the Hottentot Eve. The central irony of *Boesman and
Lena* is that Lena the earth mother, the life-giving figure, whom we
feel should be endlessly fertile, is not. Lena is so physically battered
and impoverished that her children have been stillborn. One never
really worried too much about the fate of the Hottentot Eve, because
before Fugard she had always been able to procreate so successfully
that if she herself was subjected to an humiliating and degrading life,
one always felt that her offspring would have the chance to make it
one day — a bitter observation, but a true one. Yet Lena's history has
a different result.

It's a long story [she tells the dying black man]. One, *Outa*, that lived. For six
months. The others were born dead. (*Pause.*) That all? *Ja.* Only a few words I
know, but a long story if you lived it. (p. 193)

Later Boesman, while articulating his own sense of impotence,
describes it:

Sies wêreld!
   All there is to say. That's our word. After that our life is dumb. Like your
moer. All that came out of it was silence. There should have been noise. You
pushed out silence. And Boesman buried it. Took the spade the next morning
and pushed our hope back into the dirt. Deep holes! When I filled them up I said
it again: *Sies.* One day your turn. One day mine. Two more holes somewhere.
The earth will get *naar* when they push us in. And then it's finished. The end of
Boesman and Lena. (p. 212)

Lena's moment of celebratory transcendence does not endure through to the end of the play, and the play's resolution does not point towards any sense of redemption. Fugard's pessimism is drastic and final.

In Fugard the Hottentot Eve is awarded a little life, but that life, like the bread she eats, is 'bitter and brown' (p. 199). Her greatness is that she exists beyond tragedy and beyond comedy, staring extinction in the face, but Fugard leaves us in no doubt as to her end. Possibly her death in political terms, due to a life that strips her down to a 'frail anatomy' (p. 209), is an obvious comment on current realities. But equally possibly it is because the myth of the life-giving woman of the land, the Hottentot Eve, has run its full course. It is heading for burial in the mud that Fugard says has harboured too many shrunken corpses already, and will not return them.

There are no more Khoikhoin characters in the literature. There is only the frontier, which the Hottentot Eve tried, but failed, to humanize.

4 The Imaginary Voyage through Southern Africa

In their *Theory of Literature* René Wellek and Austin Warren remark that, since 'universal and national literatures implicate each other', to discover where the universal and the national separate out would be to know 'much that is worth knowing in the whole of literary history'.[1] While stressing that with the rise of national sensibilities 'the importance of linguistic barriers was quite unduly magnified during the nineteenth century' (p. 51), they point out that any attempt to define a national literature would have to distinguish between 'questions concerning the racial descent of authors and sociological questions concerning provenance and setting from questions concerning the actual influence of the landscape and questions of literary tradition and fashion' (p. 52).

The assumption that prevails in most studies of South African literature today — that Southern African writers are those who hold, or have held, Southern African passports, or were born and bred in Southern Africa, or have at least resided for some time in the subcontinent — is based on Wellek and Warren's first category, the concept of a national literature being defined by the descent, and so on, of its authors. But Wellek and Warren raise the possibility of a literature being able also to contain writers classified less by origin than by content, less by circumstances of their lives than by their concerns in their work.

The literature dealt with in this chapter presents a test case, for the authors under consideration are demonstrably not Southern African. That none of them has even been to Southern Africa underscores what unlikely outsiders they are. That they derived their material not from first-hand experience of the subcontinent, but from works about it in their own libraries, makes them all the more interesting. If we now accept the relevant parts of Camoens as ours, there are other works that must become ours, too. If we were to think 'universally' before thinking 'nationally', we would find that the field broadened and deepened towards a greater coherence and more subtle complexity; we would see that the concept of a literature is larger than a mere sequence of literary works of an approved standard.

The first author has no name. He is a team of Grub Street journalists, the anonymous satirists deriving from Swift (whose debunking of fanciful travels has been noted) and from Sterne (who never could complete a journey without making the waylaying his objective), and a habit of pamphleteering that played the cold light of Neoclassical Reason onto man's perpetual delight in superstition. Their technique was to ridicule folly by compounding follies, and they had no trouble finding satirical targets in every quarter of the globe.

The originator of the Munchausen technique was a German refugee in England, Rudolf Erich Raspe, whose *The Travels of Baron Munchausen* was first published anonymously in Oxford (in English) in 1786. By its fifth edition Raspe's original forty pages, comprising the chapters 2 to 6 of the first volume, had been expanded by various hands into twenty chapters, to which in 1792 a second volume of fourteen chapters was added. As Carl van Doren notes of *The Travels,* this new mouthpiece belongs to 'the line from Odysseus to Trader Horn . . .[2] a highway of great liars'.[3] Although there was an historical braggart, Baron Carl Friedrich Jerome Münchhausen, from whom Raspe took his inspiration, we can assume that, on the other hand, as the Rev. S. Baring Gould states, 'Raspe took his material from any accessible quarter, and the merit of the book, such as it is, consists in the arrangement.' With reference to the second volume, the one which is of interest here, Baring Gould remarks: 'That it was intended as a sneer at poor Bruce, the African traveller to the source of the Nile, helped to give it popularity.'[4]

The popularity of this common property of Augustan journalism was enduring; the British Library catalogue lists half a dozen further Munchausen pamphlets which arose to make fun of travel news as it was reported. 'To get at the origin of the stories the Baron tells us,' according to John Carswell, 'we must follow tracks which lead back into the furthest uplands of collective memory. . . . We can chase individual tales through the pages of monkish jest-books and fifteenth-century collections of facetiae, or trace the German tradition of *Lügendichtungen* through its successive phases, until we find that the Bible, or the *Mabinogion,* or the folk literature of almost any country . . . will give us stories that the Baron might have told.'[5]

But it is the Baron as his experience becomes anglicized who is of note here. 'The English hacks tried [Munchausen] in plots lifted from . . . any topicality that was uppermost in the talk of the day, so that the Baron's successive editions became the gossip column of the day'

(Carswell, p. 187). That the gossip of the day was spurred by many highly sensationalized accounts of African travel is our good fortune.

James Bruce of Abyssinia and his suspected hokum was the catalyst, but Camoens and his many successors were enough to steer Munchausen down south as well. When he sets out on his expedition to Southern Africa, he is equipped with no caravel or frigate, but with the amphibious chariot of none other than Queen Mab:

The chariot [he tells us] was drawn by a team of nine bulls harnessed to it three after three. . . . They were all shod for the journey, not indeed like horses, with iron, or as bullocks commonly are, to drag a cart; but were shod with men's skulls. Each of their feet was, hoof and all, crammed into a man's head, cut off for the purpose, and fastened therein with a kind of cement or paste, so that the skull seemed to be a part of the foot and hoof of the animal. With these skull-shoes the creatures could perform astonishing journeys, and slide upon the water, or upon the ocean, with great velocity. . . . The creatures were ridden by nine postilions, crickets of great size, as large as monkeys, who sat squat upon the heads of the bulls, and were continually chirping at a most terrific rate. . . . You must allow [my machine] to be far superior to the apparatus of Monsieur Vaillant . . .[6]

As the mendacious Baron whips up his grotesque waggon over the reaches of the Thames for the Cape, we have our early travellers' laborious means of transport converted into a contraption of splendid and grotesque fantasy, by which their exaggerated claims are carefully satirized.

Camoens and his Adamastor are the next to receive the onslaught. One should note that in the satirist's source-book Adamastor has an alternative genealogy to the one Camoens gives him, for Rabelais forty years before the publication of *The Lusiads* (1532 as against 1572) had made him one of the succession of giants who begat no less a prodigy than Pantagruel.[7] The airborne phantom Munchausen, like a clumsy demi-urge, is intent on cutting such mythical forebears down to size:

I drove on with the most amazing rapidity; and thinking to halt on shore at the Cape, I unfortunately drove too close, and shattered the right side wheels of my vehicle against the rock, now called Table Mountain. The machine went against it with such impetuosity as completely shivered the rock in a horizontal direction; so that the summit of the mountain, in the form of a hemisphere, was knocked into the sea; and the steep mountain becoming thereby flatted at the top, has since received the name of Table Mountain, from its similarity to that piece of furniture.

Just as this part of the mountain was knocked off, the ghost of the Cape, that tremendous sprite which cuts such a figure in the Lusiad, was discovered sitting squat in an excavation formed for him in the centre of the mountain. He seemed just like a young bee in his little cell before he comes forth; or like a bean in a bean-pod; and when the upper part of the mountain was split across and knocked off, the superior half of his person was discovered. He appeared of a bottle-blue colour, and started, dazzled with the unexpected glare of the light: hearing the dreadful rattle of the wheels, and the loud chirping of the crickets, he was thunder-struck, and instantly giving a shriek, sunk down ten thousand fathoms into the earth; while the mountain, vomiting out some smoke, silently closed up after him, and left not a trace behind! (pp. 164-5)

Munchausen is bent on a course of literary demystification. As he cumbersomely labours over the details, one can feel him inventing the new lie. Reducing Adamastor in scale to the size of an insect, in the face of this new exaggerated wrecker, is to kill one tall story with another taller one. The satirist here is richly reacting to his material: the light of reason that exposes the old monster as a humbug is not meant merely to discredit him — it is meant to exorcise him. The plain fact of the matter is that Table Mountain is named after a piece of furniture, and it is made of rock. That the flying Baron should have cleaved it that way by accident is a delightful act of deflation. Yet at the same time, as the Baron reshapes the world around him, he himself remains a preposterous boaster to whose vainglory there is no end: his knowledge of rock cleavage is spurious scientific information, and his obnoxious manner of desecrating all that had been noble before him leaves us with a new kind of horror. Munchausen has no pity, no shame and no humanity. As the era of scientific practicality dethrones the age of superstitious dread, we are left with great humour; but we are also left with a mechanical maniac whose pillaging is characteristic of the commercialism to follow him.

That British enterprise in Africa in the eighteenth century meant the slave trade does not go unnoticed by the Munchausen pamphleteers. On a side-trip from the Cape, Munchausen tells us that:

. . . we fell in with a fleet of Negro-men, as they called them. These wretches I must inform you, my dear friends, had found means to make prizes of those vessels from some European upon the coast of Guinea; and tasting the sweets of our luxury, had formed colonies in several new discovered islands near the South Pole, where they had a variety of plantations of such matters as would only grow in the coldest climates. As the black inhabitants of Guinea were unsuited to the climate and the excessive cold of the country, they formed the diabolical project of getting Christian slaves to work for them. For this purpose they sent vessels every year to the coast of Scotland, the northern parts of Ireland and Wales, and were even sometimes seen off the coast of Cornwall. And having purchased, or entrapped by fraud and violence, a great number of men, women and children, they proceeded with their cargoes of human flesh to the other end of the world, and sold them to their planters; where they were flogged into obedience, and made to work like horses all the rest of their lives. (pp. 170–1)

The inversion of black for white is a cunning way of exploding the myth of the insensitive negro (among other things). So much for the theme of organized slavery, which makes few enough satirical appearances in the literature of Southern Africa otherwise.

Munchausen declares his intention of opening up the interior to the white man:

The Dutch Government at the Cape, to do them justice, gave us every possible assistance for the expedition . . . they presented us with a specimen of some of the most excellent of their Cape wine. . . . As to the face of the country, as we advanced, it appeared in many places capable of every cultivation, and of abundant fertility. The natives and Hottentots of this part of Africa have been frequently described by travellers, and therefore it is not necessary to say any more about them: but in the more interior parts of Africa the appearance, manners, and genius of the people are totally different. (pp. 181–2)

Here is the crux of the satirist's idea: he does not see why there should be a terminator dividing the known from the unknown, and thus there is no reason why the unexplored should be any different from the familiar.

Munchausen himself, however, slips into lying the moment he is over the border:

One whole day in particular we heard on every side, among the hills, the horrible roaring of . . . at least one thousand lions, approaching equally on every side, and within a hundred paces. . . . I directly ordered the whole company to stand to their arms, and not to make any noise or fire till I should command them. I then took a large quantity of tar, which I had brought with our caravan for that purpose, and strewed it in a continued stream round the encampment: within which circle of tar I immediately placed another train or circle of gunpowder; and having taken this precaution, I anxiously waited the lions' approach. These dreadful animals . . . advanced . . . growling in hideous concert, so as to resemble an earthquake, or some similar convulsion of the world. When they had at length advanced and steeped all their paws in the tar, they put their noses to it, smelling it as if it were blood, and daubed their great bushy hair and whiskers with it equal to their paws. At that very instant, when, in concert, they were going to give the mortal dart upon us, I discharged a pistol at the train of gunpower, which instantly exploding on every side, made all the lions recoil in a general uproar, and take to flight with the utmost precipitation. In an instant we could behold them scattered through the woods at some distance, roaring in agony, and moving about like so many Will-o'-the-Wisps, their paws and faces all on fire from the tar and the gunpowder. I then ordered a general pursuit: we followed them on every side through the woods, their own light serving as our guide, until, before the rising of the sun, we followed into their fastnesses and shot or otherwise destroyed every one of them: and during the whole of our journey after we never heard the roaring of a lion . . . (pp. 182–4)

The gratuitous simile 'growling . . . [like] an earthquake', with its tossed off reinforcement, 'or some similar convulsion of the world', is a hallmark of the hyperbolic Munchausen *machismo* style. His off-hand relish taken in spectacular and total warfare shows his horrendous smugness.

True to form, Munchausen reports finding in the Kalahari desert more 'gold-dust and pearls [*sic*]' (p. 184) than he could possibly carry back with him to Europe. Best of all, after the harrowing vicissitudes of crossing burning sands and boundless kloofs, he also locates the metropolis of an inland emperor whose kingdom naturally rivals that of Prester John in luxury and in wealth. '. . . how happy I was to meet so polished and refined a people in the centre of Africa; . . . I hoped to show myself and company grateful for [his Majesty's] esteem, by introducing the arts and sciences of Europe among the people' (p. 189). His Majesty, meanwhile, '[looked] upon us as a species of superior beings [and] paid the greatest respect to our opinions' (p. 193).

The source of the parody here shifts from Le Vaillant to Bruce; Munchausen's satirical commentary on how to subdue a mighty African kingdom, excel over its sportsmen in physical prowess, and reduce its might down to a bank account in London, need not concern us here: suffice it to say that in pillorying Bruce's penchant for self-aggrandizement, the Munchausen authors were also pillorying the white man's grandiose idea that he had an automatic right to assume kingship over whoever in terms of Western culture was felt to be ignorant.

Munchausen then builds the eighth wonder of the world for Africa — a marvellous bridge, from the heart of the continent all the way to London, a bridge upon which diplomatic interchange can supposedly flow.[8] In abject amazement the tottering Emperor of Inland expresses his gratitude by presenting Europe not only with every valuable he possesses, but with a gift which today seems to have had prophetic insight behind it. The gift is the kaleidoscopic Wauwau bird, the gorgeous bird of truth, which, once it flies its cage in the London parliament, draws the entire population of Europe and America after it in unsuccessful pursuit. The fantasy ends with this early illustration of the sly opinion that it is not Europe, but Africa, which might well be the home of all decency, because it is the African end of the Afro-

European bridge which provides the world not with darkness, but with light. Fielding's Mrs Heartfree had had the same observation to make in *Jonathan Wild*.

In the Munchausen saga we have many facets of the possibilities of literature in Southern Africa brought to the fore; none of these facets is commonly supposed to be there, certainly not as early as 1792. In Munchausen we have not only one set of myths replacing another (Adamastor for geology), but a fundamental reappraisal of myth-making, which is felt to be a dubious and deluding process. The martial ingenuity of Munchausen as he extirpates the continent's lion population is shown to be pretty effective, if violent, and the poor pussycats sizzle back into the dark woods of subconscious fears from which they emerged. Munchausen's conquest of the interior is utterly without redeeming features: he is a destroyer who, in order merely to glorify his boundless ego, will use his superior technological ingenuity to subdue those who are understandably hostile towards him. The miraculous invention of the Wauwau bird which eludes the Westerners' grasp flies around in the wake of Munchausen, the African conqueror, as a ridiculous portent for the literature, a reminder that imperialism in Africa can be seen as malicious and ignoble. Olive Schreiner knew this well enough when she had her Blenkins retail Munchausen stories as if they were his own (in *The Story of an African Farm*).[9]

The complete Munchausen is a compilation of immense variety and incident, applicable to almost any of the Western literatures of the world. It derives ultimately from Lucian,[10] whose *The True History* of the second century A.D. was devised to demythologize Homer and Herodotus, travellers all who started shooting lines once they were out of home waters. Lucian's traveller aspires to the moon, too, and Munchausen in his wake concurs that the moon is indeed made of cheese.

As late as 1819, Munchausen acquires a Scottish follower 'who adopted the name of Captain Munchausen because [he resembled] the celebrated hero'.[11] He is born in terms that are as knowledgeable about Southern Africa as the following:

I was scarce formed in the womb, when my mother dreamt that she was delivered of an aloe tree, whose branches ascended to heaven, and overshadowed the globe. The bitterness of this plant denoted the hardships I should have to encounter; the extension of its leaves over the earth denoted that nothing should be hid from my researches; and the well-known fact of its blossoming only once in 200 years plainly pointed one out as a prodigy with which mankind is not favoured once in an age . . . (pp. 1–2)

The coming of the British to aloe-country a year later is suitably satirized even before it occurs: the warning is — stay human size, be
content that you are perhaps as odd as any prodigy you might find
inland.

There is another work of imaginary travelling which has the same
message, one specifically designed to divest Le Vaillant's *Travels* of
their romantic appeal. It is again a hack job, probably by George
Walker (as the catalogue of the South African Library in Cape Town
has it, although on the title page Walker is credited with only the
printing). It is an extended riposte at François le Vaillant's expense,
done with a particularly British sense of stiff upper lip. The parody
is worked out in such detail that without the original on hand one is
not going to enjoy too much of its innermost subtlety. It says something for Le Vaillant's durability that two decades after he had completed publishing his travels they could still elicit such meticulous
commentary.

That the British sensibility could not absorb Le Vaillant has already
been noted; we need only to remember Lady Anne Barnard's review
of him to realize the extent to which an English writer of 1799 could
develop a national distrust for 'a Frenchman's journal':

Le Vaillant, it seems, narrates a story of his own prowess in having killed a tiger
while at [Mr Slaber's] house. Barnard asked if it was true, on which the young
Vrow Slaber, and even the old vrow, burst into invectives against him. 'He was
the greatest liar it was possible to imagine, though very civil and well-bred — but
the tiger was killed by one of their Hottentots, nor had Le Vaillant seen it till
the fellow brought it dead into the back-yard. When Le Vaillant looked at it, I
well remember what he did,' said the old woman; 'he thrust his spear through the
skin, though it spoiled it for sale — (but he did not care for that) — saying: "Now
I have to boast that this spear has been imbued in the blood of one of the most
savage animals in Africa!" ' — On points, however, where his own vanity was not
concerned, I imagine his representations are tolerably correct [she concludes].[12]

On the subject of Narina, Lady Anne Barnard concedes sceptically
that 'there might be some truth in his representation. . .' (p. 187).

It is not only rival interpretations of the African inland that are
being fought out here, but the Napoleonic Wars in words. Walker's
The Travels of Sylvester Tramper of 1813 is the literary equivalent of
the Battle of Waterloo of two years later. But if the Munchausen
Southern African pieces are part of a pamphlet war, *Sylvester Tramper* arrives as a significant step forward from the polemical slanging
of late eighteenth-century satirical realists. It is not only an extended
satire on an easily misunderstood work, but one of those lucky

examples of literature in growth, a parody that becomes a novel in its own right. To Southern African travel literature it is what Cervantes's *Don Quixote* was to the chivalric romance before it — both its demolition and its resurrection. In other words, *The Travels of Sylvester Tramper through the Interior of the South of Africa, with the Adventures and Accidents that He Encountered in a Journey of More than Two Thousand Miles through those Unknown Wildernesses, Constantly Exposed to Danger from Beasts of Prey, and the Attacks of Savages* (to give it its full title), transcends its origins in smutty journalism and libellous gossip. If it turned a few smart pennies in the four editions it went into in its first year, that is as may be. But that it created a new possibility in Southern African writing — that of the venture inland being a suitable theme for fiction — cannot be held in doubt.

Sylvester Tramper himself is a Yorkshireman, an orphan who inherits his uncle's 'gentleman's ways' and, not unlike Robinson Crusoe, another journalist's invention, he writes *in propria persona.* He shares with Crusoe a credo of economic determinism, but a century after Defoe we find our new colonizer tinged with a hopeless romanticism which in Defoe would have remained subordinate to practicality. 'My education had been hard as the rock of which our house and its boundaries were constructed; and to rove free as air, was the first and paramount wish of my heart,'[13] declares Tramper, putting English heart before English head.

Although this Tramper's aim is to puncture Le Vaillant, his book curiously picks up Le Vaillant's stylistic gestures, as if weighing them, criticizing them and ultimately condoning them; in this way the author succeeds in creating a level-headed sense of reality by replaying Le Vaillant on a smaller scale, as it were, so that while Le Vaillant's supposedly irresponsible bravura is made to appear ridiculously vain, the essential romantic spirit remains intact in a more modest key. It is a feat of great subtlety — to let a reader's sense of disbelief work critically against his desire that a grand story of adventure can nevertheless be told. With this sense of double tension the author can come up with the following:

I determined in my own mind, to explore the unknown wildernesses which compose the mass of our world; particularly as I saw, in reading works of geography, and in looking at the maps, that excepting the Continent of Europe, we were almost strangers to the interior regions of the other quarters of the globe, our researches being confined to the sea coast. (p. 9)

One feels parodic use of words like 'interior regions', 'other quarters' and 'researches', while at the same time desiring that those terms can acquire a new actuality of meaning.

At the age of his majority, Tramper settles his estate and spends a year equipping for his secret expedition. Tellingly, his most treasured item of baggage is 'my library, which was, though small, extremely costly, as it consisted of chapters and leaves cut out of books of value, which related to the country I was going to explore' (p. 15). Like Don Quixote, his points of reference are those books that contain the fanciful ideas of which life will disabuse him; they are, in sum, the literature of Southern Africa up to his departure date of 1794.

His projected route was to be from the Cape of Good Hope to Abyssinia, Le Vaillant's route to the last detail. Le Vaillant, after all, had written:

Previously to my quitting the Cape, I had prepared several letters for my family, in which I informed them of my intended second expedition. . . . It was not possible to tell them the precise route I should follow, because I was ignorant of it myself, as it would depend entirely upon local circumstances, which might happen to favour or thwart my wishes. I merely said, that my plan in general was to cross, from south to north, the whole continent of Africa, and then to return to Europe by way of Egypt if the passage of the Nile was open, and if not, by the coasts of Barbary; that this enterprise, from the best calculations I could make, would require six years; and that as, during that period, no opportunity might offer for writing to them, they ought not to be alarmed at my silence.[14]

Le Vaillant, the real man, was living an impossible dream. And now we have a book by a man purporting to be real, Sylvester Tramper, whose anonymous creator can call the real man's bluff in fiction. Le Vaillant's caravan was an extravaganza, as we know, and now we have Tramper with his crew of three Creoles, three Hottentots, five Slaves, four Horses, thirty Oxen, fifteen Dogs and so on and so forth, who comments: 'Thus, like one of the patriarchs of old, I set forward to penetrate the interior of Africa . . .' (p. 22). Le Vaillant suffers from modesty and due pride, but not the false modesty and obnoxious pride of Tramper:

It was with an extacy of pleasure I saw my little caravan on the move, flattering myself that now all the dreams I had indulged in from childhood would be realized. Indeed the appearance of my caravan was picturesque and romantic, and must, in the eyes, not only of the natives, but the planters, have appeared superb. (pp. 22–3)

His description of himself out-Le-Vaillants Le Vaillant in every particular, with the substitution of English detail for the French:

My own figure was not a little curious: I had designedly made it conspicuous, well knowing that not only ignorant savages, but even polished Europeans, pay a profound respect to external appearances. I wore blue pantaloons or striped trowsers, with half boots; a waistcoat of silk or scarlet kerseymere, ornamented with gold fringe or buttons; an open short jacket of blue cloth embroiderd, or else a silk jacket of different patterns and gaudy colours.

In my belt I always wore a brace of pistols and my dagger, whether on foot or on horseback; sometimes I had two with double barrels. On the road, during a march, I carried either a musket or a rifle. On my head I wore a white turban, with a scarlet feather [cf. Le Vaillant's white ostrich feather], which I found more pleasant than a hat, and cooler; as it at once prevented the rays of the sun from striking through and absorbing all moisture. (p. 24)

The innuendo in the last clause indicates an irresistible talent in the author for lunacy, for turning local colour into emblems of the absurd.

His method includes a devastating use of understatement as well: whereas Le Vaillant spent five volumes going round the interior in hopeless circles (as he is the first to admit), all Tramper has to say for the early stages of his voyage is that his 'singular column' was always 'moving slowly across almost endless tracts of uncultivated wastes, winding through dreary vallies, or with extreme labour creeping over and among mountains . . .' (p. 25). But where Le Vaillant turns his tramp into a daylong entertainment for himself, Tramper professes boredom. Le Vaillant's most outrageous companions on the trip, his Gallic cock and Kees, his tame baboon, are sources of endless enjoyment to him; they have their equals in Tramper's story — he keeps an ape called Clack as a court 'taster', and Clack spends his days riding their British bulldogs into the ground. Tramper's cock never crows — it sulks all the way.

At his best, Tramper can exceed Le Vaillant in over-writing, as in his parody description of the tiger-hunting incident Lady Anne Barnard has already discredited. Once, when Tramper and his scout walk face to face into an unholy monster that turns out to be a 'panther', he shoots and has the beast

. . . shaking the woods with his howling. He was about to make a second spring, when, being now ready with my double-barrelled gun, I stepped from behind the tree, firing one after the other. The balls were lodged in his body; he gave a tremendous groan; leaping perpendicularly, at least six feet, from the ground, he came down with a frightful shock upon his back, evidently in the agonies of death. He lashed the ground with his tail, tearing and scattering the dirt with long claws, in the convulsions of distraction, presenting to me a sight, at once terrible and strange. He seemed to have lost his senses, for he made no attempt to revenge himself, venting all his rage and strength upon the ground. There was no knowing what might be the termination of this scene, if we suffered him to come to; and being both loaded again, our second discharge stretched him lifeless. It was, by this time, quite dark: we were benighted in an untrod forest, and knew not a step of the way to our companions. (p. 42)

Le Vaillant's tiger, like Blake's, which was etched into all its playful, lurid colours in the same year, here bites the dust in as ornate a style as Tramper's satirical streak demands. Death agonies are shown to be desperately painful, and this senseless killing, it is implied, serves in no way to illuminate Tramper in his benighted situation. There is a genuine note of distress in this description, which, as in the Munchausen lion episode, shows the Englishman's stoic admiration for the noble denizens of the wilderness. It is a consummate piece of narrative art that has Tramper and his scout led out of the dark 'untrod forest' by the sagacity of Clack, the ape. In the next scene, Clack is taught how to shoot a revolver, but can discern no use for it.

Tramper's expedition is overwhelmed by voracious birds and voracious ants in turn. For a dozen pages he becomes mired in a rain-storm which washes all his extravagance before it, and he is on his beam-ends when he finally runs into what we have been waiting for — his first black man. His name is Prince Pooroo, and Tramper's first response is, of course, to treat the prince to a display of fireworks (brought specifically for such an occasion). Crackers, serpents, Bengal lights, rockets and the inevitable squibs explode in the unmolested sky, and the prince's awed reaction presents us with a great moment:

Pooroo laid his hand upon my arm. 'White man,' said he, 'you may travel in safety through all countries; black men are nothing.' (p. 128)

In exchange for penny whistles, jew's harps and brass wire, Tramper perseveres under a safe conduct. He has been told by the prince, however, that no native further inland will be able to believe that any European could travel to satiate his curiosity alone without also desiring riches. When he runs into a horde of Mozambique savages, Tramper loses all his worldly goods, including the quantities of specimens he has collected for the British Museum. Destitute and weary he reaches the coast, where one of the most revealing incidents of his travels occurs: his staff settle down with the local women, content to move no further, while Tramper yearns for womanly contact but cannot bring himself under any circumstances to 'go native'. He is seen to be a pathetic, unfulfilled and demoralized figure, a man whose civilizing mission is overwhelmed and who can only turn inwards on himself and his own longings, on a continent that treats him as an outcast and a joke. The same theme is implicit in many subsequent explorers' real diaries, like those of Henry Francis Fynn and Nathaniel Isaacs in Natal.

The novel is resolved by a series of action scenes on the coast of Africa opposite Zanzibar (which one remembers was to be Livingstone's point of emergence after his first trans-continental safari). They are designed to illustrate that the English navy is more humane to castaways than any French buccaneers are, for it is in pitched battle against French privateers that Tramper recovers his identity and his inherent national energy. Nevertheless, Tramper's last words are revealing and even prophetic: incredible as it may seem, the author of *Sylvester Tramper* puts the conclusion to the travel novel even before it has really come into its own as a genre. He ends:

My companions being, by my bounty, all freemen, left me with much regret, declaring they would settle in some plantation together, where they would spend their leisure in talking about me.

I reached England without any further incident, after an absence of nearly six years, accompanied by my friend Clack; and am now settled upon my own estate, perfectly cured of my desire to travel, and satisfied that the laws, constitution, religion, manners and morals of my own country are superior to those of all others on the face of the earth. (p. 216)

The point about British superiority over the French is well taken. In the same year as Tramper's return, the British occupied the Cape so that no further French revolutionary influence would spread into Dutch South Africa. As the eighteenth century phases into the nineteenth, we see Wellek and Warren's spirit of competitive nationalisms rising both in politics and in the literature. Le Vaillant, while admiring the aptness with which French theatre grafted onto Dutch at the Cape during his years there, would never have considered his culture as in competition with any other, let alone Georgian England's. Tramper does, and wins through, and after Tramper the literature will be exclusively British for a long while. Tramper knows that more than optimism and romantic notions are needed to pull the British through inland; fireworks and guns are needed. The quest for spiritual fulfilment will have to wait until a return to that dominant colonial locus in the patriotism which coalesces around the word 'home'. Yet Tramper's conclusion is that all the Englishman will bring home with him is his own intelligent trainee, his alter ego — a South African baboon.

If the scramble for Africa between French and British is soon resolved — at the Cape, at any rate — that does not mean that it is resolved in the literature. But the growing nationalism of nineteenth-century England is merely incidental to the theme we are following here — that of the imaginary voyage through Southern Africa, written by outsiders, generally for consumption outside Southern Africa. This forgotten side of the literature, its outer circle consisting of theory and possibilities, untainted by any actuality that has to do with the diurnal business of a developing British territory, does continue to be written in its own terms, parallel but not intimately related to what we might more mundanely recognize as Southern African.

As the second wave of British immigration to South Africa occurred in response to the discovery of the Kimberley diamonds, those burgeoning hopes of there being a fabulous interior became true. South Africa's new mining areas attracted the kind of media that made the bonanzas of the 1870s world-wide news. The Kimberley strike gave rise to a whole diggers' oral literature and to dozens of novels, like J.R. Couper's *Mixed Humanity* (1892), recording the struggles of Sylvester Tramper trying to turn into a millionaire. Kimberley produced in terms of stocks and shares what had only been imaginary before. Thus Kimberley meant the death of the genre of the imaginary voyage in English, as far as Southern Africa is concerned, and it gave birth to the novel of commercial enterprise. When Munchausen returned from his fantastic foray, he was welcomed back in Europe by no less a figure than the Colossus of Rhodes (and other mythological figures, from Dick Whittington to Don Quixote himself). But Kimberley created an actual Rhodes, a lumbering myth in his own turn, one of flesh and blood. To anyone versed in imaginary travels, the discovery of Kimberley might have felt like a vindication of the most notoriously mendacious imaginary voyager of them all, Sir John Mandeville, who in the fourteenth century fancied that in 'Ethiopia' diamonds 'grow together male and female. And they be nourished with the dew of Heaven. And they engender commonly and bring forth small children that multiply and grow all the year.'[15] Mandeville's images of European wish-fulfilment, dotted liberally around the medieval universe, had inspired enough paperchases; that some of them were showing themselves once more was no matter for humour. In the face of diamonds, satire is the electric spark that reduces a fortune in carbon crystals to a puff of charcoal, and no British imperialist would have found that thought anything but subversive.

But the British–French vendetta continues in terms of imaginary voyaging in the person of Jules Verne, whose twenty-sixth novel,

L'Étoile du Sud (1884),[16] persists in exploring the Lucianic genre in
terms of the South African diamond rush. In French criticism of
Verne it is a commonplace that *Star of the South* is a denunciation
of the capitalism of the precious stone industry and of Cecil Rhodes,[17]
but it reads like no such thing in its English versions to date; British
publishers who had found Le Vaillant's frankness unacceptable also
made heavy weather of Verne, not scrupling to bowdlerize most of
his novels and, in this case, excise central passages. Verne proved
acceptable to British empire audiences only in so far as he was a
glamourizer of the potential of scientific gadgetry in the service of
progress; his own complex and pessimistic view of where that progress
might take mankind proved sufficiently uncongenial to British tastes
for his work to be emasculated into a children's literature.

It begins to look, in fact, as if the Munchausen writers, the Tramper
author and Verne (with regard to the fraction of his work which involves South Africa) have suffered a common fate. Their attitudes of
distrust towards colonial expansionism, their critiques of the assumed
moral superiority of those expanding into the interior, and their basic
cynicism about those pots of gold make them anathema to a culture
unable to indulge in literary speculation against itself. If our view of
the total literature has been constricted to a British-only focus, that
must be because the national consciousness which the British brought
with them to South Africa felt it necessary to allot such supposedly
anti-British works a status that put them beyond serious consideration.

Verne's left-wing children's stories, written for right-wing adults,
have come into their own in French criticism only recently, and it so
happens that the two of his sixty-five *Voyages Extraordinaires* which
deal with Southern Africa rate centrally in his massive opus. The first,
an earlier novel called *The Adventures of Three Russians and Three
Englishmen in South Africa* (1872),[18] is a mellow tale built out of
problems of triangulation, Herschelian astronomy and means of desert
transport. Its focus is the Kalahari, but, as the action is dated 1854, it
is also a satire on Anglo-Russian enmities at the time of the Crimean
War. Its mythic substructure, as Michel Serres[19] shows, is the Mosaic
Exodus, reinterpreted in terms of a Southern African desert experience. The same sort of synthesis of such disparate ideas goes into the
design of *Star of the South*. Physics experiments on the manufacturing
of artificial gems (which threaten to reduce the diamond to the value
of that wonderfully symbolic object in Africa, the glass bead), and
French endeavours to ensure that scientific knowledge is not the property of only one privileged race, but of all mankind, are part of its

theme. That *Star of the South* is also a highly ironic adventure story about a young French engineer trying to remain morally unsullied in the ghettos of Kimberley's New Rush goes without saying. That the villain of the piece is a British landgrubber whose face was 'so flushed that you would have thought his head pumped up with red-currant jelly'[20] (the Rhodes stand-in) makes the story all the more intriguing.

Its fate within South African criticism has, however, been a miserable one. It is worth exploring local reaction to *Star of the South* to determine why the imaginary voyage as a genre has been received with such hostility. The novel was first appraised by a critic on the *Rand Daily Mail* in 1929. Dismissed out of hand as a work of preposterous fantasy (which, naturally, is what an imaginary voyage is meant to be), it was appreciated only in terms of its quaint humour. 'It was composed when oversea people knew little of Kimberley except that it contained gems by the hatful. . . . Consequently Jules could let himself go . . .'[21] remarks the *Mail,* with a great show of missing the point. (The patronizing, familiar tone is characteristic of much white colonial journalism of the time.) On the subject of race relationships, *Star of the South* obviously rankles:

> Relations between the black men and white are described with a good deal of French sentimentality. Thus, the mine magnate's daughter spends her spare time instructing an ambitious native boy in mathematics and other sciences, while the same native, 'Matakit', is tenderly laid upon the hero's bed after he has hurt himself.

That the English daughter, Alice, is actually not very well up in mathematics, and that the ambitious 'boy' has merely been dynamited sky-high while trying to save the white 'hero' is beyond the perceptions of the *Mail* critic.

Then there is Eric Rosenthal's article in the *South African PEN Yearbook* for 1955 — and considering its place of publication one must assume that such an article must have carried a degree of endorsement by South Africa's leading white writers of the time. While professing to be a 'life-long and incurable enthusiast for Jules Verne',[22] Rosenthal nevertheless manages to misread much of *Star of the South.* In plot-summarizing the novel and pointing out Verne's blunders, Rosenthal himself is guilty of blundering over more than several details: he persistently calls it *The South Star,* misnames its hero (Cyprian Meré for the real Cyprien Méré) and lets the financial interest of the various gems in the plot overrule his evaluation of character, thereby bypassing Verne's entire theme. Rosenthal is literally so blinded by the glory of diamonds that he cannot see the work's most elementary irony: the Star of the South, weighing over half a pound, is a black diamond.

The novel probably originated in a manuscript written by the radical Paschal Grousset, executive member of the committee of the 1871 Paris Commune, handed on to Verne by his publisher to polish and cut into shape.[23] So much for 'French sentimentality'. The point of the exercise was not originality, nor was it the skilful use of source material, because Verne was not really interested in South Africa per se. Kimberley was merely a common given of his time. He had only to scan the newspapers, which he did at the rate of twenty a day, and follow his intuitions through the scientific journals at the Académie of Amiens, to acquire sufficient colouring to give his tale an authentic façade. That he did not feel it necessary to voyage to the Cape to do his fieldwork should offend no one, as it offends the *Mail* critic and Rosenthal.

In an interview in 1895, when Verne was 78 and on the verge of publishing his seventieth book, he said: 'When writing my first book, *Five Weeks in a Balloon,* I chose Africa as the scene of action, for the simple reason that less was, and is, known about that continent than any other. . . . I thoroughly enjoyed writing the story, and even more, I may add, the researches which it made necessary; for then, as now, I have always tried to make even the wildest of my romances as realistic and true to life as possible.'[24] Verne's blithe assumption, however, as Roland Barthes notes, is that 'Imagination about travel corresponds . . . to an exploration of closure,'[25] an exercise that awards the researcher delight as imagination expands to contain the whole world, and illumination turns inside. Verne's universe is finite and knowable. He had already compressed a history of celebrated travels and travellers into three volumes, and dealt critically with Camoens, Velho (citing with pleasure the passage quoted earlier as a 'little fête and mutual serenade between the Portuguese and the negroes'[26]), Kolbe, Sparrman and so on, Le Vaillant, Barrow and Bruce; and in *The Adventures of Three Russians and Three Englishmen* he had handled John Campbell (1815), William Burchell (1822) and David Livingstone. The point here is not accuracy of the façade, it is the ontology of 'wild' romance.

Just as the Munchausen pamphlets amount to a parable about European superiority, and the Tramper saga to one about the quest for happiness, so Verne's second South African novel adds up to a parable about values — artificial diamond values as against the human values of courage, tolerance, forbearance and honesty. As Jean Jules-Verne succinctly puts it, the moral of the story is that 'the value we put on material things is a delusion, because they are essentially ephemeral' (p. 150). Accordingly, the plot of *Star of the South* is at least as old as Molière. It is a comedy of misunderstanding precipitated by a young destitute's falling in love with a rich man's daughter, and by the agents of wealth who try to persuade her head to take her where her heart will not go. In the miraculous dénouement true love and true fidelity are rewarded — curtain. It is Victor Hugo dressed up to look like *Popular Physics.* The key turn in the plot, one knows, will have to be, and is, the shocking reversal that occurs when the main-stay of all the greedy baddies — the ugly, the avaricious, the immoral, the miserly (and for good measure here, the racists and even the local version of the Ku Klux Klan), meet their reckoning, in this case at the moment when the most awesome diamond kimberlite has yet regurgi-tated explodes. Virtue triumphs in the comedy, as it clearly did not in Kimberley.

But it is in the seemingly gratuitous and bizarre details with which Verne decks out his plot that one feels the elements of the imaginary voyage gathering strength. Just as Munchausen and Tramper display a certain manic quality in their travels, so is there a quality of manic destructiveness about *Star of the South.* Curiously enough, this qual-ity goes by a name in the novel, and the name appears some four decades before the major moral collapse of the West in the First World War engenders it as an artistic movement — Dadaism. A dadaist illogicality and perversity operate in *Star of the South* in the shape of the heroine's ostrich, named Dada, who plays a kind of reversed Kim's game with all the objets trouvés in the novel. Darning balls, priceless deeds of sale (like the boundary dispute documents that sliced the diamondiferous part of Griqualand West out of the Orange Free State), the world's most tempting diamond, and assorted pebbles are all of equal value to the ostrich, acting like a crazed Eumenides throughout the story. In the ostrich's terms, as in the novelist's, all things great and small are no more than roughage. In ways such as these Verne plays with the phenomenon of Kimberley and its industrial values.

His gleefully anti-British way of disabusing one of the belief that a consortium of mining magnates, with all their pomp and ceremony, could have any credibility as a moral institution has its correlatives. The central relationship in the novel is not the love-bond between Méré and Alice, but the brotherhood-bond between Méré and his hired hand, Matakit, the Mosotho emaciate who stumbles onto the mine in search of work. Verne's liberal humanist sympathies for the exploited, driven off their land, find such sharp focus in Matakit that he shows us that Verne was by no means hidebound to his sources. He intuits the dilemma of the dispossessed black man as no other writer up to his time within South Africa is able to do, and he analyses the master-servant relationship under conditions of severest stress. His presentation of Matakit as the alter ego of Méré, a dark, brooding doppelganger who possesses him during his moody adolescence, but who can be grown out of with manhood, is an innovation in terms of a novelist's handling of the black–white relationship in Southern African literature, an idea that is as exciting in terms of imaginative potential as Munchausen's Wauwau bird. Matakit is not left by Méré as 'raw' as he will be by Verne's successor, H. Rider Haggard. Matakit is educated up to European standards, and his tragedy is that white society refuses to allow him a place.

The essence of the imaginative voyage, however, is in the way it establishes a vast leap of irony between the realities that we know and rely on, and the wonderland of the alternative world of the fiction. One does not expect the minutiae of actuality from an imaginary voyage any more than one does from the Wonderland of that other Victorian Alice of a decade before Verne's.[27] In Verne's hands Southern Africa turns into a land of breath-stopping potential, of quite unsuspected joyfulness. We are back to Le Vaillant's pleasure-principle when Verne really gets his Méré underway on trek — from the routine labours of the unrewarding diggings into an obstacle race of more and more fantastic transports across the Kalahari into a never-never land that conceals the true cache of man's dreams, in this case a deep treasure cave pulsing with so many gemstones that, if it were there, not only would the world's economy collapse, but mankind would be immeasurably enriched with new understanding of beauty.

The nexus of Verne's inland voyage is a trove as bountiful as any encrusted pre-Raphaelite splendour, as glimmering with energy as Fingal's cave, or the cave on Ballantyne's Coral Island. To achieve entry into this artificial paradise, Méré is compelled to abandon his laws of physics in favour of an impulsive, instinctive kind of oneiric existence that throws him into the realm of coincidence and chance. He has to divest himself of the mechanical control of the elements of nature, too, in order to learn to live in awe of, and in harmony with, the universe.

As an adventure novel, *Star of the South* fits quite comfortably into

one's preconceptions about what happens to a young hero when he is
subjected to events that fashion him into a man. But Verne's stress is
different from the stress that becomes usual in the adventure novels
of Africa that follow him; his theme is not education, but liberation.
The passages that the English publishers of *Star of the South* deleted
are precisely those passages which deal with the ambitions towards
independence displayed by non-British characters in the novel — the
Boers' attempts at escaping British domination, and the blacks'
attempts at evading white domination. It was integral to Verne's view
of the world that no man excluded from the financial power of the
day should be excluded from the right to pursue his own destiny. In
short, Verne weighed in against any power-play that disempowered
all but a monopolistic élite and, like Schreiner, ended up pro-Boer
and pro-black, backing their political struggles for independence as
an answer to the dominant nationalism that constricted not only the
politics but the literature of the times.

As Southern Africa opens up increasingly to those who record their
experiences realistically, through publication in semi-factual books
and through the press, so the potential for imaginary voyaging shrinks.
Yet if that type of fiction virtually disappears after the Kimberley
boom, that is not to say that the habit of writing in ways akin to the
imaginary-voyage genre perishes as well. An image of the magical
Africa persists in extra-South African fiction — in the Old Man's lion
dream of contentment in Hemingway's *The Old Man and the Sea,* for
example. It is there in the healing experience of Henderson the Rain
King in Bellow's novel. It prevails occasionally in the science fiction
writers Lucian, Munchausen and Verne spawned: in, for example,
J.T. Edson's Bunduki books, which transpose the South African veld,
complete with 'kopjes' and shimmering Quagga Gods, to another
planet where it can remain intact, subject to strange initiatory rituals
and paradisal promise. In Ray Bradbury's *The Veldt* (as a short story,
a play and a film), his sources, which are anachronistic, as the ortho-
graphy of his title indicates, provide an African fantasy land replete
with, in this case, vicious packs of the inevitable man-eating lions.

Since the most famous of recent explorers, Mungo Park, first entered into Africa in 1795, that recorded step from the known into
the strange, from the measurable into the infinite, has been a stimulus
to those who need a proliferation of images of the unknown as alter-
natives to their own home themes: the fiction of Wilson Harris would
be the perfect illustration of this type of dialectic in action. Beyond
the explored also lies the possibility of a superior world: in Michael

Moorcock's *The Land Leviathan* (1974), for example, South Africa can appear in 1906, turned inside out, as the world's paragon of racial harmony, a country named Bantustan conducted by one President Gandhi.

That the atlas of the continent no longer has an interior which, as Swift said, is where

> . . . Geographers in *Afric*-Maps
> With Savage-Pictures fill their Gaps;
> And o'er unhabitable Downs
> Place Elephants for want of Towns[28]

is irrelevant. It is also beside the point that South Africans themselves appear not to be amused or provoked by works which they can see only in terms of artifice and misrepresentation. We have here a case of writers who choose to wrestle with Negative Capability against those who use documentary realism. But the fact remains that early Southern African literature spawned some examples of a type of imaginative writing which, while it inevitably and persistently took off in a non-Southern African direction, nevertheless has a bearing on the body of work which engendered it. In order to assess the value of the concept of Southern African literature in an international world, one would have to dispense with an arbitrary English South African national boundary before the concept itself could become fully meaningful.

7 Artist's impression of Le Vaillant drawing an idealized Hottentot warrior and spouse.

8 Andrew Geddes Bain.
9 Stephen Black on stage as Jeremiah in *Helena's Hope, Ltd* (1928).

10   The Anglo-African connection made by the Munchausen satirists.

11   Charles Landseer's engraving to illustrate Pringle's 'The Bechuana Boy'.

5 The Rise and Fall of the Colonial Hunter

Some years ago it was fashionable for a European tourist to explore some part of Africa, and after he spent a week or two in the Dark Continent, to return to Europe and to write an authoritative work on the tribal customs, etc., of the savages who allowed him to pass peacefully through their territories. Because they didn't ask to see his visa, or offer to kill him — as would have happened to a foreigner trying to walk through any part of Europe that way — the tourist always knew that he was dealing with a lot of savages.

And the funny thing is that Africa has been uncivilised like this for a very long time. Look for how many years Livingstone walked about all over Africa as a spy. And whenever he came to a village the savages, with studied brutality, would set before him food and drink. When he got fever, the benighted heathen even nursed him back to health without pay — just so that he could go and spy on them some more. There's this continent for you, sunk in absolute abomination.[1]

Colonial life is simply a substitute to those who are obscurely drawn to a world without men — to those, that is, who have failed to make the effort necessary to adapt infantile images to adult reality.[2]

IN HIS SURVEY OF LITERATURE IN SOUTH AFRICA UP TO the end of the nineteenth century, W. Basil Worsfold, sometime editor of the Johannesburg *Star,* has these definitive remarks to make of the work that had grown up about him:

What gives individuality to authors of the class we are proposing to consider is the capacity to reproduce the spirit, and not merely the letter of colonial life, or better, of the life of the English outside of England. In its broadest aspect this will be the life of the Anglo-Saxon race, when the blood of its sons is stirred with strife, and their faces are flushed with victory over the forces of nature and alien races, or their teeth set tight in defiance of the inevitable. The fiction which reflects this life is marked by a note of freedom with which is associated a certain natural materialism, born of cloudless skies and virgin lands; its poetry, by a fierce realism which glorifies in the worst, whether that worst be the result of physical conflict or mental anguish. For in this struggle our race is at its best and its worst; and the eyes of the spectators are quickly opened to the realities of existence.[3]

Worsfold's date of first publication was 1895. This paragraph deals in a unique way with the functions of the literature of South Africa in the phase stretching from the first British occupation of the Cape to the event which, within months of his going to press, would herald a new phase — the Jameson Raid and the turn-of-the-century Anglo–Boer War. In his survey of the Colonial administration and development in which this chapter on South African literature occurs, Worsfold was not to know that the era he was dealing with — a period of exactly one hundred years, 1795 to 1895 — was about to end, or at least to transform into a new one. His assessment, therefore, has a certain unintentional conclusiveness about it. It outlines the manifestations of colonial life in literature which it is the purpose of this chapter to define further and to discuss.

Where Worsfold then proceeds to retrospect ineptly is in finding the works to qualify his claims about nineteenth-century British Colonial South Africa — he plumps for Pringle and Schreiner, who exemplify quite other aspects of the literature; he overlooks the obvious illustrations of his case because he feels they are too sub-literary to grace his overall plea for a belief that this outpost of progress has had a vital artistic life of its own.

Worsfold is by no means the only critic to dismiss the nineteenth-century material that must be examined here, whether it is sub-literary or not. Francis Brett Young, in his 1929 survey of South African literature, is more explicit on the nineteenth century, and yet he too misses the point of his own argument:

In the literary evolution of what condescending Europeans are pleased to call 'new countries' there appears to be a recognizable similarity of progression. As far as literature is concerned, the earliest stages are usually barren; which is natural enough. The pioneer has no place for art in his life; his energies of body and of imagination are absorbed to the uttermost in his conflict with untamed nature. His women, of necessity, play their part in the same struggle, bearing children to supplement the available force of labour, protecting them against strange diseases and unfamiliar enemies to life. In a pioneer community romances are lived, not written; leisure and contemplation are frowned upon as being vicious. Books there are none, or, if any, only that epic of the pioneer life which is the Old Testament. Here and there, a man of action, impressed by the strangeness and dignity of his adventure, or a man of religion inspired to bear witness to his missionary faith, sets down, with the economy which, under these conditions, straitens all things, bare records of what he has seen, done, or desired. Such are the chronicles of the Pilgrim Fathers, the voyages of early navigators. Their writers handle the pen as they would a flint-lock or an axe. A certain stark integrity gives vividness to their records; the abundant material, the virgin curiosity, the exaltation of perils faced and survived, atone for the lack of what we call literary quality. Reading them, we feel ourselves participators in a lived romance. When literary art appears, as sometimes it will, we are startled and exclaim: 'These men could write!' But the surprise is a significant comment on our attitude.

The pioneer epoch of South Africa affords some examples of this stirring, artless romance. There are the early travels of Le Vaillant; there is that classic of Big Game Hunting, Harris's *Wild Sports of Southern Africa* — a rare book which every sportsman who wants information straight (as one might say) from the lion's mouth may be advised to acquire. Harris, an army officer on leave, as keen an observer as any good soldier should be, records a hunting-trip to the Orange River and beyond it. His writing is that of a good despatch: clear, business-like, economical. He might have been taken as a model and a tradition in the literature of sport, which has degenerated, alas, into those flushed catalogues of slaughter with which the modern Big Game Hunter bores us. *Wild Sports of Southern Africa* is probably the best book of that kind in existence.

After the hunter comes the missionary . . .[4]

Young's assumptions about early Southern African literature are common ones; it is one purpose of this book to show that they are also mostly fallacious. The early stages of Southern African literature were by no means barren; neither Camoens's nor Herbert's records could by any stretch of the imagination be assessed as lacking in literary artistry, nor could one say of them, or of the other writers of the seventeenth and eighteenth centuries, that they wield a pen 'as they would a flint-lock or an axe'. This kind of presumptuous claim reveals not only Young's lack of broad reading, but that he actively wishes the origins already described here to have been uncomplicated and uncouth. 'A certain stark integrity' might be said to characterize the nineteenth-century records of a man like Pringle in his *Narrative of a Residence in South Africa* (1835) or of Andrew Smith in his *Report* (1836), but it does not, in general, characterize very much of the early non-fictional literature of South Africa. One could go on picking holes in Young. He is concerned to assert that the early literature was a pioneer literature and nothing more. His own implicit definition of a pioneer makes him exclude anything but the Old Testament as a source of pioneer experience. With his pioneer spectacles on, Young is not equipped to perceive, as many critics in his wake are not equipped to perceive, that the literary origins of much Southern African literature might have been quite other than the vacuum that he must posit as the explanation of the pattern he wants to maintain exists. He requires those origins to be artless. If he allows the local writer no literary predecessors, his unprecedented native genius is all the more miraculous, one supposes, and the inborn pioneer ability to make literature directly from raw experience is given its supposed come-uppance. That this is merely another myth in Southern African literature is beyond Young's perception.

There is virtually no document of literature written during the century of British colonialism under discussion which is not without its very obvious literary precedent. Although the literature from 1795 does take on a particularly British cast, it is also a continuation of an extensive and complex literary tradition which, far from being spontaneously generated, is a further modulation of the already established into 'British' terms. If Young had read Harris with more care, he would have seen how heavily indebted to his pre-British forebears even a patriot like Harris is, and how he in turn merely gives a new twist to a set of givens which have been operative in the field for far longer than Young would care to know.

However, two pertinent concepts arise out of Young: the first is the idea that the pioneer phase is an opening one, characterized by its own fresh, exciting sense of discovery, and the second is its connection with the hunter-figure, the man whose style is ostensibly 'clear, business-like and economical'. Laurens van der Post, in his introduction to the re-publication of William Plomer's *Turbott Wolfe,* concurs with Worsfold and Young in believing that the first phase of English literature in Southern Africa reads approximately as they describe. What he analyses is, of course, the first intensive *British* phase:

The first begins [according to Van der Post] with the appearance on our scene among the 1820 Settlers of a crippled Scot, Thomas Pringle. It is true there was the talented and charming Lady Anne Barnard, a daughter of the gifted house of Crawford and Balcarres and author of the ballad 'Auld Robin Gray', whose letters from the Cape written some twenty years before Pringle have a technical claim to be called the beginning. But I overlook these because they might have been written anywhere in the world, their local colour going no deeper than the colour of its surroundings into a chameleon. But in the six years that he spent in Africa Pringle took the nature and the problems of the country deeply upon himself: he took the blow as it were not over the head but in the solar plexus of his sensitive, imaginative and courageous nature, and as a result left us a record in prose and verse of his single-handed encounter with South Africa. He wrote among other things a poem which Coleridge himself described as 'among the two or three most perfect lyrics in our language'. For all that, no matter how closely his wide-open nature enabled him to identify himself with the country, Pringle remained a foreigner writing about Africa in English.[5]

Apart from the quite extraordinary remark about Lady Anne Barnard and her chameleon-like adaptability (which one would have assumed to be a crucial virtue in a pioneer writer), and apart from his somewhat tangled account of Pringle's solar plexus, Van der Post's feelings about this first phase are basically sound: we are dealing with a century of colonial writing which is marked, as Worsfold and Young omit to mention, by its writers being committed to engaging and changing the land, but not to belonging to it. The writers here, as Froude would say of them, are those 'English colonists [who] go to South Africa to make money, and come back with it'.[6] The colonial writer retains a tourist view of things; like Sylvester Tramper, once his adolescent yearnings are allayed, he returns 'home' to enjoy the fruits of his labours. Our area here is that part of Southern African literature which epitomizes the pioneering, frontier-type experience; the literature which is written frequently in the romance genre, and which frequently features the hunter, the hunter who came before the missionary. Its authors are those who are raiders rather than stayers, ones who use Southern Africa as a projection of certain sentiments within the British psyche, ones who, when all is said and done, consider themselves British writers out on an experiential spree from the great body of English literature.

Sir William Cornwallis Harris is indeed the hunter with whom to start. His experiences on furlough from India over the years 1836–7 provided him with the material for three Southern African books. In the third, *Portraits of the Game and Wild Animals of Southern Africa* (1840), he wearied of the criticism levelled at his two previous works:

Of those who have taken up the unpretending Narrative of my recent adventures in the wilds of Southern Africa, to which the present volume may be considered to form an amplification, few will deny that to wander through a fairy-land of sport, among the independent denizens of the wild wilderness — realizing, as it were, a new and fabled creation amid scenes never before paced by civilised foot, — is in itself so truly spirit-stirring and romantic, that in spite of the many hardships and privations which are inseparable from a campaign directed against the ferae naturae, the witchcraft of the desert must prove irresistible. Nor will any one who reflects that the regions I traversed were either totally depopulated, or very sparingly inhabited, complain, that my attention should have been so exclusively directed to the brute creation. . . . It seldom fell to my fortune to have opportunities of studying the natural history of those primitive children of the desert.[7]

Harris is myth-making about himself without realizing it; his *Narrative* suggested that he had more than ample chances to 'interview' the 'wild races of the human species' (p. 1), and no one who experienced endless receptions at the hands of Mzilikazi in the heart of the Matabele Empire could pretend that what is now the Western Transvaal was then underpopulated. Like all the hunters in his wake, Harris is not interested in people.

His scrupulous interest in animals, however, is his saving grace, for Harris's 'portraits' are among the wonders not only of nineteenth-century South African zoology, but of its art. Harris's assumptions about hunting become stock in the literature: the hunt is a 'campaign' which involves 'hardships and privations', and these in turn lead to a well-earned victory; the military rhetoric is endemic not only to Indian Army captains, but to the writers in the genre as a whole, deriving as it does from a school-room exposure to works like Caesar's *Gallic Wars*. What is also mandatory to the hunter is that as he crosses the divide into the unknown, or the barely known, he discovers a 'fairy-land', one that derives in essence from the school-room as well, for it is a fairy-land peopled more with the hobgoblins and ogres of the British nursery than with anything observably African.

I have beheld [continues Harris] the venerable and half-reasoning Elephant browsing in native majesty among his own contemporary trees, 'in his huge strength impregnable;' — have torn the much-prized ivory from his giant jaws, and plucked the horn from the saucy nose of the Rhinoceros. I have stripped the proud *spolia* from the shaggy shoulder of the 'king of beasts, who clears the desert with his rolling eye;' — have humbled the haughty head of the forest bull; — and though 'she scorneth the horse and his rider,' have despoiled the fleet Ostrich of her costly plumes. More — I have dragged forth *Behemoth*, 'whose ribs are like bars of iron,' from his hiding place under the shady trees, in the covert of the reed and fens, — and have ridden familiarly by the side of the towering *Zamor*, the colossal glory of the wilderness, long classed with the wild chimeras of man's brain. (p. 3)

Young is at least partly right about the Old Testament — if ever Harris can prove that an obscure phrase of the Bible has a living origin, he takes a splendid joy in exhibiting that Biblical verses and schoolboy poetry texts can be about poetic reveries coming true.

Linked with this endearing, but nevertheless spurious, habit of literary footnoting is the British concept of sport. The wilderness becomes a playground for inflated bullies who measure fun in terms of the humbling of brutes greater in size than themselves. Hunting is seen as a contest, to be won by the small man with the big weapon. In case the implications of this sporting spirit miss us, Harris tells us what to think about him:

if I am occasionally charged with lavish slaughter, I must e'en shelter myself behind the renowned deeds of bold Robin Hood and his gallant yeomen in the 'greene forrèst of Sherwood' . . . (p. 3)

One takes the hunting connection in the spirit in which it is offered, and, like Harris, recalls the proud tradition of the chase in Europe in all its most elaborate formality. One concedes that there is a Chaucerian glory to Captain Harris, ' "pricking at a right merrye pace" with my fellow-voyageur, over the broad bosom of the flower-decked prairies of South Africa' (p. 3), and one appreciates the cult aspect of his dedication of the book to 'my brother votaries of the Chase' (p. 3). That the rural English stag or fox could proliferate into a subcontinent of verminous quarries is a fact. That a young Englishman could regard the Cape Colony as a magnification of the ritual dream in which he is blooded by the bucketful — and thus becomes a man, a member of the club — is an irony. And that the whole exercise should be conducted in terms of a literary tradition traceable back to Nimrod is not surprising at all. The fruits of the cult of the hunter are maturity, the by-products are the endless trophies which clutter the dark stairways of Victorian manor houses. Its meaning is that of a prolonged and venerable ceremony which, by definition, is mainly of interest to those who are due to go through it — the British boys whom society wishes to make adult through ritual. When Harris drops the name Robin Hood, he has no thought of robbing the rich to feed the poor.

With the above kind of consideration in mind, this whole pioneer literature begins to take on some meaning. When Worsfold talks of 'the life of the Anglo-Saxon race, when the blood of its sons is stirred with strife', and when Young talks of romances being 'lived, not written' because 'leisure and contemplation are frowned upon as being vicious', and when Van der Post talks of a 'single-handed encounter with South Africa', they may all be using a slippery kind of literary jargon, but they are, in fact, trying to define this type of literature which features the theme of hunting as initiation. Young himself lived it out in romances like *They Seek a Country* (1937) and Van der Post, in writing works such as *A Story like the Wind* (1972), is mining the genre to this day. The patterns of the hunting romance are crucial in Southern African literature and, because of its central characteristic of a rite of initiation into adulthood, it remains a literature written for the young, or — to give it its full Victorian flavour — a literature for 'boys'.

In his *Portraits* Harris is exceedingly concerned to back up his sporting games with literary precedent, and not only the Biblical and British ones already suggested. He is, for example, a chronic quoter of Pringle, one of whose lines we should refer to in passing: 'St. George! he's upon us! — Now, fire, lads, for life!'[8] — a specimen of anapaestic zeal

which puts paid to the lion of Eildon. What happened to the carcass
of that lion we know is not without interest:

The skin of this lion, after being rudely tanned by our Hottentots, was, together
with the skull, transmitted to Sir Walter Scott, as a testimony of the author's
regard; and these trophies have now the honour to form part of the ornaments of
the lamented Poet's antique armoury at Abbotsford. (Wahl, p. 136)

Harris finds a new niche of glory for Le Vaillant as well in the hunter's
gallery.

Like Le Vaillant before him, and like Burchell (with his zebra),
Harris on his return from the frontier leaves behind him one species
of game named after himself — the buck now known as the Sable
Antelope — so that it is an incidental characteristic of the hunter
narrative that it also has an onomastic function.

If one were to doubt the continuity of this genre, one would only
have to go to the next sportsman-hunter to record his adventures in
order to check if the origin of his inspiration were not perhaps more
literary than actual. In his anthology, *The Great Hunters,* Geoffrey
Haresnape concedes the literary interest of hunters' records, but he
does not mention that the role of the hunter is so sacred to him that
it has to be passed from one man in the field to the next, as if there
were an unspoken, secret fraternity to which they all in turn belonged.
Haresnape notes the splendour of these pioneers 'who went into un-
charted places with their twin-grooved muzzle-loaders, solar topees
and volumes of Byron',[9] and shows how their era in effect terminates
as the sport goes out of it, as their weapons become too efficient and
as the sentiment for conservation takes over from the compulsion to
kill; but he does not note their direct line of succession — Le Vaillant
to Harris, and then Harris to Cumming, to Baldwin and to Selous.
When Gordon Cumming arrives in South Africa, his authority for his
five hunting expeditions in the 1840s is Harris, and as he leaves with
his thirty tons of trophies and Cape waggon (and his 'little Bushman')
he crosses paths with William Cotton Oswell, who is to sponsor Livingstone in his great push for Lake Ngami. William Charles Baldwin finds
that his reading of Cumming 'settled me at once'[10] on the idea of
going hunting in Africa, and he carves his initials in a tree overlooking
Victoria Falls alongside Livingstone's. Frederick Courtenay Selous in
turn, according to Baldwin's publisher, 'was greatly influenced in his
decision to go out to Africa by the impression made upon him by Mr
Baldwin's work' (p. 3). Selous himself is rated as 'the last of the big-
game hunters of South Africa; the last of the mighty hunters whose

experiences lay in the greatest hunting ground which this world has seen since civilised man appeared therein' by none other than President Theodore Roosevelt,[11] the first of the twentieth-century heirs of the Great White Hunter — the safari-goer.

It is worth dwelling on these accounts for what they reveal of how the hunters view themselves, because their self-image hardly alters throughout, and their sentiments are virtually interchangeable.

I remember even to-day [writes Selous], and with perfect distinctness, though I have not seen it for many years, a certain picture of Gordon Cumming's well-known book on African hunting, and the fearful fascination it always had for me when I was a small boy. That picture presented a great gaunt lion in the act of seizing one of the hunter's Hottentot servants — poor Hendrick — as he lay asleep by the campfire; but it left to the imagination all the horror and agony of mind suffered by the poor wretch, when so rudely awakened at dead of night and swiftly dragged away in the darkness to a cruel death, in spite of the gallant attempts of his comrades to save him.

During the sixty odd years that have elapsed since this tragedy was enacted on the banks of the Limpopo, many a similar incident has taken place. . . . As a rule, I think, a lion seizes a sleeping man by the head, and in that case, unless it is a very old and weakly animal, death must be usually instantaneous, as its great fangs will be driven into the brain through the thickest negro skull. (*Notes*, p. 47)

The Cumming engraving which acted as an ikon for Selous is one sub-titled 'The Fate of Poor Hendrick', Hendrick being Cumming's faithful servant and shadow, given to drunkenness and 'fits of sulkiness'.[12] Cumming's own account of the incident shows that at daybreak he

proceeded to inspect the scene of the night's awful tragedy. In the hollow, where the beast had consumed his prey, we found one leg of the unfortunate Hendrick, bitten off below the knee, the shoe still on his foot; the grass and bushes were all stained with blood, and fragments of his pea-coat lay around. Poor Hendrick! I knew that old coat, and had often seen some of its shreds in the dense covers where the elephants had charged after my unfortunate after-rider. Hendrick was by far the best man I had. He was of a most cheerful disposition, a first-rate waggon-driver, fearless in the field, very active, willing, and obliging, and his loss to us all was very serious. I felt sick at heart, and could not remain at the waggons, so I resolved to go after elephant to divert my mind. (p. 279)

Cumming the military man, who had hunted in Canada and the Far East, never declares a moratorium against death. His reminiscences read as a vivid and incessant action sequence without much of the cir-cumstantial interpolation that usually makes hunting adventures co-herent. The resort to action whenever luck deals one a bad turn is always made on the reflex at the intrusion of even the most formal emotion. In the literature one becomes familiar with this arrival of an unwarranted death, its dismissal in cursory funeral meditations, followed by renewed obliterative action. Poor Hendrick's virtues, never remarked upon while he was alive, are the virtues that Cumming admires in himself.

In their study of the sociology of colonialism in Africa, *The Africa that Never Was,* Dorothy Hammond and Alta Jablow make this analysis of the Arnoldian concept of sporting behaviour:

> The ethical import of sportsmanship and the code of fair play are extended into all aspects of life. If life can be thought of as a game, then profound emotion is uncalled for, and the English distrust of emotion and its repression are justified. Whether in sport, war, or all of life, there is, therefore, every need for good form and very little need for strong feeling.[13]

Generation by generation these same hunter–sportsmen, each a replica of the last, recur with these same responses. 'Poor Khiva' in *King Solomon's Mines* dies on behalf of another of them, Sir Henry Curtis.

The hunters' motives for writing are always identical: in their preface they each unequivocally declare that, because each one of them has pushed further into the hinterland (Harris to beyond the Orange, Cumming to beyond the Limpopo, Baldwin to the Zambezi and Selous into equatorial Africa), their accounts of the extra territory covered might at least have the value of adding to man's storehouse of knowledge, as indeed they did. When Darwin needed to know about the ecology of inland, he made an excursion into the Karoo briefly enough to discover only that it was a 'sterile country'[14] and then turned to an explorer like Smith for evidence of grazing habits; such accumulating evidence would take him further along the network of scientific data for him to evolve the theory of natural selection, in which his axiom about the survival of the fittest would lend an incidental glamour to the whole matter of British supremacy over the animal kingdom.

Although each hunter emphatically claims for himself the right to have no literary pretensions, he makes no end of use of literary techniques. Each account is invariably based on a ramshackle field diary or journal and, as Cumming says, and as they all say:

> Whatever on these occasions I witnessed worthy of attention, I noted in my journal whilst the impression was yet fresh in my memory — from this journal the following work is almost literally transcribed. Written under such circumstances, the reader will not look for the graces of style. The hand, wearied all day by grasping the rifle, is not the best suited for wielding the pen. If I have in simple language given pleasure to sportsmen, or added one page to the natural history of Southern Africa, or to our knowledge of its tribes, I shall think myself amply repaid for my

many wanderings and watchings in a wild and savage land. (p. 6)

But this assumed modesty and pretended naivety does not hold up to scrutiny, for these accounts, by their very acts of selection and omission, are frequently as calculated works of prose as any fiction. The hand that is 'wearied all day by grasping the rifle' is usually capable enough of dealing out machine-gun prose which, in its sparseness and directness, is, if nothing else, designed to duck the return fire of literary criticism. This pretence at being a literary hamhand, which is part of the hunter's acute self-defensiveness, is as cunning a technical ploy as any wielded by a Dickens or a Hardy and, as we have seen in the case of Young's rating of the hunters, one which has succeeded in taking in most readers.

None of these writers is unaware of how to shape action sequences, for example, as they are all habitual readers of adventure stories themselves. Baldwin writes:

Sent away four *Blackwood Magazines,* which I almost knew by heart, and begged something in the shape of print in exchange from two Englishmen. (p. 197)

As for the others, Baldwin's patron writer is Sir Walter Scott, whom none of them is averse to adapting to African scenery. When Baldwin comes across a secret kraal, he sees nothing incongruous in remarking that: 'It is, verily, the queerest place I ever saw in my life, just as Walter Scott describes Ben Venue' (p. 206). Their reading of Scott, as much as their direct experience, conditions their views of the landscape and its people. As Susanne Howe notes in her *Novels of Empire* (1949), the Scott link is appropriate, since to his enthusiastic readers Scott is the glorifier of muscular action and (in a novel like *Ivanhoe*) of the clash of cultures. The game of 'playing the Nimrod' (Cumming, p. 5) is inspired by Scott's attempt to recreate a disappearing chivalric spirit in the face of modern progress. Thus the pure action of the hunter takes on a glorious, honour-saving dynamic of its own.

The following passage shows how this spirit works out in a South African situation, and to read it for its full effect one has only to see Cumming, complete with kilt, as a latter-day knight at arms:

I took the sea-cow next to me, and with my first ball gave her a mortal wound, knocking loose the great plate on the top of her skull, when she commenced plunging round and round. . . . I feared that she would get into deep water, and be lost like the last two. To settle the matter, therefore, I fired a second shot from the bank, which, entering the roof of her skull, passed out through her ear; after which she kept constantly splashing round and round in a circle in the middle of the river. I had great fears of the crocodiles, and did not know whether the sea-cow might not attack me; my anxiety to secure her overcame all hesitation, so, divesting myself of my leathers, and armed with a sharp knife, I dashed into the water . . . seizing her tail, I attempted to incline her course to land . . . as the only means of securing her, [I] cut two deep parallel incisions through the skin of her stern, and lifting this skin from the flesh, so that I could get in my two hands, I made use of it as a handle; and after some desperate hard work, sometimes pushing and sometimes pulling, the sea-cow continuing her circular course all the time, and I holding on like grim Death, eventually succeeded in bringing this gigantic and most powerful animal back to the bank . . . and moved Behemoth to a tree; I then sent a ball through the centre of her head, and she was numbered with the dead. (pp. 395–6)

The passage is worth quoting at such length for what it reveals of the hunter's view of his purpose in life. Basically Cumming is exulting in a game of physical prowess, but, though this hippopotamus is no force of evil threatening mankind, in Cumming's terms the contest takes on an element of Beowulf's civilized arms overcoming some floundering Grendel. A popular variation on this theme is of course the hunter of man-eaters story, like *The Man-eaters of Tsavo* by Colonel J.H. Patterson, the Anglo–Boer War veteran, whom Selous rated as a masterpiece of 'pluck, tact and determination'.[15] Cumming conceives of the hippopotamus as a metal beast, she has 'plate on the top of her skull' and her backside is a 'stern', as if she were an ironclad ship. The little metal of bullets can overcome the whole of the vast steely monster who has to pay tribute to the strength of the fighter's arm. That the whole scene is also an exhibition of sadism acquires a grim humour when one learns that the caption to the engraving is entitled 'A Waltz with a Hippopotamus'.[16]

Cumming is by no means naive in his deployment of literary tricks. The entire passage, by overstating the grossness of the victim, reflects back on his own heroism; in Cumming's case particularly, the modesty is a disguise for self-glorification. He slips into seeing himself as the agent of 'grim Death' itself, as his pride urges him to have a moral duty to kill. None of the hunters mentioned here is ever hypocritical enough to frame his acts to look as though they were meant to be deeds of self-defence; as a man of action he holds it his right to be a naked aggressor. If this were not so, Cumming would not write the scene as if he had anything but his honour to lose, and he is honest enough about it as he presents the Behemoth as trying her damnedest to get away from him. In converting a tranquil river scene into an outpouring of blood, Mars the god of war smoulders over Cumming, relentlessly and unrelievedly. He always did: 'Long before I went to

Eton [Cumming remembers] I took pride in the goodly array of hunting trophies which hung around my room' (p. 7). His Nimrod game is merely a prelude to what will come in his wake on the playing-fields of South Africa.

In his survey of the heroes of popular Victorian fiction, Patrick Howarth traces the progress of what he wryly calls Newbolt Man through the public schools with their muscular Christianity, and abroad where the mad, vengeful dogs of England act out the concept of the White Man's Burden. Here is Baldwin, assuming that weary burden with an exasperation that betrays no doubts about the validity of his mission abroad:

[Day's entry] I saw a troop of old buffaloes in thin hackthorns, where there was no shelter in case of a charge. I took a circle, however, and came at them from below the wind, two only standing, and eight lying; they were very bare; I got within eighty yards, and one bull stood well and I took a steady pot, hearing the bullets clap beautifully. . . . They all tore away, and I should have given up, had not Juno taken the blood-spoor, and I heard her baying him 300 or 400 yards ahead, and when I got up he was just expiring, the bullet in the exact place and right direction. This will save one nag a hard day's work, as otherwise, I must have gone to shoot an eland or giraffe, for I have to support daily eighteen men. I could, had I been so disposed, have killed four or five bráce of pheasants, thus making rather a good morning's work of it. I have nothing to amuse myself with but a pile of *Illustrated News,* the latest bearing date 1856, but most of them 1854. (p. 317)

Baldwin is saying that the hunting is the business, the reading the amusement. If he had no staff of eighteen he would not have to shoot for them, and the sanctity of his role forbids his letting that staff hunt for themselves, which presumably they had been capable of doing for centuries before the arrival of the white man.

David Livingstone himself spots the irony of the white man's assumption of this burden of being the great provider when, in his *Travels and Researches in South Africa,* he describes the natives' reaction to Mr Oswell:

I sometimes felt annoyed at the low estimation in which some of my hunting friends were held; for, believing that the chase is eminently conducive to the formation of a brave and noble character, and that the contest with wild beasts is adapted for fostering that coolness in emergencies, and active presence of mind, which we all admire, I was naturally anxious that a higher estimate of my countrymen should be formed in the native mind. 'Have these hunters, who come so far and work so hard, no meat at home?' — 'Why, these men are rich, and could slaughter oxen every day of their lives.' — 'And yet they come here, and endure so much thirst for the sake of this dry meat, none of which is equal

to beef?' — 'Yes, it is for the sake of play besides' (the idea of sport not being in
the language). — This produces a laugh, as much as to say, 'Ah, you know better;'
or, 'Your friends are fools.' When they can get a man to kill large quantities of
game for them, whatever *he* may think of himself or of his achievements, *they*
pride themselves in having adroitly turned to good account the folly of an itiner-
ant butcher.[17]

Livingstone's insight into the ironic distance between the alternative
concepts of the hunter as hero and as butcher is appropriate to a man
of peace, but Livingstone's double vision could not be operative in the
hunting tradition.

On the other hand, the hunter's ethic did require a kind of openness
and frankness, geared to unquestioning confrontation and bashing
ever onwards; at a touch of irony such impulses would have had to
crumble. Hence the literature that flows from our hunting fathers has
for its own preservation to be utterly without humour. The stress is
on the accumulation of new knowledge, and titles vie with one another
in advertising experience; E.F. Sandeman's *Eight Months in an Ox-
Waggon* (1880) is superseded by Andrew Anderson's *Twenty-Five
Years in a Waggon* (1888). In his preface, Anderson remarks of the
fruits of exploration:

Such information is imperative to a commercial nation like Great Britain, particularly when we look round and see such competition in trade with our continental
neighbours, [which] necessitates corresponding energy at home if we wish to hold
our own in the markets of the world, and this cannot be done unless the resources
and capabilities of every quarter of the globe is thoroughly known.

The essence of the hunter–explorer's world view has to remain an external one; it probes ever forward, it never probes inward.

Their pose that they are constitutionally professional in everything
but literature, in relation to which they claim amateurism as a virtue,
is thus part of the pioneer myth. This pose persists right through to
the last great pioneer work that Southern African literature has produced, J.P. Fitzpatrick's *Jock of the Bushveld.* There, as late as 1907,
we still find this kind of disclaimer:

The writer is well aware that . . . there are grave inequalities in style and system,
and in plane of phrase and thought, in different parts of the book. . . . It is not a
diary: incidents have been grouped and moved to get over the difficulty of blank
days and bad spells, but there is no incident of importance or of credit to Jock
which is not absolutely true. . . . Little by little the book has grown until it has
come perilously near the condition in which it might be thought to have Pretensions. It has none! It is what it was: a simple record, compiled for the interest and

satisfaction of some Little People, and a small tribute of remembrance and affection offered at the shrine of the old life and those who made it . . .[18]

One would hesitate to accuse Fitzpatrick of misrepresentation of himself as a literary artist, yet it is indeed strange that a convention could arise which forces the author to deny himself any claim to artistic merit, when he himself knows that in cutting and shaping experience (in getting over the 'blank days and bad spells') he is pretty deeply involved in the business of turning life into art, of writing not factual documentation but for fictional effect. This obstinate refusal to admit to the use of well-tried and highly effective artistic techniques in writing about the frontier life is an illuminating part of the pioneer's make-up: he feels that art bamboozles (instead of clarifying). He adopts this stance because he believes that life itself should be shown as the reality and the educator. Most hunters are self-made men, and it is their supposed greater rapport with life that made them.

The records we have of hunting experiences comprise a low-key literature all of its own. It is generally written in the service of an expanding imperialism, and the hunter himself, because he is always a day's ride ahead of the imperial standard, becomes the literature's true frontiersman. The moment he feels his function being pre-empted by the farmer whose land he has cleared and by the more sedentary members of Her Majesty's Service, he becomes gloomy and resentful. As the towns displace Swift's elephants, the hunter is accordingly obliged to relocate his frontier. When he is finally displaced by the colonial bureaucrats — the traders, magistrates, police and military, whom he resists and despises — he becomes dispossessed and dies.

All these tensions are operative as early as 1860 in a man like John Bisset. In his memoirs entitled *Sport and War* — and the concepts of sport and war become inextricably linked here — this 'regular soldier' writes his own elegy. The tone is indeed that of the 'good despatch: clear, business-like and economical', as Young would have it, but the effect is altogether the opposite. Bisset recounts the triumphal progress of the somewhat simple-minded Prince Alfred, the fifteen-year-old son of Queen Victoria, through the Eastern Cape, the heart of Boerdom in the Free State and Transvaal, and into Natal Colony on a mission of goodwill that prefigured the unification of the four provinces under a British flag half a century later. When he comes to describe the ceremonial grand battue which marked not only the royal adolescent's baptism in blood, but perhaps the greatest — and last — hunt of its kind ever staged, he tells us more about the frontier

than he means to. The advent of the Prince himself, although Bisset is
magnificently respectful towards his Royal Charge, is to him a kind of
charade. When Chief Moroka and his obliging citizens drum up every
head of game there is left in the entire Free State, and drive them together for confrontation with Prince Affie, it is as if all the scattered
hunter's records have accumulated into a grand finale, one which is
symbolic of ultimate regal power over the animal kingdom, but one
which is nevertheless dehumanizing:

. . . the battue commenced by the Prince bringing down a great wildebeast, or
gnu. This ferocious-looking beast turned on His Royal Highness on being wounded,
and received a second ball, which rolled him over. This was the signal for a general
onslaught.

The hunting party advanced up the plain in extended order, a few yards apart,
and masses of game kept breaking through as the pressure of the coming streams
of antelopes, quaggas, zeebras, bles-boks, eelands, ostriches, hartebeasts, wilde-
beasts, koodoos, &c. &c. came pouring on towards us, and checked by our fire,
commenced to whirl. The plain in which we were was of vast extent — I dare say
nearly a hundred miles in circumference — and the whole of this extent was one
moving mass of game. The gaps between the mountains on all sides of this plain
were stopped by a living line of men, and we were in the midst of this whirling throng firing at great game at not twenty-five yards' distance as fast as we
could load. The Prince fired as fast as guns could be handed him, for Currie rode
on one side and I on the other, and we alternately handed guns to him as he discharged his own. As the circle narrowed there really was a considerable danger
from the game breaking through, for when a stampede took place so much dust
arose that you were in danger of being trampled to death. It became very exciting
to see great beasts larger than horses rolling over from right and left shots not ten
paces from you, and also charging down with their great horns lowered as if they
were coming right at you and then swerving to one side or the other. . . .

During the great slaughter of the day the circle of natives was closing in; and
the mass of game became so dressed together at last, that the Prince and Currie
took to their hunting hogspears and charged into the midst, driving home the
'Paget blades' into the infuriated animals. . . . This great destruction of 600 head
of large game was no wilful waste of God's creatures; some thousands of natives
had been employed to drive the masses together, and they had brought 600 pack-
oxen to carry away the carcasses for their winter supply of food. . . .

Most of the sportsmen looked more like butchers than sportsmen, from being
so covered in blood. His Royal Highness and Currie were red up to the shoulders
from using the spear. I cannot myself boast of many trophies, as I generally
handed my double gun to the Prince as fast as I could load it; nevertheless I
could not resist now and then bowling over a couple of great antelopes as they
whirled past me. It was a very exciting day, and were His Royal Highness to live
for a hundred years I do not believe he could ever see such a scene again, for the
game in South Africa is fast disappearing.[19]

Bisset's account is quite extraordinary, if read as a piece of literature, for it reveals all the stock responses of the hunter operating under maximum pressure. The jest that if the Prince were to be virtually immortal (which even his being the living impersonation of an heraldic lion cannot make him), he could never again behold such splendours, contains the nub of an inexpressibly grand truth: youth dies. A word like 'game' itself takes on a new resonance of meaning here. The general confusion in Bisset's terminology between hunting and military terms is characteristic: 'extended order' facing up to 'hordes' and 'masses' and 'whirling throngs' are phrases which could equally well be, and were, used to describe many a 'Kaffir' War.

Bisset shows in two details that he senses the demise of his own kind: he feels the horizon closing in on him like a noose that winds in all infinity; there is no more room for sport. He feels himself displaced as the etiquette of the ceremony demands of him that he abjure his individuality into playing a subordinate role in a hierarchical situation. Once this, his individual heroism, is denied him, as personal endeavour is turned into systematic slaughter, he is good for no more than a nostalgic tale about the good old days, when men could behave like boys for ever.

This relentless spirit of individual go-getting accounts for the type of tunnel vision characterizing the boy's adventure literature which derives directly from the documents discussed here. The boundary line between fact and fiction is blurred, as the hunter narrative moves into mass production with the advent of boy's fiction. It is quite mandatory in this kind of fiction that the world view of the protagonist must be limited by the bounds of his ethic. Thus, what we call 'wild life', and they called 'game', can be seen only in terms of its potential brutish hostility, never in its pacific contentment; the mildest, most sunny nook turns into a raging jungle, the most pastoral savannah into a threatening and aggressive hell-hole. That attitude to nature which was endemic to Rose's interpretation of Le Vaillant transfers holus bolus into the British pioneer's view of nature's other 'denizens' as well, the people whom with an unconscious acknowledgement of their rights the British named 'natives'. Rose can no more conceive of a possible relationship with a 'savage' human being than with a wild animal. The love-bond is subordinated to the war-bond, whereby relationships become a matter of subduing, of reducing equal but opposite forces into tributaries or, if that fails, wiping them out in a holocaust of retribution. This inherent urge to dominate, the Prospero complex, as Mannoni calls it, becomes unrepressed in a colonial situation.

This is demonstrated very precisely in one of the first South African novels, E.A. Kendall's *The English Boy at the Cape* (1835), a work that has almost as much space devoted to footnotes as to the text itself. The English boy's adventures are written for the vicarious enjoyment of other English boys not fortunate enough to be out on their travels yet. The boy of the title, however, exhibits many unconvincing characteristics, as boys in Victorian fiction are wont to do, since the idea that a mere boy could engage one throughout a tripledecker novel (as this one is) turns into a gross overworking of a simple pretext. Nevertheless, the boy himself is merely an excuse for an educational lecture, an exercise in didacticism which uses the novel form to sugar the pill of the instruction manual within.

Having identified the 'Black Caffres' all down the east coast of Africa as the Macrobian Ethiopians of Herodotus, Kendall instructs as follows:

The Black Caffres are gentle or rugged according to the occasion; but this admission does not vindicate them from the charge of savageness. It is not how soft and amiably [*sic*] a people can behave when they are pleased, or when they are not offended nor excited, that stamps them as civilised, or as morally estimable; for those things are natural to the human character, and need no cultivation, and confer no distinction. But the test of the cultivated man is, his moderation in resentment, his forbearance towards his enemies, his mildness even in his anger, his incapability of cruelty; – the length, in short, to which he can go, or beyond which he will not go, under circumstances the most adapted to bring into action the violence of his temper. The command of temper, – this is breeding; and breeding is civilization. . . . The great business of improvement of human character, both in civil and savage life, is the restraint of its ferocity, and the increase of its sweetness.[20]

For all that, Kendall's concept of civilization includes allowing his hero, Charles, the once-in-a-lifetime occasion to lapse into being a little 'savage' himself, on the grounds that it is part of the Englishman's acquisition of experience that will mature him into being able to use his 'breeding'.

During the course of the action what Charles is put through includes:

his adventures with hunting parties, his escapes among the rocks, his share in tracking and killing a leopard, his investiture with a *carosse* of its shining spotted coat; (his hair and skin, at the same time, being properly ornamented with red clay;) his gambols, and songs, and dances, with the merry and black-eyed children; his admission even to the evening ring, among the taller girls and boys; or of his acquisition of a Caffre bow and arrow, and little Caffre assegay, and ivory armlets; and his success in often spearing a fish, or bringing down, from a tree, or out of the air, the bird upon which, an hour after, he made a hunter's dinner! (vol.3, p. 31)

All that, before going home not only to the Mother Country but to mother herself.

The equation does not work the other way round. No 'Black Caffre' youth in the literature is permitted to romp his way through a Settler household, is given a place of honour at the dinner table and permitted not to say his prayers before tumbling into bed. Although this specimen of British boyhood has the privilege and the 'breeding' to be allowed to contain all that is finest in the savage, no savage, because of lack of 'breeding', is allowed to aspire to a state of civilization. In the literature the pattern is of English boys being encouraged to become men (and the boy's literature of the time is their rite of passage, their initiation school), while 'Black Caffre' men are encouraged to become boys.

Enumerating the ramifications of this literary idea, which remains essentially unchanged from Kendall through Captain Marryat and R.M. Ballantyne, Haggard and Bertram Mitford and G.A. Henty, through John Buchan to Stuart Cloete and Wilbur Smith, would be a tedious business, because these authors' works of adventure fiction conform so rigidly to established patterns that technical advances in ways of story-telling or of dramatization are minimal. The very solidarity and unchangingness of this genre is an index of its stability, of its awesome power and undying appeal. Invention, it seems, is no great necessity when churning out the same old goods for an insatiable and constant market that can maintain an illusion that things do not change. No Southern African work of hunting and adventure has received its reverse image, as Ballantyne's *The Coral Island* did in Golding's *Lord of the Flies* in 1954.

One remarks of this genre that it does have a direct link with the raw material out of which it is shaped. All the authors mentioned here, with the exception of Marryat, produced factual works about Southern Africa as well as their boy's adventures. One remarks also that it has to be a comment on the nature of Southern African English literature that this genre alone is the one that has produced the most works, and endured the longest. Therefore, in trying to define it more closely, one would arrive at a more clear definition of the literature as a whole.

In Frederick Marryat's *The Mission, or Scenes in Africa,* first published in 1845, the young hero is not as youthful as he behaves: he is twenty-two, 'a tall, handsome young man, very powerful in frame, and very partial to all athletic exercises; he was the best rower and the best cricketer at Oxford, very fond of horses and hunting, and an excellent shot; in character and disposition he was generous and amiable, frank in his manner, and obliging to his inferiors'.[21] He makes his first entry after breaking in ('conquering') a horse, whereupon his grand-uncle clarifies the groundwork of what is to become Alexander Wilmot's mission:

'I think I see my poor Elizabeth [his daughter, lost in the wreck of the *Grosvenor*], the wife or slave to some wild savage; her children, merciful Heaven! my grand-children, growing up as the brutes of the field in ignorance and idolatry. It is torture, my dear Alexander — absolute torture, and requires long prayer and meditation to restore my mind to its usual tone, and to enable me to bow to the dispensations of the Divine will.' (p. 5)

The mission itself is to confirm that the missing daughter cannot have been ravished by a black man and — worse still — have borne him children. Mission is accomplished when the young Alexander, conqueror of not only a considerable tonnage of the remaining wild life of Southern Africa, but of imperialism's deepest fears, returns to the old man with the reassuring news that the lost Elizabeth did not survive to live a fate worse than death. As Russell J. Linnemann observes, the purpose of the book is to teach the message that 'it is better to be dead than to be a savage'.[22] The Prospero complex, as defined by Mannoni, requires that there is total severance between the civilized and the savage. This, however, is merely the general drift of the novel, for Alexander's education is compounded of even stranger moral dilemmas.

What makes Marryat's work so interesting is that he, unlike the others, writes without first-hand knowledge of South Africa; for this reason Oliver Warner labels it Marryat's 'one fiasco'.[23] But, being a compilation of scattered bits and pieces of printed records about South Africa, painstakingly researched and skilfully assembled, the novel can proceed as pure theory, untouched by any intrusion of any particular reality which might catch it off balance, and for our purposes it is by no means a fiasco. For Alexander Wilmot the Cape of Good Hope presents an alternative to the Grand Tour of Europe, of which his grand-uncle has this to say:

in the present high state of civilization there will be found little or no difference in the manners and customs of people; in the Courts, none; very little in the best society, in which you [would] of course mix; and not so very much as people may imagine among the mass of population; but the scenery of the countries and the remains of ancient times are still interesting . . . (p. 13)

This is a vast oversimplification of the state of Europe in 1828, but it is of interest in the way in which it reveals the Wilmot family's own attitude to history — the remains of ancient history with all their various significations are lumped together as stony evidence of some vague generalization that there once was immeasureable greatness in Europe. This attitude, antipathetic to the most basic tenets of modern-day history and archaeology, is transferred directly to Africa, where the young Wilmot is to receive an alternative education in life: no ancient ruins, therefore no history, thus uncivilized.

By the time of Haggard, when ancient ruins are indeed found to exist in Southern Africa, they have to be explained away as yet further manifestations of ancient 'European' grandeur (for example, Zimbabwe turned into Ophir, and King Solomon transported bodily from the Negev Desert to some mythical Kukuanaland). When in 1871 the German explorer Carl Mauch becomes one of the first white men to 'discover' Zimbabwe, his explanation is as follows:

All [the local population] are absolutely convinced that white people once inhabited the region, for even now there are signs of habitations and iron tools to be found which could not have been produced by the blacks. . . . Veni, vidi and God be praised for it. To Him be the glory! [24]

Any historical sense is extremely manipulated, not to say distorted, in Marryat and his successors; all the history the young Wilmot is allowed is the hazy notion that once there was a Roman Empire, complete with crested helmets and gladiators, whose garrisons fell to an invasion of barbarians. This tragedy the border-guards of the new frontier must somehow avenge.

Marryat manipulates literature no less skilfully for his ends. All Wilmot needs to know about English literature is that it has a poet or two; he remarks to Mr Swinton, the naturalist who accompanies him on his tour, that: ' "The proper study of mankind is man,' says the poet' (p. 24) — *which* poet being unimportant (or unknown). In Marryat's books, all of English literature from the tribal *Beowulf* poet through to Pope conflates into 'the poet', and the fact that barbarian culture does not have 'the poet' (or at least a succession of poets who wrote books) is proof of their inferiority in that field, too. Mr Swinton replies to that apophthegm: 'Poets deal in fiction, Mr Wilmot . . . to study man, is only to study his inconsistencies and his aberrations from the right path, which the free-will permitted to him induces him to follow; but in the study of Nature, you witness the directing power of the Almighty' (p. 24). Man's freewill, according to Swinton, virtually absolves him from conforming to any precise sense of divine law, which is an ironic belief to hold in the face of the fact that all Marryat's characters automatically, like Herbert, presume that lawlessness is a defining quality of the savage. The disbelief expressed in the interest of the marks of individuality (those 'inconsistencies' and 'aberrations' are the normal province of realist fiction) explains why the entire literature can – and must – function on the level of stereotype. To propagate the notion that all poetry is 'fiction', too, is characteristic, for, if fiction is defined as pulling the wool over a reader's eyes, how much greater can the effect of fiction be if it forewarns the reader against the propagandistic skills of art, only in order to be free to wield those skills all the more effectively.

As Tony Harrison establishes in his introduction to the modern re-publication of *The Mission,* it contains an early version of a Victorian concept of there being a hierarchy of nature, a sort of revised Great Chain of Being, a 'scale of creation, with man at the summit, in two kinds "enlightened" and "savage", and then down to the "brute species" and by means of the list of natural sciences through the animal, vegetable and mineral kingdoms' (Harrison, p. viii, quoting Marryat, p. 24). This periodic table of values dictates which way one's human sympathies flow, which, as Harrison remarks, is a system that has hardened into today's ranking order of apartheid. 'The hunters feel remorse at killing only when the creatures transcend their status on the scale of creation and display some anthropomorphically attri-buted characteristic, like the "sagacity" of the elephant or the "human motions" of the baboon' (Harrison, p. xi, citing Marryat, p. 206 and p. 234).

This scale of feeling is operative at every level of the text. For example:

'What magnificent animals!' exclaimed Alexander.
'They are enormous, certainly,' said the Major. 'Look at the beautiful dying eye of that noble beast. Is it not speaking?'
'Yes, imploring for mercy, as it were, poor creature.'
'Well, these three beasts, that they say are such good eating, weigh more than fifty antelopes.'
'More than fifty springboks, I grant. Well, what shall we do now?'
'Let our horses get their wind again, and then we will see if we can fall in with some new game. . . . Does Swinton want to preserve one of these creatures?'
'I believe not, they are so very bulky. He says we shall find plenty as we go on, and that he will not encumber the wagons with a skin. . . .' (p. 250)

The animals referred to are not impressive enough to deserve mercy and preservation; they are merely quaggas. One notes in passing that the last quagga at liberty was shot outside Kimberley in 1884, the year of publication of Verne's *Star of the South.*

If in Marryat the message is that God is ultimately lenient to the landed gentry, because they have been chosen to have right of way, the same cannot be said of his view of the lot of the landed gentry's womenfolk. Although the ship that Wilmot travels over on is fairly loaded with nubile Englishwomen (for whom no adventure literature was ever written), they never impinge upon the consciousness of the Anglo-Saxon hero in his pre-initiate condition. Shooting becomes the substitute for sexual activity. Although Marryat is ready to temper the onslaught with a softening power known as philanthropy (represented by Mr Fairburn, cf. the Cape journalist John Fairbairn, whom he is given to quoting verbatim), the preliminary sallies of love are not permitted to engage and weaken the hero. Mars reigns uncontested; Venus is the one who gets the trophies back home.

Adolescent mother-love has to be filtered through nationalism prior to its post-adolescent emergence as love of woman, and the glow of nationalism cossets Wilmot as tenderly as could be desired. As he first sees England sinking out of view from the quayside, Marryat's Mr Swinton imparts this information:

' . . . we [are] both indulging in similar thoughts as we [take] leave of our native shores. Every Englishman does the same, and indeed every true lover of his country, let the country be what it will. We find the feeling as strong in the savage as in the enlightened; it is universal. Indeed, we may fairly say that it extends lower – down to the brute species, from their love of localities.'

'Very true, Sir,' replied Alexander, 'but with brutes, as you say, it is merely the love of locality; with men, I trust, the feeling is more generous and noble.' (p. 17)

Once Wilmot returns to the object of his love, it will be to prove it peopled with suitable ladies, skilled in inspiring that generosity and nobility in a more down-to-earth fashion. The fear that a fair daughter of England, like Wilmot's cousin Elizabeth, could be ravished by the Calibans of the Transkei has to be allayed, before the true ravisher, the Ferdinand of this functional tale, can claim his Miranda as his rightful spoil.

The reference to Shakespeare's *The Tempest* is not made fortuitously; its themes of the superiority of the white man maintained by superior magic, of the unlettered barbarity of the devilish savage and of the sanctity of the virgin daughter-figure caught between the two reverberate through the adventure works for boys. In the Shakespeare allegory of colonization, as Mannoni says, 'the "inferior" being always serves as a scapegoat; our own evil can be projected onto him' (p. 106).

The usefulness of *The Tempest* in this context appears to be not the parable about art and artistry that it is, but the way in which it also encapsulates and perpetuates patterns that are integral to the English self-image abroad.

Like *The Tempest,* many of these adventure novels commence with a shipwreck — a threatening enough reality to a nation that can proceed out of itself only by way of perilous sea voyages — but a shipwreck which symbolizes an unleashing of chaos. Terra firma (be it the Cape, or the Eastern Province or, later, the 'happy hunting ground' over the Orange River, as Harriet Ward calls it) is then awarded the psychic equivalence of another island with all its enchantments (an island in a sea of savagery, etc.) and a shore that is in fact a succession of tidemarks, of borders against the dark and formless inland, frequently seen as a turbulent mass of stormy tribal currents (headed by a Shaka or a Mantatisi), as potentially overwhelming as tidal waves. Marryat's characters are neurotically worried about the girl left floundering after the wreck of the *Grosvenor* because they conceive of her as still being adrift; although they know she has made a landfall, they cannot conceive of her as having completed any voyage — she has not come home. In actual history, white women who were stranded after that same wreck (like Lady Lambert and her daughter, who married the Pondo Chief Sango and his chief adviser) lived on in Kaffraria, producing children apparently without many qualms. In the Prospero eyes of the English islanders, however, they have as good as died; they must be as obliterated as if they had been lost at sea, so that the challenge their compromise with savagery poses to Prospero's dominance is avoided.[25]

In her adventure novel for young readers, 'A Boy's Own Story' called *Hardy and Hunter* (1858), Mrs Harriet Ward writes in her preface, which inevitably is 'Not a Preface, but a Few Words to the Reader', that:

there is scarcely an incident in the book which is not founded on fact, and though some may seek to accuse her of harshness in delineating Kafir character, she has no fear of being mistaken in this matter by those confident to judge. The late accounts from the Cape of Good Hope show that these Savages have been reduced to a pitiable condition through their own folly and superstition; and that the Colonists, forgetting all old grievances, have come forward nobly to their assistance. Time will show what return the Kafirs will make to their benefactors; in the interim, Colonization, with her trusty hand-maidens, Commerce and Agriculture, will, by God's blessing, be the best antidotes to those evils which have been the stumbling-blocks to Emigration.[26]

The frankly propagandistic intentions of Ward's fiction are common to all the novels. But what is less obvious, from the perspective of today, is how the novels, one after the other in rapid succession, also served the function of a continuous news service from the front.

In preparing the novel that was to be published in 1851 as *Jasper Lyle,* Ward wrote to her publisher:

Dear Sir,

This war drags its slow length along — The last passage in each chapter always contains the latest news — and therefore there is no occasion for me to write you a long history of what the troops are doing. . . . England seems greedy now of any kind of information, if we may judge by the pictures from *imagination* in the Ill. London News. . . . Please God this land may yet be a safe refuge for our famine-stricken population. *Now* is the *time* to emigrate.

And in another letter she beguilingly writes: ' . . . you see, dear Sir, I am working very *very* hard — No joke in this untempting illiterate country. . . .'[27]

There are many such novels, born to satisfy the same needs: hunger for in-depth background to the news, desire for evidence of possible adventures in the furtherance of Britain's civilizing mission on the frontier, the yen to know 'how to' achieve, and so on. In Thomas Forester's *Everard Tunstall: A Tale of the Kaffir Wars* (1851) and E.W. Phillips's *Richard Galbraith, Mariner, or Life among the Kaffirs* (also with the subtitle *Wrecked in Caffraria*) (1872), although they are a generation apart, the effect is the same: more potential for the white man, more practical lectures with abundant examples in the lessons of life, learned in the raw. The only essential difference between the two is that the doubts of an outcome of successful conquest in the former are dispelled by the time of the latter, when that conquest is virtually complete.

By 1876, when R.M. Ballantyne visits the frontier, the sensations of exhilaration and relief that the white man is, at last, safe are paramount:

Oh! it was a glorious burst that first race over the wild Karroo, on a spirited steed, in the freshness of the early morning — *'With the silent bushboy alone by my side,'* — for he *was* silent, though tremendously excited. His brown rags fluttered in the self-made breeze, and his brown pony scrambled over the ground quite as fast as Rob Roy.[28]

As for Pringle, so for Ballantyne; the hunter's servant holds his peace. One realizes why: the hunter and his servant share no earthly language. But there are other barriers to communication formed of ideology. Ballantyne, for one, does not expect talk of anyone who is not English.

On coming upon a hut in the Zuurberg, he remarks:

> Close beside it stood a little black creature which resembled a fat and hairless
> monkey. It might have been a baboon. The astonished gaze and grin with which
> it greeted me warranted such an assumption, but when it turned and bolted
> through the hole into the beehive, I observed that it had no tail — not even a
> vestige of such a creation, — and thus I discovered that it was a 'Tottie' . . . (p. 42)

Ballantyne's perceptions, as displayed in his boy's adventure novel of
the next year, *The Settler and the Savage,* admit no questioning of any
of his most Prospero-like assumptions:

> I use the term savage advisedly [he notes], because I wish to call things by their
> right names. A savage *is* a savage, and in my experience among the natives of
> different parts of the earth I have never met with what is styled the 'Noble
> savage', nor even heard of a genuine specimen, except in cases where individuals
> have embraced the civilising Gospel. . . . Nobility of a kind the Kafir does indeed
> possess. God has given him a noble frame and physique. . . . But the uneducated
> savage Kafir is an intellectual child — and a very bad child too. To put him on an
> equality with civilised whites is equivalent to granting, in England, the franchise
> to boys. (pp. 43–5)

Compared with Kendall, Ballantyne exhibits a hardening of attitudes
and a tastelessness which derive from overbearing self-confidence. His
reasoning is so pat and cliché-ridden that it is not reasoning at all; it is
blunt statement of entrenched dogma.

The dogma is the same, but more fearsome, in a writer like Parker
Gillmore, himself a noted hunter. In his novel, a rare piece called *The
Amphibion's Voyage,* the hunter's confidence is so overweening that
the novel is an extended exemplification of how destructive and how
merciless these imperial parables can be towards societies that have
not yet given in to British control. The narrator here is a man called
Johnny Bull, no less, and he, too, subscribes to the idea that:

> Education is a grand thing, no doubt, but if a man never goes beyond his own
> state or county-line, he may have ancient history, the classics, Euclid, and the
> deuce knows what at his finger-ends, and still be an egotistical fool.[29]

That he can go abroad and be educated into being an even more ego-
tistical fool is not within Gillmore's understanding.

The amphibion itself is an invention which is an automated steam-
roller, a juggernaut of a paddlewheel, complete with steering turret,
and its effect is literally to crush whatever it crosses. Due to imperfect
steering, it occasionally runs amuck at 60 m.p.h., which makes its
tank-like depredations cause for mirth. Its inhabitants, a Professor

Ubique and the to-be-educated Mr Attwood, blaze forth from the amphibion's turret. The novel appears to be accumulating a certain ironic promise when the amphibion on its voyage from New York runs aground on Ichaboe Island and the professor is hurled headlong into an age-old deposit of guano — a product that is a fine quarry for those hunting treasure instead of game — only to emerge 'like a whited sepulchre' (p. 47), but Gillmore's humour is meant chummily, not ironically. The conquering mentality has gone so rampant in Gillmore that the fact that they mistake a Bushman for an 'ostrich with elephantiasis' (p. 63), and shoot it, is meant as another joke.

In Gillmore the boy's adventure novel seems to complete a small cycle of its own. The purpose of the amphibion's expedition into the Chobe area of Botswana seems to be not only to glamorize the concept of sportive camaraderie for the reader back home, but to ensure that those same values are imposed on the natives as well. Christianity, in this case, carries with it its own spirit of open competition, of stress on healthy manly virtues that the 'savage', for all his marvellous prowess, now has to learn in turn. If we may say that the heyday of the British Empire stretched from the 1880s to 1914, this novel is a herald of its most aggressively dominating phase.

In order to terminate their visit suitably, and 'to give *éclat* to their departure':

it was decided by our heroes to get up a series of races, in which beads and other trinkets should be the rewards of the conquerors. These were of three descriptions: the first to be competed for on ox-back, the second for warriors and hunters, and the third for all comers irrespective of sex. The course was about half a mile long. Jacob [their general factotum] was instructed in the duties of starter, which he performed admirably; and this is not so much to be wondered at, as he had witnessed several scratch races at the Diamond Fields. At the winning-post, on a raised dais, the King, Professor Ubique and Mr Attwood, attended by a large staff of Indunas, and waited on by a whole crowd of Court beauties, took their seat, that they might witness the termination of each event, decide who was the winner, and also award the prizes. . . . Ere the royal party had been seated many minutes, a shout from many lungs rent the air, which required no interpreter to translate into 'they're off!' Never was such a scramble seen since the days of Donnybrook Fair. . . . The whole affair was so ridiculous that gravity for the moment was forgotten; and His Majesty . . . was graciously pleased to relax his usual immobility, and laugh till the tears ran down his fat cheeks. (pp. 342–4)

This Homeric gymkhana, this parody of a school sports day, conceived as if it were the only means of containing chaos, is illustrative of the state of race relations in the heyday of the genre. When Harriet Ward, thirty years earlier, had her black characters stage ox-races in tunics and jodhpurs, there was still some grace to it; in Gillmore, the grace has turned into patronizing jibes which leave us in no doubt as to whom he conceives of as the only people *capable* of sportsmanship. In the course of his novel the intruders assume kingly roles as instructors and judges, two to one against the tribal chief, and the only reasonably 'admirable' savage is Jacob, the Bushman peppered in jest, now wise to the white man's ways and willing to imitate his most lowly functions. The scene trembles on the brink of becoming a jolly rumpus, a ludicrous free-for-all that could have been cathartic and a breakthrough into genuinely interracial camaraderie, but Gillmore has his umpires remain stonily unimpressed. It is the Old Chief who understands laughter, laughter before the new social routine settles down into another great ritual, the hearty English 'tiffin'.

The quintessential example of the genre, at its very best and at its very worst, is Haggard's *King Solomon's Mines* (1885). It is so because Haggard's one stroke of genius was to make his narrator different from those we have had before. Allan Quatermain is everything all the previous heroes have been, with the exception that he is an older man. From the English boy at the Cape through to Johnny Bull we have been dealing with adolescents performing adolescent feats for adolescent readers. Now, in Haggard, we have a mature man. The book remains dedicated to 'all the big and little boys who read it',[30] but Quatermain himself is not dedicated to remaining a British boy. With Quatermain, one feels, the genre itself has begun to grow up.

In his biography of Haggard, Morton Cohen tells the story of how Haggard came to write *King Solomon's Mines* in six weeks as the result of a wager that he could not outdo Robert Louis Stevenson's *Treasure Island* in the excitement of a mystery adventure.[31] In placing Haggard and his numerous works in the context of the 1880s and on, Cohen is meticulous in showing that Haggard was in the forefront of a revival of romance (as against the naturalist novel) which lasted for over a generation; Haggard's work is part of a fashion which involved Kipling, Stevenson, Lang and others as originators of an alternative Victorian literature. Haggard codified it, and mass-produced it to the delight of his readers back home, starved of surrogates for action, avid for exotica, yearning for some kind of transcendent experience, and so on. The romance Cohen has in mind, with its dubious roots in medieval chivalry and in the Anglo-Saxon mystique of racial superiority, catered for escape from mundanity and offered a sense that glory could be easily won. All that is well and good, and one would not wish to disagree with Cohen; nor would one in any way want to discount his observations that this was a global British phenomenon — romance poured back into London from all corners of the world. Although Haggard's stamping ground was most frequently Southern Africa, he was by no means restricted to it as a backdrop. Anything extra-insular, one might say, served to feed Victorian adventure romance.

But the point to observe here, and one which Cohen does not make, is that a work like *King Solomon's Mines* is also situated at the focal point of what is here postulated as a tradition in Southern African literature which had been in evidence for close on a century, every nuance of which was Haggard's for the taking. Perhaps the map device — whereby Quatermain and his cronies are lured across burning sands into the heart of a fantastic African kingdom — is an ironic nod on Haggard's part at the pirate map in *Treasure Island,* but that is not to say that it is not also a map which derives from intense and accumulating Southern African experience in literature as well. Significantly, the map was bequeathed to Quatermain by a Portuguese explorer who thought he had located Monomatapa. *King Solomon's Mines* incorporates and reaffirms, and to some extent transforms, every element of the genre that has been examined piecemeal here. It may be a manifestation of a vast colonial network which interconnected all parts of the known world during one era of history, but it is also a work that could not have existed if the two or three generations of British writers in Southern Africa before Haggard had not worked at knocking the genre into shape for him.

That this is the case is implicit throughout *King Solomon's Mines.* The form itself is used as a given; Allan Quatermain has merely to flesh it out, making variant stresses here and there, insinuating his own amusing demurrals every so often, but basically leaving it alone to work for itself. *King Solomon's Mines* is no great fictional innovation; it is a work that derives its strength and its assuredness from thoroughly tried predecessors. It has an unerring certainty about it, an unfaltering sense of fictional rightness. It is an act of supreme self-assurance.

As Graham Greene comments on Haggard's works:

They seemed so straightforward to us once, those books we first encountered behind the steel grille of the school library, casting a glow over the dull neighbouring H's. . . . We did not notice the melancholy end of every adventure or know that the battle scenes took their tension from the fear of death which so haunted Haggard.[32]

The straightforwardness, the apparently cut-and-dried quality of the Haggards was inherited, and it is Haggard's virtue that in endlessly repeating his exercises in the genre, counting on its built-in stock responses and its readily workable formulas, he was able to give it an emotional underpinning which was more resonant than the genre had theretofore required.

The strength of *King Solomon's Mines* lies in its being an inventive (as opposed to innovative) exercise in fiction. This is apparent from the first page. It comes as a jolt that many of the conventions of the genre are to be questioned, not in order that they be discarded, but that they be reasserted with renewed strength. The very questioning is the beginning of a subtle kind of artistic sabotage: what before was taken for granted becomes merely conventional, and what before was asserted in earnest becomes a cosmic joke. Quatermain himself is the main joke: he is short in stature, lethargic, more animated by money than by myth, and at almost all times a coward. Alexander Wilmot would have cringed. Whereas his predecessors at least had some honesty on their side when they apologized for crudities in narrative technique, Quatermain seems genuinely distressed that he is such a numbskull. Once again he offers 'my apologies for my blunt way of writing. I can only say in excuse for it that I am more accustomed to handle a rifle than a pen, and cannot make any pretence to the grand literary flights and flourishes which I see in novels' (p. 8), which is an elaboration that seems tongue in cheek; he adds that 'the sense of [the book's] shortcomings, both in style and contents, weighs very heavily upon me' (p. 7).

Quatermain's introduction to his record also apologizes for its not being a hunter's documentary, replete with day-to-day notes about game ('I discovered eight varieties of antelope', he asides in a skilfully placed footnote [p. 7], which is a nod at Harris) and improvised anthropological speculation about the tribes (Quatermain alludes 'only incidentally' to the 'magnificent system of military organization in force in that country, which is, in my opinion, much superior to that inaugurated by Chaka in Zululand, inasmuch as it permits of even more rapid mobilization, and does not necessitate the employment of the pernicious system of forced celibacy', p. 7). Haggard is rupturing the easy and direct bond of identification which has existed in the genre to date: one can no longer assume that the narrator is a flimsy façade speaking on behalf of the speechifying author. There is an immediate disparity between the two here, as Haggard warns the reader implicitly that while Quatermain, the seedy hunter, thinks he *should* be writing a novel along established lines, and supposedly tries to, Haggard himself is set on a different course — he is using the genre merely as a pretext for a different kind of novel. Thus *King Solomon's Mines* has a high parodic content. Part of its enjoyment lies in the fact that as one reads along with Quatermain in this doubting but nevertheless keen spirit, one finds Gillmore, Ballantyne, Ward, Marryat, Kendall and so on being used against one. Haggard feels that Quatermain's forebears often ramble too much, are too frequently waylaid by false trails, and are fatally given to inserting into the narrative gobbets of local colour which always appear unassimilable. In streamlining the previous novels, he is turning what has always been a sloppy form into its logical artistic refinement.

It would be labouring the point to stress how much of a literary creation Allan Quatermain is — his every reflex is, in fact, thoroughly predictable. But whereas no reflex in the previous novels was ever explored past the point of nascence and first action, in Quatermain we have each one assessed and, to some extent, evaluated. 'Let me set down my reasons [for writing the book of the expedition] just to see if I have any' (p. 9), he remarks, undermining some of the confidence we have had in the genre to date.

First reason: Because Sir Henry Curtis and Captain John Good asked me to.
Second reason: Because I am laid up here at Durban with the pain and trouble in my left leg. Ever since that confounded lion got hold of me I have been liable to it, and its being rather bad just now makes me limp more than ever. . . . It is a hard thing that when one has shot sixty-five lions, as I have in the course of my life, that the sixty-sixth should chew your leg like a quid of tobacco. It breaks the routine of the thing. (pp. 9–10)

Haggard's subtlety appears in the slight exaggerations; 'more than ever' opens up a life of pain which is unexpected in a hunter and 'the routine of the thing' shows us the hunter figure going sour, one who acknowledges that even he has become the subject of mechanical reactions, and that life does take its heavy toll.

An apparently gratuitous detail that recurs throughout *King Solomon's Mines* is that it is written by Quatermain expressly for his son, 'my boy Harry' (p. 10). For the first time in the genre we have an author who personalizes his audience. Harry, who is studying to be a doctor, is, incidentally, not planning to return to South Africa to emulate his father. Here we have the spectacle of a father attempting not to instruct his son, but to explain himself to his son — that is rather a shift in emphasis. When the sequel to *King Solomon's Mines* opens with: 'I have just buried my boy, my poor handsome boy of whom I was so proud, and my heart is broken,'[33] the reader is indeed confronted with a reversal that is unprecedented in the genre. That Haggard and others like Fitzpatrick were to bury their sons in the First World War and break their hearts is one reason for the genre having had to come to an end. 'It is very hard having only one son to lose him thus, but God's will be done. Who am I that I should complain? The great wheel of Fate rolls like a Juggernaut, and crushes us all in turn, some soon, some late — it does not matter when, in the end it crushes us all' (p. 11), Allan Quatermain continues on Haggard's behalf. This attitude is more than funeral sentiment, and it serves to raise the concerns of the genre from a mere colonial rough and tumble with Lady Luck into a dicing with imperious death herself.

When Haggard has his hero swear himself in as narrator ('I, Allan Quatermain, of Durban, Natal, Gentleman, make oath and say — ' (*King Solomon's Mines,* p. 10)), he means him to testify in a court which is no mere colonial one. The evidence he is to furnish is of an entanglement with hardships that have tempered him, to be sure, but which are also killing him off. He says: ' . . . it is a cruel and wicked world, and, for a timid man, I have been mixed up in a deal of slaughter. I can't tell the rights of it, but at any rate I have never stolen, though I once cheated a Kaffir out of a herd of cattle. But then, he had done me a dirty turn, and it has troubled me ever since into the bargain' (p. 11). It would seem that while Haggard is asserting the illusions that the genre is so conspicuously successful in trading in, he is at the same time seeing that those illusions come to disillusion the reader. In reading Haggard one feels that his own experiences in South Africa, conditioned by the very reading-matter which was geared to make him a success at handling them, have given him a desperate feeling of let-down. He sees that the genre he teethed on taught lessons that were gauche and over-optimistic; he intends to mature it, to let it contain its own inner contradictions and its own inner sense of futility and disbelief. In the light of what has been established in this chapter, it was virtually blasphemous of Haggard to admit a timid man into the field at all, a man who by all the rules was an incompetent. Quatermain's low profile reduces the heroic to the real, and Haggard's intentions are to turn the outward bound inward.

That Haggard was not able to drive his intentions as a novelist through to a successful fictional resolution is an unfortunate fact. The let-down for the reader comes as soon as Haggard's trio are underway; the account of their journey proves to be a refinement in the genre, but not its transcendence. In *King Solomon's Mines,* Haggard defeats his own ambitious aims, as he turns the work into no more than yet another saga of conquest and blood-letting. In his desperate attempt to add new vitality to the pale and fading genre, Haggard can only set about outdoing his predecessors in 'special effects'. Gagool the witch-doctress, for example, is an insanely over-inflated character: her role as evil utterly personified, her baboon-like racial memory and her staggering longevity are details that overstep the enlargements of fantasy into the merely silly. The carnage, which is equivalent not to that of an Mfecane or two in the hands of a few berserkers, but to genocidal holocaust, mounts up until it rivals earthquakes and floods (of blood) in proportion, and is sickly sensational.

Haggard's characterization of Quatermain is effective, but not effective enough. During the Kukuana Civil War, he notes:

Warlike fragments from the *Ingoldsby Legends,* together with numbers of sanguinary verses from the Old Testament sprang up in my brain like mushrooms in the dark; my blood, which hitherto had been half-frozen with horror, went beating through my veins, and there came upon me a savage desire to kill and spare not. I glanced round at the serried ranks of warriors behind us, and somehow, all in an instant, began to wonder if my face looked like theirs. There they stood, their heads craned forward over their shields, the hands twitching, the lips apart, the fierce features instinct with the hungry lust for battle, and in the eyes a look like the glare of a bloodhound when he sights his quarry. (p. 146)

But, although Quatermain resists his own blooding, and he perceives the lusting savagery within himself, there is no doubt that Haggard ultimately condones what the expedition actually does, which is to cause an entire black nation to be so divided that it all but exterminates itself, and thus can be ruled. Quatermain's doubts here are caused by personal squeamishness, not by political insight. Even though he may not like what he has been reduced to, he will still do his hunter's duty. The vivid metaphor of doubt ('mushrooms in the dark') gives way to the inevitable cliché (blood running cold). Haggard counteracts his flagging faith with greater and greater spectacle, covering up his own doubts with an over-emphasis that amounts to bathos. The media's revenge on *King Solomon's Mines* for this has been no less than four feature movies which reduce the work to a matter of campy cardboard vulgarity. One is tempted to deduce that here, behind the convincing façade, we find no author; there is only wind. Haggard tries to control the genre, but the genre wins over him in the end.

The measure of Haggard's failure can be seen in how he introduces a potentially fruitful refinement only to let it peter out. When he split his main character into three, he had the idea that could have given the genre a new creative energy; Quatermain, the doer and scribe, is only one facet of the three-in-one character of the expedition itself. Ballantyne had done it with respect to youths in *The Coral Island* and in other lurid African blood-letting adventures, but Haggard lets his trio be of mature adults. Sir Henry Curtis, the noble classical scholar, landlord, muscular warrior and curly-haired ancient Dane incarnate, a quite absurd conflation of all that is aristocratic and to be aspired to, and Captain John Good, the earthy, blaspheming (though not on the page), sensual animal, a figure of low comedy with his trousers perpetually off, his hairy white legs and monocle, are foils to Quatermain, his upper and lower selves. Although there are occasionally situations which cause one or the other to come to the fore, they are never shown to march out of step with one another, nor are any wider personality-cleavages exploited. The agreeable interfaces they maintain are no more than a symbol of solidarity; they never diverge into expressing the doubts Haggard professes to feel.

A key illustration of this is in the way Good is observed by Quatermain when a threatening love interest arises. Despite the fact that Quatermain states there is 'not a *petticoat* in the whole history' (p. 10), it is full of scant peltries and curvaceous hips. When Foulata, the beautiful maiden of Kukuanaland, saved by the trio from a grisly tribal sacrifice, nurses Good back to health, pouring her own warm life force into his waning body, Quatermain pulls himself up at the prospects:

Women are women, all the world over, whatever their colour. Yet somehow it seemed curious to watch this dusky beauty bending night and day over the fevered man's couch, and performing all the merciful errands of the sickroom as swiftly, gently, and with as fine an instinct as a trained hospital nurse. (p. 160)

Yet, as Quatermain repeatedly says, as if echoing a slogan, and, worse still, as he has his Florence Nightingale say, 'the sun cannot mate with the darkness, nor the white with the black' (p. 182). This is mere doctrinal assertion, for no fictional reasons are given. When Good's carnal temptations become too apparent, Haggard does the dirty on him by having Foulata killed off. 'Looking at the thing from the point of view of an oldish man of the world, I consider her removal was a fortunate occurrence, since, otherwise, complications would have been sure to ensue' (p. 194) — which is one of the least gentlemanly sentiments ever expressed in the genre. Nothing of any import, nothing that might unbalance the harmony of the three, is ever pursued.

In *King Solomon's Mines,* when all is said and done, Haggard offers only one excuse for the disruption of Kukuana tribal life that his invaders effected. For Kukuana read Matabele, and the historical allegory makes sense. Quatermain says:

> I remarked, that Ignosi [the puppet they instal in place of the supposed usurper of the Kukuana throne] had swum to the throne in blood.
>   The old chief shrugged his shoulders. 'Yes,' he answered; 'but the Kukuana people can only be kept cool by letting the blood flow sometimes.' Many were killed, indeed, but the women were left, and others would soon grow up to take the places of the fallen. After this the land would be quiet for a while [at least until *Prester John*]. (p. 159)

The cosmetic improvements on the old order they leave in their wake are expressed in Quatermain's farewell words to Ignosi:

> If thou art grateful to us, remember to do even as thou didst promise; to rule justly, to respect the law, and to put none to death without a cause. (p. 197)

That is, 'no man's blood should be shed without trial, and . . . witch-hunting should cease in the land' (p. 162). Their legacy is a framework of European law and order which is geared to maintaining a friendly alliance with those who obey the constitution of Greater Britain. When our heroes are given a conqueror's farewell, Quatermain remarks: 'It really was very affecting, and not the sort of thing one is accustomed to meet with from natives' (p. 199), and he speaks more truth than he knows. In return, Kukuanaland has given our heroes not only a rattling good time, but diamonds 'of the finest water', enough of them to 'flood the market' (p. 206). Not one of the three characters feels that the effects of their actions call for comment.

The last work of consequence in the genre, John Buchan's *Prester John,* happens to have been first published in 1910, the year of Union between the four provinces of South Africa, the year of consolidation of territory under the British flag which had waved all the way from the Cape, if not to Cairo, at least up to Mashonaland. That date does not mean, however, that in *Prester John* Buchan was to betray much interest in the results of the Anglo–Boer War, the event which called for his arrival in South Africa as one of Milner's 'kindergarten'. Although *Prester John* is set post-1902, its main concern is the fear of black mutiny. The Boers, in Buchan's book, play no role in the balance of power, being shown as no more than shady, distant takhaars who get massacred in their nagmaal waggons somewhere off stage. As has been remarked before, one characteristic of the genre is its ability to see through Good's eye-glass, as it were, to view the world as a cyclops would.

The genre completes another internal cycle in *Prester John,* as what had previously been the problem of how to divide and rule turns into the new problem of how to suppress the broken tribes if they reassemble. Buchan's canvas is a larger one than in the works that deal with day-to-day experience; his intention is to assemble the whole of the history of African resistance to colonial domination into one last suicidal bid to drive the English back into the sea from which they came. Buchan's theme of rising Ethiopianism pulls together all the threads of African history into a revival movement, Christian American in inspiration, which dates itself back to the sixteenth-century Prester John who, supposedly, has counted Shaka, Dingane, Cetshwayo and others as his direct successors. They are all reborn in the person of his black hero, the Rev. John Laputa. Buchan had the Bambata Rebellion of 1906 in mind as an example of recent historical precedent; certainly he had his own mission in mind in the creation of his 19-year-old hero. Against Laputa Buchan pits this all-time wonder of British (actually Scottish) boyhood, Davie Crawfurd.

The difference between a Haggard and a Buchan is that in Haggard (the man who in 1877 ran up the flag in Market Square, Pretoria, with the annexation of the Transvaal) we have a man who, like Quatermain, raided but finally retreated; in Buchan the flag is there to stay. Everything in Buchan's novel is more conclusive. Laputa's last jump into oblivion, when it comes, complete with the symbol of all African might around his neck, is a terminal act. In *King Solomon's Mines* Ignosi could reserve the right to remain African:

If a white man comes to my gates I will send him back; if a hundred come, I will push them back; if an army comes, I will make war on them with all my strength, and they shall not prevail against me. None shall ever come for the shining stones; no, not an army, for if they come I will send a regiment to fill up the pit. (p. 198)

Yet in Buchan the white men have prevailed. Laputa's massed chiefs, once they are defeated, are either hanged or turned into 'members of our county council'.[34] Where the war-making indabas were held is now 'an institution for giving the Kaffirs the kind of training which fits them to be good citizens of the state' (p. 235).

Buchan senses his role as chronicler is of the last stages of the 'opening up' of the dark continent and of the battle between the colonizer and the indigenous population. His concern is to let his novel be the summation of a wave of history which, after *Prester John*, was to take a new direction. Thus *Prester John* is, in effect, the genre's crowning achievement, and its ending. Davie Crawfurd epitomizes all that we have had to date in the hunter-figure, but in John Laputa Buchan creates for him an adversary who is far beyond the demands of the genre — its first individualized black character. In a real sense it is Laputa's book, and one notes that Buchan chose not to call it *The Adventures of David Crawfurd.*

Crawfurd is no news to us. In a matter of eighteen months he is able not only single-handedly to take on the entire accumulated insurrectionary tribal forces of Africa but, having utterly dispersed their last centre of power, to escape back home 'centuries' older, his initial investment of twenty sovereigns into his African adventure having multiplied into no less than 'a trifle over a quarter of a million pounds' (p. 233) — no mean achievement for a semi-literate fellow.

He has someone to emulate in style: when, after Laputa's agonizing plunge, Buchan's plot contrives to have Davie the one to address the captured chiefs, he has 'to do as Rhodes did in the Matoppos, and go and talk to them . . . to strike when their minds were perplexed and undecided' (p. 227). His down-to-earth skills are amazingly brought to the fore by life on the frontier: the boy who was condemned to 'acquiring a taste for philosophy and the dead languages' (p. 15) which would lead to no more than a clerking job, finds that at Blaauwildebeestefontein he can pick up 'Dutch' ('The Dutch is easy enough. It's a sort of kitchen dialect you can learn in a fortnight', p. 32) and a fluency in 'Kaffir' (no particular language specified) in less time than it takes to learn to be 'a really fine shot with a rifle' (p. 36).

In acquiring a dog we see the entire hunter saga re-enacted in miniature:

the owner [of the dog] departed with injunctions to me to beware of the brute's temper. Colin — for so I named him — began his career with me by taking the seat out of my breeches. . . . It took me a stubborn battle of a fortnight to break his vice, and my left arm to-day bears witness to the struggle. After that he became a second shadow, and woe betide the man who had dared to raise his hand to Colin's master. (p. 36)

Colin, one should note somewhat ruefully, is Crawfurd's only consolation throughout the action — when the night-drumming presaging the revolt is at its highest frenzy, Crawfurd remarks: 'It was a real comfort to me to put out a hand in the darkness and feel Colin's shaggy coat' (p. 60). When the villain shoots Colin, Crawfurd's terrible outbreak of distress proves to be one of the truest moments in the whole literature. That the entire uprising is interrupted for Colin to receive what is tantamount to Christian interment is an irony, and his epitaph reads as follows: 'Here lies buried the dog Colin, who was killed in defending D. Crawfurd, his master. To him it was mainly due that the Kaffir Rising failed' (p. 231). Like all of black power, Crawfurd's dog, responsible for several feats of crucial derring-do in the action, has to be buried for Crawfurd to grow up. Of the mopping-up operation after the aborted rising, Crawfurd remarks (although he specifically notes that such technical details fall outside the scope of what he calls his 'romance'):

it was an experience for which I shall ever be grateful, for it turned me from a rash boy into a serious man. I knew then the meaning of the white man's duty. He has to take all risks, recking nothing of his life or his fortunes, and well content to find his reward in the fulfilment of his task. That is the difference between white and black, the gift of responsibility, the power of being in a little way a king; and so long as we know this and practise it, we will rule not in Africa alone but wherever there are dark men who live for the day and their own bellies. (p. 230)

So much for Crawfurd, and so much for the genre of which he represents the culminating phase.

The novel itself, however, demonstrates point by point the contradiction of what Crawfurd wants to believe, in a way that is unprecedented in the genre. For a start, in taking all the risks he does in the novel, he simply never has a reckless feeling for his life and fortunes; one of Buchan's strengths is in the way in which he dramatizes the acute distress Crawfurd undergoes when he is subject to physical pain or has to cross a crocodile-infested river. Furthermore, he does not appear to feel all of 'the difference between white and black' that he claims he does; he is constantly filled with a sneaking, though unacknowledged, affection and admiration for Laputa, played out in a father-son bonding that he is too gauche to see exists. Laputa's downfall, like Lobengula's to Rhodes, is to Crawfurd a far more personal affair than a matter of colonial conquest — it is the obliteration of the father whom the stripling has to overturn in order to survive. Crawfurd becomes the heir to Laputa in more than a commercial sense.

We are familiar with the provenance of the ritual:

The words meant nothing to me; they must have been in some tongue long since dead. But the music told its own tale. It spoke of old kings and great battles, of splendid palaces and strong battlements, of queens white as ivory, of death and life, love and hate, joy and sorrow. It spoke, too, of desperate things, my.teries of horror long shut to the world. No Kaffir ever forged that ritual. It must have come straight from Prester John or Sheba's queen, or whoever ruled in Africa when time was young. (p. 113)

Yet Crawfurd's accession by no means makes him 'in a little way a king'. Laputa keeps telling him quite accurately that he is no more than a trader. He is not called Mr Hunter throughout the book, but 'Mr Shopkeeper'. Buchan tells us that this is his true role, as the entire focus of the romance, the heirloom of Prester John, flashes before the boy:

The priest raised the necklace till it shone above his head like a halo of blood. I have never seen such a jewel, and I think there has never been such another on earth. Later I was to have the handling of it, and could examine it more closely, though now I only had a glimpse. There were fifty-five rubies in it, the largest as big as a pigeon's egg, and the least not smaller than my thumb-nail. In shape they were oval, cut on both sides *en cabochon,* and on each certain characters were engraved. No doubt this detracted from their value as gems, yet the characters might have been removed and the stones cut in facets, and these rubies would still have been the noblest in the world. (pp. 115–16)

In *King Solomon's Mines* Haggard contrived to leave the treasure chest of all Africa buried under a mountain the size of Sheba's breasts, which in turn left the reader with the promise of suckling on further romance. But in Buchan the body of romance is given its hysterectomy, as it were; Crawfurd dynamites into smithereens the cave that was his entry into manhood, and he has no compunction about hocking everything but the most sacred of the 'fetiches' in which all of Africa's power is (supposedly) invested. The mopping-up operation is, then, also a general mopping up of the raw material of romance. Just as the novel itself goes past the normal resolution in the genre into a general pamphleteering about how to pull the savage through into civilization, so Buchan takes the romance reader to his last threshold. Crawfurd says as much:

The hunters had become the hunted, the wheel had come full circle, and the woes of David Crawfurd were being abundantly avenged. (p. 197)

In Buchan the vengeance that civilized man wreaks upon the savage has its clear motive. Crawfurd says to Laputa: 'You want to wipe out the civilization of a thousand years and turn us all into savages.' The theme of his own maturation is transposed into an unshakeable political axiom. When Laputa replies that it is because 'I have sucked

civilization dry that I know the bitterness of the fruit' (p. 173), Crawfurd can make no reply. The romance of the hunter has no answer to
the supposition that civilization could, in fact, be savage, and that
'savagery' could be a form of civilization.

But Crawfurd's resolve remains unshaken, even if Buchan's betrays
signs of the opposite. His hero has a sense of fate having conditioned
his actions and, even if he does not know why or how, like Bunyan's
Pilgrim, he achieves entry to the 'Delectable Mountains' (p. 29):

Perhaps the Calvinism of my father's preaching had unconsciously taken grip of
my soul. At any rate I was a fatalist in creed, believing that what was willed
would happen, and that man was but a puppet in the hands of his Maker. I
looked on the last months as a clear course which had been mapped out for me.
. . . It was foreordained that I should go [it] alone . . . and in the promptings of
my own infallible heart I believed I saw the workings of Omnipotence. Such is
our moral arrogance, and yet without such a belief I think that mankind would
have been content to bide sluggishly at home. (p. 107)

Buchan's hero was the last in the gallery to return 'home'. The inevitable process of imperial expansion is personified in him. After Buchan
we find that the wave of history, which washed ashore and drew back
a literary genre of its own, had left other forms of writing in the hands
of those who stayed behind.

12 Cornwallis Harris in his 'fabled creation' of the hunter's wonderland.

13 'The Fate of Poor Hendrick' from R. Gordon Cumming's *The Lion Hunter*.

14   An engraving by Harrison Weir from Harriet Ward's *Hardy and Hunter*.

15   In silent movies, Rider Haggard's projection of a white Africa inland came in for the full Hollywood treatment, in the Johannesburg-made feature of *Allan Quatermain*.

6 Schreiner and the Novel Tradition

Perhaps the time is already come ... when the sluggard intellect of this continent will look from under its iron lids, and fill the postponed expectation of the world with something better than the exertions of mechanical skill. One day our dependence, our long apprenticeship to the learning of other lands, draws to a close. The millions, that around us are rushing into life, cannot always be fed the sere remains of foreign harvests. Events, actions, arise, that must be sung, that will sing themselves.[1]

EMERSON'S DECLARATION OF INDEPENDENCE FROM British culture of 1837, made on behalf of the American writer, took four decades to find a sympathetic response in the South African context. When Olive Schreiner opened her 'iron lids' in the 1870s, called herself 'Ralph Iron' and invented a hero called Waldo, and proceeded to celebrate life in the Cape Colony from inside, the South African writer too had taken the vast leap from dependence on 'foreign harvests' to harvesting his own that Emerson's New England romanticism recommended. That the harvest in the 'New England' of the Cape was to prove a somewhat bitter one shows how the literary histories of the United States and South Africa diverged thereafter.

Since the life and works of Schreiner have occasioned most of the literary criticism in English by South Africans, dealing here with some of her work in detail can conveniently summarize some of the prevalent attitudes that typify criticism in this, the first truly South African area of the literature. If one were to read Buchanan-Gould, Hobman, Friedmann, Partridge, Krige, Laredo, Rive, Beeton and Marquard[2] on Schreiner through in sequence, one would discover a painful circumstance within South Africa: none of these critics has made the leap that Schreiner made over a century ago. Those who have chosen to write on Schreiner have almost all used similar 'colonial' critical approaches, which release ever more sterile and anachronistic literary assessments.

Furthermore, in the case of Schreiner the matter of the missing context of the totality of Southern African literature is also so aggravated that judgements of her work become increasingly irresponsible as research techniques and critical standpoints offer the critic more and more of the necessary equipment to deal with an author of her type. If, in the end, Schreiner is one of the world's minor writers, recent scholarly attitudes, which have been applied to other English writers of the Third World and of other parts of Africa (that is, English writers generated outside the British mainstream), have shown that criticism of so-called minor writers does not have to be minor as well. One thinks of Lawrence on Cooper and Poe, of Olney on Mphahlele, Coetzee on Alex la Guma, and Soyinka on Lewis Nkosi.[3]

One turns to the survey-type critics to find an outside view of the contours of realist fiction in Southern Africa.[4] But the survey-critics tend all too frequently to mistake bibliographical description for the genealogy of a literature; they tend to start with *The Story of an African Farm* and then step the stepping stones across a gully marked repository of 'great works', delivering an appreciative word here, an admonishment there, a bit of attention everywhere. On the whole they never make more than minor re-alignments, nor do they manage to take off from the subject sufficiently to command the necessary overview. A sample route is as follows: *African Farm* (1883) to Sarah Gertrude Millin's *God's Step-children* (1924) to William Plomer's *Turbott Wolfe* (1925) to Pauline Smith's *The Beadle* (1926) to Peter Abrahams's *Mine Boy* (1946) and/or Alan Paton's *Cry, the Beloved Country* (1948) and/or Doris Lessing's *The Grass is Singing* (1950) and/or Nadine Gordimer's *The Lying Days* (1953) and/or Dan Jacobson's *A Dance in the Sun* (1956) and/or Ezekiel Mphahlele's *Down Second Avenue* (1959), after which comes Jillian Becker's *The Keep* (1967), or Bessie Head's *A Question of Power* (1974), or J.M. Coetzee's *Dusklands* (1974), dependent on taste and preferences. The survey critics are often unaware of how bizarre their systems of literary classification can be, since all these works have in common is the Southern Africanness of their authors and their fortuitous choice of the English language as a medium in which to write a novel. The Millin and the Head apart, they are all first novels, which would apparently seem to award such a list some spurious glamour. Of such repeated listings is literary history made. One might as well summon up a tradition within a tradition, that of the promising first novel by a woman, for all the greater logic it would display. Yet the enumerative technique with all its thoughtless deformations persists; Southern African critics have become so accustomed to accepting the fixed patterns in critical works on the novel in Britain that they assume the same easy pattern-making can be operative in the field of Southern African fiction as well.

Schreiner herself implicitly warns us of the danger of importing behavioural patterns from Britain and applying them directly to Southern African cases like this. She showed that her Southern Africa consisted of a polyglot mixture of peoples about whom common British responses would be difficult to make: among the 'white' characters in *African Farm* we find various English- and Afrikaans-speakers in juxtaposition, and a main character who is German in origin, and, although the novel happens to be in English, one should not be deluded into imagining that English was the sole, or even the most helpful, medium of communication within her locale. Tant' Sannie and Blenkins, we must remember, could not understand one another. *The Story of an African Farm* symbolizes the polylingualism of the whole. The true pattern of what the course of the novel in South Africa has been since then should, perhaps, finally be determined by comparison translingually. The Englishness of these novels is no guarantee of continuity.

The second fallacy to which the generalists are prone is that mere fame, determined by a sufficient consensus of favourable reviews in the U.K. or U.S., combined with a certain historical memory, automatically means that there is a meaningful sequence. Many writers, like Millin, for example, systematically counter in their works major facets of Schreiner's fiction; others, like Head, for example, probably have no use for Schreiner, and feel no need to respond to her. No survey, then, should tick off such works one after the other, lest fundamental variations within the development of the realist novel in Southern Africa should be diffused out of all recognition.

To locate Schreiner, and to determine whether or not she is the fountainhead of a certain continuity in Southern African fiction, one would have to be more precise and demanding in one's attitude towards the conditions which supposedly generate a new literature. It is not, perhaps, until one has sufficient quantity of literary matter in a particular genre that one can be confident enough to do the kind of heaving aside of historical markers that F.R. Leavis does with the English novel in order to discern his 'Great Tradition'. Like Leavis, one is obliged to re-align, polemically, and with a desire to make sense of the otherwise unshaped mass of novelistic proliferation on hand, before elementary patterns begin to cohere. Such determined tradition-plotting is desirable in the field of Southern African literature as well, even if Leavis's moral certainties may not be entirely helpful here, and even if one feels that in Southern Africa 'tradition' is a word that is relatively undefined.

For the purposes of argument, then, it will be sufficient here to demonstrate that the logical and coherent tradition of the realist novel in South Africa is a very narrow, but highly organized one. What begins with Schreiner's novel as the liberal tradition in Southern African English fiction does continue in *Turbott Wolfe*, is endemic to *Cry, the Beloved Country*, is reviewed in Lessing's *The Grass is Singing*, and meets its culmination in later novels. But this is not a development in the normal sense of the term; it is not a case of one work influencing the next, which in turn influences the next, for here each work takes *The Story of an African Farm* as a sole common origin without significant regard to intermediate variations.

The liberal tradition and realism go hand in hand here, for realism in the novel implies a certain capaciousness that can admit a variety of styles, from the symbolical and allegorical to the naturalistic, which is felt to be necessary to deal with the stresses of the liberal debate. Although early editions of *The Story of an African Farm* published by Chapman and Hall were subtitled 'A Romance', that term should be reserved to describe other uses of the novel form in Southern African literature. The animatory word here is 'liberal'. In criticism of the English realist novel, the word is implicit in the very descriptive term 'novel'. In Southern Africa 'liberal' has a flavour and cast of its own — no liberal tradition of the arts has been a mainstream occupation in Southern African life. One might say that in Great Britain the liberal tradition of the novel has been part of the fibre of British history, which in recent times has led to the achievement of an open society; in Southern Africa, the liberal tradition has been maintained by habitual outsiders who, as Gordimer has chronicled in novels like *Occasion for Loving* (1963) and *The Late Bourgeois World* (1966), have always played a marginal role. Given these precise limits, one excludes Millin from this tradition (on the grounds of illiberality), one partly excludes Smith (on the grounds of her unleavening neutrality), one has to exclude Abrahams and Head (on the grounds that, although they match up politically beside Schreiner, the origins of their fiction are at a distance from Schreiner's origin), one excludes even Coetzee's *Dusklands* (on the ground that he uses other than realist fiction techniques). Thereafter one is left with a pattern of stimulus and direct response which is knowable and verifiable, a pattern which makes good sense in its own bleak terms.

One has to describe the false starts which have been made in attempts to establish this pattern, before the true pattern can be shown to have its special meaning. One begins with 'Olive'.

There is a curious nervous tic that Schreiner causes in her sympathetic interpreters. Almost all the critics down the line, all the way to Rive, have this familiar manner of lapsing into calling their subject by her first name. This error of critical protocol is deeply symptomatic of the type of commentaries we have in hand; one would not, in the normal course of events, habitually refer to Jane or Iris, unless one were writing a personal memoir of Austen or Murdoch. Yet there she is: everybody's friend, Olive. The Olive school of critics make an initial tactical error in their work, one which needs to be isolated so that its unfortunateness may become apparent. Those who enter on Schreiner with such amiability are inclined to mistake the author for the work. In reply to this tendency one need make only one observation: when Schreiner published her *African Farm,* she did so pseudonymously, and the true concern of the critic should be to define the personality, not of the Schreiner we have in a copious spate of letters, memoirs, diaries, biographies, and so on, but of the 'Ralph Iron' who wrote the novel. It is not in order, then, to quote Schreiner on 'Ralph Iron' in justification of some minor quibble about characterization, plot or narrative in *The Story of an African Farm.* It is not in order to assume that Schreiner lurks within Lyndall merely because author and character share some common views, and that therefore Lyndall acquires some special interest within the novel. It is not in order to deduce that, because the farm of the novel resembles the Klein Gannahoek and other farms at which Schreiner wrote it, it is so very autobiographically based. In determining the persona of the novelist, it is the *differences* between the author's life and the novel's life which become liable to critical commentary.

Schreiner herself has always been subject to facile typecasting. When in 1894 W.T. Stead hailed her as 'the Modern Woman, par excellence, the founder and high priestess of the school',[5] and excerpted Lyndall's entire speech on the lot of women (in chapter 6 of Part Two) as illustration, he made a false start at defining Schreiner, because he failed to mention that the obverse view to Lyndall's is structured into the scene which apparently allows her such a free rein. While expatiating in her quotable manner, Lyndall is placed by Schreiner in a Cape cart that is going nowhere. Off stage, meanwhile, Tant' Sannie is dancing herself into a lather at her thoroughly admirable wedding feast. When J.C. Smuts pays Schreiner (and other noble souls, like Emily Brontë) a fulsome compliment in describing her as living 'beyond good and

evil, in the pure atmosphere of the spirit which we ordinary mortals
so seldom breathe',[6] he rather neglects to mention that Schreiner was
also, for example, a rabid polemicist, and one who used the soul only
in order to demonstrate how soulless it was. One indulges in paradoxical speculations of this kind only because Schreiner's critics do; such
biocritical props are perhaps amusing, but ultimately fruitless.

Allied to this is the type of criticism which hinges on a moral lesson
or on an artistic generality to be derived from Schreiner's work. In the
piece called 'An Infinite Compassion', for example, Rive implies that
Schreiner's breadth of humanitarian spirit is one to emulate today.
(Schreiner's breadth of fictional techniques is more to the point, one
must reply.) In a piece that threatens to unleash new possibilities in
approaches to Schreiner, Marquard also spoils it all by drawing to the
conclusion that she was, once all reservations are duly made, a 'great
artist' (*Standpunte,* p. 47) after all. These matters should never be in
doubt; that they are is merely an index of colonial critics' worryings
about the status of their own culture. The real questions are: how
does Schreiner's humanitarianism work in her prose, and what kind
of an artist was she? With those questions in hand, one would be tack-
ling the nature of the culture which produced her. Once one were in
a position to elaborate on her 'Southern Africanness', one would be
more confident about the artistry, the 'greatness', the power and the
effect of this literary termagant.

In another sense, an equally unhelpful position to start from is
Christopher Heywood's in a paper like 'Olive Schreiner's *The Story of
an African Farm:* Prototype of Lawrence's Early Novels'.[7] Naturally
it is of great interest that the importance of Schreiner for the novel in
English in late Victorian and Edwardian times might be said to be unexplored, and absorbing to discover that she did palpably influence
Lawrence and other British novelists in turn, that Lyndall is an Ursula
Brangwen in embryo, and that when Birkin fingers a brutish African
carving in *Women in Love* we might well have to make acknowledgements to Schreiner's Waldo for his earlier crude attempts at hacking a
meaningful totem out of a post of Karoo wood. One watches Heywood
comparing Schreiner's early images of dissected nerves running their
branches through the limbs of biology specimens with the systematic
vivisections of Lawrence's rainbow-enclosed modern woman. One
applauds as a footnote to the history of metropolitan English literature
acquires an importance greater than news from a far colony is normally
accorded. One concludes that the culture of the Victorians and Edwar-
dians was indeed expansive enough to absorb, and even to be minutely

modified by, what the media drew in from the furthest tentacles of the English-speaking octopus.

Yet for the critic whose concern is not primarily the broadening of the complex sources of the British mainstream, but Southern African literature per se, the adoption of an opposite perspective is obligatory. The novelist who is a footnote to Lawrence, however significant she might be in that context, is subject to overwhelmingly different interpretation when the poles are reversed for Lawrence to become the footnote to her. The question of which perspective is preferable should not arise, for the point here is obviously that *both* should be operative for Schreiner to have her full meaning. She should not be reduced to a matter of having to choose between one or the other, and literary studies need not be so monolithic as to insist that the view of an African farm from London must exclude an internal and complementary view.

When Schreiner set about writing *The Story of an African Farm* she had few precedents to fall back on. There had been earlier attempts to depict life in Southern Africa through realist rather than romance eyes. There was the now utterly lost three-decker novel, *Makanna, or The Land of the Savage* (1834), for example, in which its anonymous author forged a detailed, if somewhat windy, style of effective realism with which to convey the essential feelings of his individual human characters with all their mythic overtones. But his setting (the Grahamstown frontier) and date of action (1817) were hardly propitious in creating the necessary in-depth explorations, since the life he wished to fictionalize had not yet stabilized into patterns of well-worn experience. The adventure romance, as we have seen, was ideally suited to conveying the colour and vigour of a complex society in flux, with its ill-defined parameters in a constantly-changing century of activity.

But by the time of Schreiner and her *Story of an African Farm,* the introductory phases of the colonial search for a settled society were complete. Schreiner's main character, Waldo, is not a settler, but the son of a settler. Her Lyndall and Em are the stranded children of British parents who either passed in the night or died young, wrestling a young country, and they are born into and brought up in the most settled matrix of Afrikanerdom, the agrarian establishment, supposedly rooted there since time immemorial, resistant to change, isolated and a complete world unto itself. On his one exploit out into the larger movement of Southern African progress (into the British world of storekeeping, transport riding and so on), Waldo finds that the life of the common, meandering adventurer is no substitute for being at home in an environment which he cannot, in fact, escape. The basic plot structure of the novel must be seen to have undergone a radical change.

The contrast between romance and Schreiner's realism is apparent if one considers that in all the romances, and in the remarkable *Makanna*, a prelude at sea leads to a series of actions deeper and deeper inland. In *Makanna* the full implications of this pattern of action are tellingly considered as the author devotes his entire first volume to poising his characters pregnantly in the doldrums and in shipwreck on the verge of the shore. Yet, in *African Farm*, when the shoreline is used at all, it acts as an outer limit rather than as a threshold:

the sea is always moving, always something deep in itself is stirring it. It never rests; it is always wanting, wanting, wanting. It hurries on; and then it creeps back slowly without having reached, moaning. It is always asking a question, and it never gets an answer. I can hear it in the day and in the night; the white foam breakers are saying that which I think. I walk alone with them when there is no one to see me, and I sing with them. I lie down on the sand and watch them with my eyes half shut. The sky is better, but it is so high above our heads. I love the sea. Sometimes we must look down too.[8]

The sea is symbolic merely of Waldo's own perpetually confused mumblings; it is no gateway, no exit. Although Waldo has no historical sense, Schreiner has, because the effect of this passage in the context of the entire literature is truly anticlimactic. The poles of Southern African experience have been reversed, for, in the eyes of the brooding inlander, it is Europe which represents the distant, unattainable core of mystery, and the once mystically exotic inland is no more than the datum of his existence.

Thus, in some senses, Schreiner has no need of predecessors except in so far as she can parody them. One of her subsidiary themes in *The Story of an African Farm* is that the available books are pretty useless to her characters. One key scene of Waldo's young days is his discovery of a crate of books in the loft, as a result of which discovery he is not ennobled or edified, but beaten flat. To Tant' Sannie there is only one book — the familiar Bible — and to Blenkins books are anathema, since they might expose his subterfuges. Blenkins's rule is simple:

Whenever you come into contact with any book, person, or opinion of which you absolutely comprehend nothing, declare that book, person, or opinion to be immoral. Bespatter it, vituperate against it, strongly insist that any man or woman harbouring it is a fool or a knave, or both. Carefully abstain from studying it. Do all that in you lies to annihilate that book, person, or opinion. (p. 104)

Whenever Waldo manages to dwell on the pages of a book, Schreiner makes quite sure that he is distracted by events on the farm. Even Lyndall in her dying days discards the books which have sustained her:

'Will you open the window,' she said, almost querulously, 'and throw this book out? It is utterly foolish. I thought it was a valuable book; but the words are merely strung together, they make no sense. Yes — so!' she said with approval, seeing [Gregory Rose] fling it out into the street. 'I must have been very foolish when I thought that book good.'

Then she turned to read, and leaned her little elbows resolutely on the great volume, and knit her brows. This was Shakespeare — it must mean something.

'I wish you would take a handkerchief and tie it tight round my head, it aches so.' (p. 257)

Even Shakespeare, Schreiner implies, cannot save Lyndall from a gruesome death — a death caused by the claustrophobic conventions of a staid morality, desertion, traumatic childbirth and the indifference of a hostile universe — all matters which, quite simply, had never before fallen within the scope of books about Southern African life.

Schreiner is not advocating that all books should be flung out-of-doors; she is merely dramatizing the dilemma which she and her characters find themselves facing: how do books contain relevant experience (or, ironically, in Blenkins's case, how can the right books be kept at bay)? In her rejection of the books generally available to her, she was creating all the possibilities of a new type of literature, born out of new areas of life. In short, she was, with *The Story of an African Farm*, the first author to think out a blow-by-blow answer to the question: what can Southern African literature be?

On this matter she was notably specific. In her preface to the second printing of *The Story of an African Farm*, she wrote:

It has been suggested by a kind critic that he would better have liked the little book if it had been a history of wild adventure; of cattle driven into inaccessible 'kranzes' by Bushmen; 'of encounters with ravening lions, and hairbreadth escapes'. This could not be. Such works are best written in Piccadilly or in the Strand: there the gifts of the creative imagination untrammelled by contact with any fact, may spread their wings.

But, should one sit down to paint the scenes among which he has grown, he will find that the facts creep in upon him. Those brilliant phases and shapes which the imagination sees in far-off lands are not for him to portray. Sadly he must squeeze the colour from his brush, and dip it into the grey pigments around him. He must paint what lies before him. (pp. 23–4)

That is the realist's manifesto. But Schreiner by no means squeezed all the colours from her brush; *The Story of an African Farm* is one

of the gaudier works of world literature, and since its first appearance
it has been remembered by its devotees as much for its colouring as
for its realism. Schreiner means that no spectacular colouring is to be
done gratuitously. Her contrasting 'grey', sombre underside of the
African Karoo, is as much in evidence as the multihued splendour,
which is generally reserved for the dream sequences, and a balance is
maintained.

Although Schreiner has no direct predecessors, she makes quite sure
that even the indirect predecessors the circumstances of three-quarters
of a century of British literature in Southern Africa have provided her
with are overthrown. Where the adventure reader, as exemplified by
her 'kind critic', might have had a desire for the appearance of further
Bushman raiders, Schreiner commences her novel with a description
of Bushman cave paintings which, unless understood in terms of the
context suggested here, would appear merely decorative. She means
to show that the Masarwa on the African farm are well and truly dead.
Their immortal art on cave walls has, by the 1860s, become an historical relic, incomprehensible to the three children who play hide and
seek beneath them:

> They sat under a shelving rock, on the surface of which were still visible some old
> Bushman-paintings, their red and black pigments having been preserved through
> long years from wind and rain by the overhanging ledge; grotesque oxen, elephants,
> rhinoceroses, and a one-horned beast, such as no man ever has seen or ever shall.
> (p. 37)

The wild animals, Schreiner means to say, and the chimerical unicorns
of inland, have gone, too. In a few introductory paragraphs she establishes that her novel will be different from the usual fiction of her day.

Those same children toying with crystals are also oblivious of the
implications of the fact that other Karoo farm children in their gambols with the stones beneath their feet were turning up the diamonds
which would precipitate the new rush of adventure fiction. Yet Schreiner uses those pebbles to spur her children to discuss marriage, education, inheritance and disillusionment — Schreiner's new themes for old
South African situations.

The surface of *The Story of an African Farm* may be a microscopi-
cally persuasive documentary about life down on the farm, but its
essence is something refreshing in Southern African fiction. It is still
about that chestnut of colonial fiction, self-education, but here the
education is acquired under the most harrowing circumstances and
with different results. It is not unreasonable to view the whole of

The Story of an African Farm as a broad parody of its educative fellow novels, for Schreiner shows that the matter of gaining the personal skill to wield experience in the business of growing up to adulthood is no matter of certificates and easily-won wealth. Life's education so garbles Waldo that the last paragraphs of the novel imply that he understands no more about life than the chickens that crawl over his sleeping body. Life's education so constrains Lyndall that it kills her. Education does not liberate, in Schreiner's view of the colonial world; it is merely part of a general oppression of the spirit which irrelevant texts reinforce. The flights of the imagination which Ralph Iron's critic reproached her with for lacking are by no means out of evidence in the novel, but Schreiner has uses beyond local colouring for the word 'imagination', and she shows in the abundant flights of imagination she has her characters indulge in that flight itself is unattainable. Suffering, not wishing, brings experience, yet those who do not suffer gather it in just as well. When fact and fiction meld, as she says, the 'trammelling' begins. She knows she has the right to create a book about that trammelling process, if she sees it as the essence of the colonial experience.

The Story of an African Farm is structured out of broad and breathtaking paradoxes like these, which give it its daring and its moral courage. It is at once a novel about how to live which denies that living is entirely worthwhile. It is about the quest for knowledge, when that knowledge is seen to be unprocurable and even irrelevant. One is to take Schreiner's own view of life as reflected in the novel scrupulously, for Schreiner meant it:

Human life may be painted according to two methods. There is the stage method. According to that each character is duly marshalled at first, and ticketed; we know with an immutable certainty that at the right crises each one will reappear and act his part, and, when the curtain falls, all will stand before it bowing. There is a sense of satisfaction in this, and of completeness. But there is another method — the method of the life we all lead. Here nothing can be prophesied. There is a strange coming and going of feet. Men appear, act and re-act upon each other, and pass away. When the crisis comes the man who would fit it does not return. When the curtain falls no one is ready. When the footlights are brightest they are blown out; and what the name of the play is no one knows. If there sits a spectator who knows, he sits so high that the players in the gaslight cannot hear his breathing. (Preface, p. 23)

Schreiner's view of life, which is the second, random one, the one that needs the conventions in order to be felt to be unconventional, and needs the built-in sense of form in order to express formlessness, is integrally operative within *The Story of an African Farm*. As she remarks in the same preface:

> Life may be painted according to either method; but the methods are different.
> The canons of criticism that bear upon the one cut cruelly upon the other. (p. 23)

The assumption that life in the novel ought to be judged as belonging to the first category, when the work itself subscribes to the second, is responsible for most of the half-truths and miscomprehensions which have become the standard dogma of Schreiner criticism. In choosing the second method Schreiner set up a trauma in the white South African mind. That the South African mind has not been able convincingly to come to terms with her at face value, and work out of her, is a pointer to the fact that the condition she defines as inherent in colonial culture still prevails.

The Story of an African Farm appears within the context of Southern African literature exactly between two watershed points, neither of which seem to exist for her critics.[9] Both are clearly beaconed in the opening and closing chapters of the novel. The preliminary chapter establishes Schreiner's theme of revolt against God and against time — embodied in the merciless landscape and the tickings of the 12-year-old Waldo's watch — the tyranny of both of which is to crush her characters year by year, chapter by chapter. She dates the beginning of the action of the novel to 1862, 'the year of the great drought' (p. 37). The drought, one remarks, lasts until chapter 11 of Part Two, by which time, incredible as it may seem, Waldo is in his early twenties; that is, the novel covers the time from two years before 1862 to quite close to its date of first publication. Quite unfalteringly she is concerned to conflate into the period of her novel the beginning and end of a major transition that occurred in rural South African culture, so that the novel is a precise model of the historical process at work.

The action of the novel begins with a self-contained community of landed Boers whose cemeteries are full of the blood and the bones of Englishmen. Into this sheltered paradise, firm in its own sluggish but stable growth-patterns, comes the new type of British intruder, Bonaparte Blenkins, opportunist and pseudo-aristocrat. No matter what the characters in Schreiner's paradise feel about Blenkins's blarney, the fact is that they do not know how to cope with it. Schreiner knows he is a lethal new Munchausen; Blenkins systematically exploits the farm dwellers and, as more than one commentator has observed, the first to go is Waldo's good, impractical father whose defence against the intruder is no more than a God-fearing amiableness. Blenkins finds the African farmers only too credulous, too defenceless; we are amused by and amazed at his cunning fraudulence, and we are made to see how unable to counter him his victims are.

Yet, in the end, Schreiner shows us that Blenkins is not really alien to the African farmers, for his machinations can, surprisingly, be accommodated. He is content, when all is said and done, to marry a local and to settle down to a life of sweet indolence in the capacious arms of Trana. In his wake he leaves Waldo's one attempt at mechanization, the shearing machine, in smithereens, and sufficient scars on the boy's back for him never fully to recover from abasement. When Blenkins is caught out by Tant' Sannie, he moves on down the neighbourhood; he neither returns home nor ventures further inland. For all his Napoleonic airs of conquest and vanquishment, he is no more than a lazy British 'shopkeeper', out for a good life; a retrogressive parasite, but not a transformer. Blenkins plays a very standard role in South African history and in the novels which deal with it — the role of the wandering *meester* or travelling schoolmaster. He is more on the inside of South African life than any of the characters who appear in adventure fiction, for he was there in Lichtenstein and there as a straggler in the train of the Great Trek. He survives today as a key character in bushveld fiction, notably in the Marico stories of Bosman. He plays a role that the English could play with some success in predominantly Dutch-Afrikaans communities.

Given that the period of Schreiner's novel is the heyday of the adventure novel, it is not surprising that *The Story of an African Farm* also subsumes the story of the adventure hero into its fabric as a strand of the larger whole. In *African Farm* this role is played by Gregory Rose, the youth to whom Schreiner's contemporaries were devoting whole scenarios. Schreiner's cool and blatant ironies centring on the figure of Rose come into their own only when one sees him in this context, transposed into a community which was more actual than the adventure writers could devise. The result is Rose's ceremonial defrocking, conducted in a subtle undertone which gives the portrait power, and which makes the novel all the more meaningful in the context of Southern African literature in general.

At first Gregory Rose is so much of a conventional adventure hero that his mere banality fails to make much impact on the more involving and individualized characters in the novel. Schreiner is forthright and even bitter about him:

And sometimes what is more amusing . . . than tracing the likeness between man

and man, is to trace the analogy there is between the progress and development
of one individual and of a whole nation; or again, between a single nation and the
entire human race. It is pleasant when it dawns on you that the one is just the
other written out in large letters; and very odd to find all the little follies and
virtues, and developments and retrogressions, written out in the big world's book
that you find in your little internal self. (pp. 185-6)

Rose the individual is a stand-in for the romantic British hero in a
South Africa that is its own 'nation', for as Schreiner dryly remarks:

the Roses since coming to the [Cape] colony had discovered that they were of
distinguished lineage. Old Rose himself, an honest English farmer, knew nothing
of his noble descent; but his wife and daughter knew — especially his daughter.
There were Roses in England who kept a park and dated from the Conquest. So
the colonial 'Rose Farm' became 'Rose Manor', in remembrance of the ancestral
domain, and the claim of the Roses to noble blood was established — in their own
minds, at least. (p. 163)

Rose's first rapturous love for Em is soon proved to be baseless;
Schreiner wastes little time in showing him up as being of little substance and less moral endurance. The youth, who in the tradition is
a would-be conqueror, becomes content only as Lyndall's slave, a role
which is humbler in Schreiner's scheme of things than that of Dross
the dog, and that of the 'Kaffirs' who stride around the background
of the novel.

Rose comes into his own attending Lyndall on her deathbed, when
the only way he can satisfy his utterly confused desires and physically
touch Lyndall is sneakily under the bedclothes. It is typical of Schreiner's satirical method that in order to have him reach the bed of his
life's desires, deep inland, she has him shave off his beard and dress
as a woman. This is the ultimate downfall of the virile English frontiersman and ranger, a humiliation that must rank as blasphemous to hard-
core adventure readers. That this is indeed Schreiner's intention is
shown by her continuing fascination with this theme in *Trooper Peter
Halket of Mashonaland* (1897), in which the psyche of the bushveld
colonizer is given its sharpest dissection. Rose returns to the farm a
loser, no richer than when he set off on his quest; and he is spiritually
broken.

If the period of Schreiner's novel allots its characters specific roles,
roles that are different from those assigned to characters in the hands
of authors with an outside point of view, it is also clear that Schreiner's
intention is to show that period slowly drifting towards a vague but
nevertheless final close. In the last chapter of the novel, when Tant'
Sannie makes her farewell appearance on the scene, complete with her

'pudding-faced, weak-eyed child' (p. 274), asserting that 'Marriage is the finest thing in the world' (p. 274), we have this monument to nineteenth-century isolationism at her finest — broad, gauche, blissfully ignorant of the outside world and committedly superstitious, so certain in her certainties that she appears to be one of the world's great survivors. Tant' Sannie contains a motor energy within the novel that is the mainspring of the pastoral life and its perpetual renewals. She represents a dogged and unstoppable continuation of communal peasant living, and although Schreiner is sometimes pretty vindictive towards her as she lifts the skin off her most sanctimonious pretensions, we can have no doubt that her attitude towards this suppressor of youth, of endeavour and of intellectual ambition, is one of wry admiration.

Schreiner has Tant' Sannie frequently give herself over to this kind of denial of individuality:

'There's nothing like being married,' said Tant' Sannie, as she puffed toward the door. 'If a woman's got a baby and a husband she's got the best things the Lord can give her; if only the baby doesn't have convulsions. As for a husband, it's very much the same who one has. Some men are fat, and some men are thin; some men drink brandy, and some men drink gin; but it all comes to the same thing in the end; it's all one. A man's a man, you know.' (p. 274)

If one were to take a deathcount on the characters in *The Story of an African Farm,* one would have to agree with Tant' Sannie: Lyndall's moral and feminist 'convulsions' wipe her out, Waldo drifts out of existence and becomes a perch for chickens, Old Otto the German putters to death like the last gentleman Christian, while Tant' Sannie, the conventional Em and Rose are the ones to pull through. Schreiner's own admiration for stolid Boer virtues, extolled in such vital terms in her essays in *Thoughts on South Africa* (written over the period 1891 to 1901), demonstrates that a central part of her engagement with the land was a tacit endorsement of all the qualities which most of her critics maintain she abhorred: tenacity, peasant virtue that will sacrifice individuals for the cause, and a laager-like group confidence which is unassailable. Schreiner, one finds, is no radical libertarian when it comes to the matter of endurance; she echoes John Stuart Mill, but she enacts Darwin.

But the direction in which Tant' Sannie's fearsome community was going, Schreiner knows, for all her defence of it, was, like all things, towards change and transformation. That this view is a source of comedy for her is remarkable enough; but that it is a source of acute

social comment as well is our pleasure. When in the final chapter Tant'
Sannie is faced with a new technological gadget, a soap-pot which Em
is becoming adept at having the servants wield, Tant' Sannie concludes:

'It's with all these new inventions that the wrath of God *must* fall on us. What
were the children of Israel punished for, if it wasn't making a golden calf? I may
have my sins, but I do remember the tenth commandment: "Honour thy father
and thy mother that it may be well with thee, and that thou mayst live long in
the land which the Lord thy God giveth thee!" It's all very well to say we honour
them, and then to be finding out things that they never knew, and doing things
in a way they never did them! *My* mother boiled soap with bushes, and I will
boil soap with bushes. If the wrath of God is to fall upon this land,' said Tant'
Sannie, with the serenity of conscious virtue, 'it shall not be through me. Let
them make their steam-waggons and their fire-carriages; let them go on as though
the dear Lord will follow them. I don't know how such people read their Bibles.
When do we hear of Moses or Noah riding in a railway? The Lord sent fire-
carriages out of heaven in those days: there's no chance of His sending them for
us if we go on in this way . . . ' (p. 275)

Tant' Sannie is a little drawn to the soap-pot, nevertheless. In this
marvellously ironic speech, she free-associates from the formula for
the continuation of the tribal life (what to her is the tenth commandment, actually the fifth) into a vision of apocalypse which we see as
fundamentally quaint. Yet Schreiner's tactics in this novel are highly
oblique, and the passage does portend more than the merely superficial satirical snigger one has at Tant' Sannie's expense.

Once the chain of generational continuance which the fifth commandment ensures is ruptured, as it will be, by the railways marching
inland, and by further events that the railways will precipitate – the
arrival of the Khaki soldiers, the Long Toms and lyddite and flame-
throwers which, by the turn of the century, will literally have burned
down the African farms (as Schreiner took care to show in a short
story like 'Eighteen Ninety Nine') – the wrath of the Lord will des-
cend on the pastoral ways which Schreiner treated to a gentle, if
mocking, elegy. As *The Story of an African Farm* draws to an end,
we feel that it was indeed 'Well to die then!' (p. 279) when a perception of Herbert Spencer's underlying unity in all Nature was almost
within grasp.

If the cycle of history in *The Story of an African Farm* is clear
enough, one must go further and say that, although one does note
the working out of a view of history which is thoroughly explored
and complete, Schreiner's world cannot, and should not, be reduced
down to that one elementary cycle alone. Schreiner's own inner

tensions within the novel are complex and even contradictory; one cannot see them resolved unless one arrives at a view of the novel as constructed out of paradoxes which are, on the face of it, baffling and exasperating. The novel's own force is derived from pitting Mill against Darwin, one feels — how does the indivisibility of human freedom apply to evolving African society? — and pitting Emerson's commitment to social change on the part of the artist against Spencer's *First Principles* which, whatever else it might stand for, offers the novelist the theme that all men aspire from the known towards the unknowable, which is unchangeable. These four writers, who are commonly labelled as Schreiner's sources of inspiration in early reading, set up such antipathies within the fabric of the novel that part of its liveliness is derived from her attempts to resolve them into a total whole. She tries, but it is perhaps her enduring strength that she fails. However, in a profound sense the working out of themes from Mill, Darwin, Emerson and Spencer are part of the superstructure of *The Story of an African Farm,* not part of its essence.

Schreiner tries to allay these countercurrents within the novel. It has as its theme the failure of man to achieve transcendence, although the work itself, we must assert, is a demonstration of transcendence (over the mean, over the elemental, over the unimaginative) at work. Yet it is also a work which is so acutely pessimistic and dubious of transcendental values that one can only resort to a theory of ambiguities in order to make sense of it. Such ambiguities, also at work in a novel like Laurens van der Post's *The Face beside the Fire* (1953), are so crucial to an understanding of Schreiner's method that when an editor like Thurman[10] begins to excerpt handy quotes from *The Story of an African Farm* in his *Olive Schreiner Reader* one needs to observe that a system of contraries worthy of a Blake is being violated: every quotation that Thurman has her make has its own riposte within Schreiner's own work. Schreiner, who is usually compared to George Eliot and D.H. Lawrence, actually demands comparison with the Stephen Cranes and Melvilles of extra-insular English fiction.

When a survey critic like Raymond Sands, in his paper 'The South African Novel: Some Observations', makes the remark that landscape often looms too large in South African fiction, that 'background has to give at all points significance to the transactions taking place before it, and not mountainously muscle into the front',[11] he is exercising a judgement which is too conditioned by the conventions of the realist novel of Victorian England; one might as well say there is too much whale in *Moby Dick*. The landscape looms large in South African fiction because it looms large in the South African psyche: for Schreiner it is monstrous, unformed, inimical and crushing. One cannot say that she should not use it that way, if that is the way she felt it to be. When the railways come to Middlemarch in the 1830s, they are resisted with pitchforks and a millennium of the agrarian establishment's interests. When the railways come to Schreiner's African farm, they are resisted by chains of mountains, by 'a certain colossal plenitude, a certain large freedom in all its natural proportions. . . . If Nature here wishes to make a mountain, she runs a range for five hundred miles; if a plain, she levels eighty; if a rock, she tilts five thousand feet of strata on end. . . . There is nothing measured, small nor petty in South Africa.'[12] Except, she implies in her novel, its people, who are not enlarged by their landscape and who fail to live up to it. The railways are resisted by Tant' Sannie who, complete with a new soap-pot under her arm, will nevertheless board the whites-only carriage to escape the dustbowl which her pastoral paradise is becoming. When Will Brangwen carves his crude totems, his actions are a pleasant relapse into a pseudo-primitivism which Lawrence hopes will charge his fiction with a new energy; when Waldo carves his Karoo post into a spiral of ascending figures, he does so because African ritual art is the only form of art he knows at first hand. When Dorothea is edged into a marriage that allows her romantic notions no fulfilment, Eliot allows her to outlive the dead hand of learning; for Lyndall there is no way she can reach the blue mountains of her release, and there is no liberal Will for her beyond them. Schreiner's interest is severely diminished by the kind of ready comparisons that are made without taking into account the fact that her Southern Africanness sets its own concerns, and those concerns are fundamentally different from those of her fellow novelists in British Victorian fiction. If this were not so, she would be of little interest to us.

The overwhelming intransigence of the landscape in Schreiner, which is one of her major themes, is a reality, and it finds its echo in several major Southern African works that follow Schreiner without any significant alteration in attitude: it is virtually a cliché of Southern African fiction that it depicts vast natural forces at work on puny beings in a way which is degrading and humiliating to human ambition. Landscape, in South African realist fiction, never merely sustains and magnifies man; it dwarfs and overwhelms, it remains unyielding and destructive. Out of Schreiner's single vision of that landscape comes this enduring vision of it, common to many white novelists: one follows it through *Turbott Wolfe, The Beadle, Cry, the Beloved*

Country, The Grass is Singing and *A Dance in the Sun* to Gordimer's
The Conservationist, unchanged, as a basic given of the genre. There
is no point in complaining about it. The evidence of these works is
that all these authors concur with Schreiner that the land itself dries
the vital juices out of its inhabitants, stunts them and — worst of all
— disallows them from achieving man's most sacred desire, the desire
to take root in the land and belong. Thus, although one trembles to
say it, the literature of this kind has as a basic tenet the theme that its
characters do not — cannot — belong. We are confronted with a coherent and continuous stream of fiction that is about permanently
alienated beings, white beings who are not part of, and can never be
part of, a land which offers them no harmonious, sympathetic growth.

In situating her African farm in the Karoo, Schreiner established a
major precedent in the literature. From her flows the most abundant
and unending stream of images of aridity, impotence, deformity, isolation and rootlessness that one associates only too readily with a desert
landscape. Post-Schreiner, the hardened, double-crossed white man,
trapped in a rootless condition, will become a standard posture struck
by the novelists of the most impressive current of Southern African
writing. The condition is not located in the Karoo alone, for the Karoo
condition becomes transportable to almost any area of the subcontinent, be it the actual semi-desert of Millin's Northern Cape, of Smith's
Little Karoo, of Lessing's Southern Rhodesia or of Jacobson's Kimberley, or the figurative desert of Plomer's Zululand, Paton's Natal and
Gordimer's Transvaal. The condition remains the same.

A common factor of this condition is that when landscape is used
dominantly, it is most usually used *against* the drift of the novel.
Schreiner saw such possibilities first, and others have responded with
the same reaction. When the appallingly tense drought which resonates
throughout *The Story of an African Farm* finally breaks, it breaks in
a way which seems sublimely irrelevant to its main characters. As one
feels the surge of new life penetrating down to the roots of the meanest
milk-bush outside, the storm delivers up a soaking Waldo. Sands would
maintain that background material, like storms, should be kept in the
background, where it can highlight character. Schreiner maintains that
her storm is a participatory enemy: as the whole of central South Africa comes back to a fecund new life, Sands, one supposes, would prefer
to have Waldo regenerated at the same time. But Schreiner is not so
deterministically romantic. At the height of the deluge she makes
Waldo discover that Lyndall, his potential new life, is utterly dead,
and that he might as well die too. Schreiner positions her key dramatic

moments exactly at points where they would not occur in Emily Brontë, for example. Floods incapacitate and demoralize Turbott Wolfe. Dust clogs Jacobson's hitch-hikers in his novel. Mary Turner, in *The Grass is Singing,* is stabbed to death in an apocalyptic storm which promises relief to everyone but her. In *Cry, the Beloved Country,* erosion and waste is symbolic of spiritual bankruptcy. When Gordimer's expense account farm outside Johannesburg, in *The Conservationist,* runs awash in a storm which heaves in all the way from the Mozambique Channel, it delivers up mud and skulls and crossbones which promise no comfort to its white hero.

Thus one can establish that the use of landscape in Southern African realist fiction is a constant which defines that century-old part of the literature. Schreiner discovered it, and her successors have followed her. She is the literature's fountainhead, and, one must hasten to add, its limits. For that reason one must pay respectful attention to what her heirs have made of her, by way of tribute and as a source of inspiration. One turns to the strongest documents in the criticism of the literature: the comments by the novelists who succeeded her on the influence she has been on their own creative impulses.[13] Those who have chosen rural settings, farm life, as their fictional bases in one or another work, have, without fail, been eloquent on the subject of their indebtedness to Schreiner.

Dan Jacobson, for example, in his introduction to the Penguin edition of *The Story of an African Farm,* makes the unavoidable point about

the initial difficulty Olive Schreiner had to overcome as a novelist: when I read her novel for the first time, some sixty years after it was first published, I had to struggle with my own incredulity that the kopjes, *kraals* and cactus plants she mentions were of the same kind as those I was familiar with; so little experience had I had of encountering them within the pages of a book. For it isn't only the hitherto undescribed, uncelebrated, wordless quality of the life around him that makes it seem implausible to the colonial as a fit subject for fiction; it is also (no matter how bright the moonlight may be) its appearance of drabness, its thinness, its lack of richness and variety in comparison with what he has read about in the books that come to him from abroad. (pp. 18–19)

Doris Lessing has written of *African Farm:*

this was the first 'real' book I'd met with that had Africa for a setting. Here was the substance of truth, and not from England or Russia or France or America, necessitating all kinds of mental translations, switches, correspondences, but reflecting what I knew and could see. (Schlueter, pp. 98–9)

The debate about Southern African literature, then, cannot proceed with much depth unless these kinds of personal testimonies about an internal continuity are taken into account. One's points of reference may well be British culture, as they were to Gregory Rose's sister, Jemima, but one's perspective must be Southern African as well for the literature to be seen to have its own internal cohesion.

For the British Isles, then, Schreiner substitutes a different island — the island of a circumscribed and cut-off part of Southern Africa. As it is the largest of the 'islands' in what this introduction has chosen to call the archipelago of Southern African literature, it would be well to examine the effects of isolation on it in some detail.

Before her *Götterdämmerung* in the last chapter of the novel, Schreiner comments: 'Our fathers had their dreams; we have ours; the generation that follows will have its own. Without dreams and phantoms man cannot exist' (p. 272). Yet, when those dreams and phantoms prove to be deluding or inadequate in the formulation of a world-view, the result is death, death prematurely, death without redemption. This theme of constriction breeding despair, which finds its analogue in the landscape and the action of the novel, is perhaps a manifestation of the general limits of life in the colonies. If Schreiner is to be typified as a major colonial writer, this must be because she has defined the effects of stultification and oppression that the mental life is subject to in a lost quarter of the globe. *The Story of an African Farm* remains pre-eminently a colonial novel. Its characters may be born in Africa, and are put to death by Africa, but that is not the same thing as being African.

According to her husband, one of the many working titles Schreiner adopted for *The Story of an African Farm* during the writing of it was *Mirage,* to which was to be added the epigraph: 'Life is a series of abortions'.[14] This discarded subtitle, which had shock value if nothing else, was certainly central to *African Farm.* The most poignant event in the novel is the birth to Lyndall, at the age of seventeen, of an illegitimate baby, conceived on her by a shady lover whom she persuades to desert her so that she might live out her role of independent woman. Schreiner goes that far against the grain of public decency in plotting her novel, and the baby dies after a few hours. (It would also seem curious that those critics who are keen to show parallels between Lyndall's and Schreiner's lives do not remark on the coincidence that some twenty years later Schreiner's own baby suffocated within hours of its delivery.)

As Lyndall's landlady describes it to Rose:

Six months before a lady had come alone to the hotel in a waggon, with only a coloured leader and driver. Eight days after a little baby had been born. If Greg-ory stood and looked out at the window he would see a blue gum-tree in the grave-yard; close by it was a little grave. The baby was buried there. A tiny thing, only lived two hours, and the mother herself almost went with it. After a while she was better; but one day she got up out of bed, dressed herself without saying a word to any one, and went out. It was a drizzly day; a little time after some one saw her sitting on the wet ground under the blue gum-tree, with the rain dripping from her hat and shawl. They went to fetch her, but she would not come until she chose. When she did she had gone to bed, and had not risen again from it; never would, the doctor said. (pp. 251–2)

Because of Lyndall's pride and her obstinacy, her unrelievable grief can and must lead to her own death. Schreiner leaves no room in her scheme of things for a catharsis and a recovery. The earth in the novel, the 'red sand' that Waldo lies on on his stomach (p. 127 and p. 145), from which he cannot take off, sucks man and woman down, reduces all to organic matter. There is a macabre aura of decay throughout the novel, in the landscape and through to the souls of the characters, which is illustrative of a death wish, a fatalism which is relentlessly extreme. This brooding kind of desire to die in the red, rich earth is where the root of South Africanism in this stream of novels begins. We are not dealing merely with a young girl's morbid fantasies, for Schreiner, contrary to the usual amazed claim, was hardly young when *The Story of an African Farm* was first published — she was a fully-grown woman 28 years old. What we are being shown is the first ap-pearance of a struggling but implacable fatalism which has taken its place in the fore of the South African English mentality, an uneasy lack of identity which, in the last resort, can only die on the land to prove that it has lived above it. Mulch, Schreiner implies, is the lowest, and first, form of belonging.

Schreiner's symbolism in this regard, like her use of landscape, echoes and re-echoes through the fiction derived out of her: Turbott Wolfe's death-laden phantasmagoria (the only stable element within a novel which is otherwise confused with uncertain impressionism), the steely living deaths of Smith and Lessing, the murdered liberal and the noose in Paton's allegory, the corpse that unburies itself and floats through Gordimer's *The Conservationist,* these are all signs of a felt state of zombiehood which characterizes the English South African at the innermost level. If Africa may be said to spook its white English inhabitants, the walking dead who stalk the pages of their fiction are the inevitable concomitant. Schreiner, the left-wing reformer, knew that she was only one against an entire capitalist society that never could, and never would, afford her thoroughly civilized and liberal sentiments much currency. The great liberal British tradition, once it was applied to an African colonial situation, had to battle against extraordinary tensions in order to survive at all. We know that in *Heart of Darkness* Conrad's Marlow is reduced to a state of meditative stupor, which is a sorry and ghastly conclusion to the quest for moral sharpness and re-definition. The adventure novel offered easy solutions to every African dilemma. The tradition of the liberal realist novel in South Africa offers few.

Thus the centre of Schreiner's novel is quite elsewhere from where the critics to date have looked for it. In a George Eliot or a Hardy one finds the focus of the entire moral and aesthetic universe at the core of their fictions; in Schreiner one finds — nothingness. It is only once one feels the Southern African novel in the imitative liberal mode to be a game played about a void, a vacuum, that it can be seen to emerge as a fundamentally different type of novel from those with which it, to its discredit, is constantly forced to bear comparison.

The truly and unutterably shocking truth about Schreiner's first novel is that at its heart there is the shadowy figure of Waldo's Stranger, and that he says the following about himself:

I am a man who believes nothing, hopes nothing, fears nothing, feels nothing. I am beyond the pale of humanity; no criterion of what you should be who live here among your ostriches and bushes. (p. 148)

Yet the drift of the criticism to date is to see Waldo's Stranger in the terms in which Waldo sees him, as a source of rapturously escapist and romantic riddles. It would be more to the point to see him as Schreiner sees him: he is a man who, while delivering our favourite passage in the book, the Allegory of the Hunter, is a deceiver, a liar and an illusionist whose own self-honesty shows up the fatal allure of the vision while denying its potency. If *The Story of an African Farm* is, in the final analysis, about the desire for faith, Schreiner means to state through her system of ironies that faith is merely an easy escape from the horror of numbness. In this sense, Schreiner's true heir is a writer like Bosman who, in works like 'Unto Dust' or in his novelized autobiography, *Cold Stone Jug* (1949), dances an ironic turn or two with death. The English Southern African writer as an outsider has lived within the panic-stricken void of the absurd for so long, and so unrelievedly, that one may say that moral paralysis has become his stock-in-trade. Schreiner gives one the picture: ice-plants, plants blistered with sacs of water, held aloft in case the rain does not come.

When it comes, of course, it comes at the wrong time and wrecks everything.

Since the society out of which Schreiner wrote simply was not a homogeneous, stable one (as, for example, one could call Emma's Hartfield stable and homogeneous), the novel that represents it could not be either. Since the even stratifications of English life underwent an unpredictable and diverse set of variations once they were re-arranged by the Southern African experience, the old compartmen-talizations of the society reflected in the fiction Schreiner knew had to be reassessed, frequently with bizarre results. One has to say that, if in the British nineteenth-century novel it is bad taste to mix farce with tragic downfall, in South Africa it was a matter of everyday life. Thus, what appear to be some of Schreiner's most incongruous mo-ments are in fact her most true moments: why should she not have a Blenkins being terrified out of his wits by being pecked on the bald pate by an ostrich, or a Rose stuffing his male garments into an ant-hill? Why not, as Fitzpatrick and Buchan will, write a novel which has as its most adjusted character a dog?

In finding her structure in *The Story of an African Farm,* Schreiner has taken the outstretched glove of hunter-adventure fiction and tried to turn it inside out. That some of the fingers have remained stuck in the old positions, and that the glove does not look as polished on the inside, is part of the fascination of the work. That this is indeed her method in building up her novel is exemplified in the Allegory of the Hunter which Waldo's Stranger tells. He is a dismal failure as a hunter, he cannot find his quarry, he cannot bring it home. The plain physical occupation of professional huntsman is rudimentary to him — he sets off at a tangent from a man like Harris or Selous, and, instead of bag-ging his trophy, fails to bag the reflection of the bird of truth. While the real-life hunters paid their way and returned home replenished, this dream-life hunter dies trying to scale a mountain which his real-life counterparts had not even noticed. The reward for his life's strug-gle is the silver plume, Schreiner's emblem as a novelist. The central irony of Schreiner's relationship to the literature around her is com-plete.

We must take Schreiner's word for it:

And it was all play, and no one could tell what it had lived and worked for. A striving, and a striving, and an ending in nothing. (p. 99 and epigraph to Part Two, p. 125)

And, in conclusion, one should quote the following:

A confused, disordered story — the little made large and the large small, and nothing showing its inward meaning. It is not till the past has receded many steps that before the clearest eyes it falls into co-ordinate pictures. It is not till the 'I' we tell of has ceased to exist that it takes its place among other objective realities, and finds its true niche in the picture. The present and the near past is a confusion, whose meaning flashes on us as it sinks away into the distance. (p. 159)

The sooner the 'I' that blurs the perspectives of her readers is allowed to be dissolved out of the artwork, the sooner the artwork will be allowed to stand on its own as a seminal document in Southern African realist fiction, out of the plangent ironstone breast of which a century of memorial stones have been bred, stretching like a wall against the Africa that threatens to overwhelm some of its authors.

Yet, at present, we are left with the Olive school, whose recommendations to the dead include the following: that Olive should cut out the digression of the Allegory of the Hunter because it disturbs the narrative of the work, that Olive should excise chapters like the Emersonian 'Times and Seasons' because generalized accounts of growing older by the calendar should be concretized within character; that Rose should be more robust (because we like our heroes that way) or Uncle Otto a bit less vulnerable, and so on. Marquard goes as far as declaring that the limitation of Schreiner's political vision, which disqualifies *The Story of an African Farm* from being quite the Great South African Novel, is her inability to see blacks as more than part of the landscape, when, in reality, the role that blacks have always played in Karoo society has been marginal; the Karoo belongs to the Hottentot Eve, who here translates for the main characters, acts as a go-between and attends Tant' Sannie's Sunday services — she is integral to the process of that society's perpetuation. One detects the itch to sub-edit even today, a century after Schreiner received the manuscript back for her own revisions.

In reply one can only list the following: the very abundance of Schreiner's fiction, its variety, its incongruities and its peculiar uneasinesses, has proved a vessel out of which her successors have comfortably managed to select the streams which they need to channel for their own uses. From *The Story of an African Farm* comes Smith's hellish stasis in a convention-bound community in *The Beadle*, comes Plomer's theme of demoralization and disintegration in *Turbott Wolfe*, come Bosman's ironies as he took her use of the Biblical phrase 'Seed-time and harvest' (p. 268) as his *leitmotif*, come Paton's manipulations of Old Testament allegorical symbolism in *Cry, the Beloved Country*, comes Jacobson's absurdity when Fletcher, like Waldo, bites his fists and tears his hair in frustration while dancing under a bright and copper sky, comes Lessing's psychological study of a woman fighting for a romantic role to play in a system which denies her her basic rights as a human being and as a woman, comes Becker's assurance that a *Bildungsroman* can be the measure of a society's growth, comes the farm that evicts its tenants in favour of its true occupant, the giant under six feet of the country who is the main character of Gordimer's *The Conservationist*, Adamastor resurrected.

Furthermore, there are other streams of novels which flow out of Schreiner, but which run outside this obvious pattern of liberal realism, based as it is on the uneasy feeling of the white man's failure to belong to the land, and his guilt at being an interloper, a colonizer. During the period after the Anglo–Boer War there emerged two novelists who were also more than here today and gone tomorrow: Douglas Blackburn and Perceval Gibbon, both of whose fictions, if paid any attention at all, are undervalued because the context of their work has never been recognized. Blackburn's Sarel Erasmus trilogy — *Prinsloo of Prinsloosdorp* (1899), *A Burgher Quixote* (1903) and *I Came and Saw* (1908) — written in a naturalist picaresque style, refutes the assumption that no English writer in South Africa can write in depth about the back of the non-English mind, for these three works stand as the only convincing registers (in English) of the Boer's tribulations during the conflict that delivered him into the twentieth century. Blackburn satirizes the Boer from within, as he collides with the commercial mining culture of the British conquerors, and comes to terms as an Afrikaner with his first place in the white urban establishment. In another novel, *Leaven: A Black and White Story* (1908), Blackburn brings the rural black man to the fore with his portrait of Bulalie, which is a calculated parody of Haggard's portrait of Umslopagaas, the faithful servant. Blackburn's passionate sociological interest in the changing patterns of Southern African society engendered in *Leaven* the theme of black labour recruitment and the drift to the towns which *African Farm* was too early to have felt. *Leaven*, nevertheless, acts as a bridge from Schreiner to the later novels about labour and urbanization, like Plomer's 'Ula Masondo', in *I Speak of Africa* (1927), and *Mine Boy*, which were to become known as the 'Jim Comes to Joburg' type, after a film of that title on the same theme made in 1949.

Gibbon's *Margaret Harding* (1911), also derived from Schreiner's *African Farm*, was to initiate another direction taken in the Southern African novel, the work with love across racial barriers as a key theme.

As Michael Wade remarks with respect to Abrahams's *The Path of Thunder* (1952): 'It is apparently quite obligatory for all South African novelists to try their hand at least once at the theme of miscegenation.'[15] In *Margaret Harding* the love between a TB-patient recovering her health on an African farm and a black man repatriated back to South Africa after the finest education in England symbolizes a deeper quest for identification, on the white character's part, with black Africa than had appeared possible to Schreiner, and it heralds a series of novels which analyse the precise and tragic compromises the colour-bar society forces on individuals from both sides of the tracks, a theme which Schreiner tried to launch in embryonic form in *From Man to Man* (first published only in 1926).

If Schreiner has remained a Southern African writer's Southern African writer, that is as her declaration of independence intended it to be. That her Southern African critics have not observed this is less than fortunate.

7 The Emergence of Black English

Run Rabbit-Man run
The hunter's coming with his gun.[1]

It is only by the successive testing of hypotheses and rejection of the false that truth is at last elicited. After all, what we call truth is only the hypothesis which is found to work best. Therefore in reviewing the opinions and practices of ruder ages and races we shall do well to look with leniency upon their errors as inevitable slips made in the search for truth, and to give them the benefit of that indulgence which we ourselves may one day stand in need of . . . [2]

IF THE STUDY OF THE ENGLISH AND AFRIKAANS WRITTEN literatures of Southern Africa is at present not conducted on a comparative basis, and the literatures together with their critics may be said to have hived off in their own directions, the study of the origins of black literature in Southern Africa and its manifestations in English is equally fraught with organizational difficulties. There is as yet no established discipline whereby literature in indigenous languages can be studied in relation to its English and other offshoots. Scholars who embark upon the study of literature in, say, Zulu, Sotho or Xhosa frequently approach such work in translation, as do most English-language creative writers. Mofolo's *Chaka* (1925) is the prime example, for, although it has always enjoyed a large Sotho reading-public, it has travelled with influence in its English, French, Italian, German, Yoruba, and more recently its Afrikaans, versions.[3] Commentators like Daniel P. Kunene, who examine Sotho literature in the original in extensive detail, have not yet yoked together the heterogeneities of a comparative approach between Sotho and English literature in Southern Africa to arrive at a new critical metaphysics.

A three-way comparative study undertaken along the lines of Gérard's teamwork proposal, discussed in the introductory chapter, would seem beyond accomplishment within South Africa at present, because the society which advocates the separateness of races also tends to enforce a separateness of cultures. Although the total Southern African culture would seem most interesting precisely where there is intercultural con-

tact, and a resultant ripple effect of influences, the three camps that
South Africa's political and educational system has created ensure
that no academic within the country is educated very far beyond
specialization in his own field. If the motivation for cross-cultural and
translingual studies is, therefore, lacking, owing to political happenstance, that is not to say that political habits make for sound literary
habits. Southern Africa may be seen as one of the world's most di-
versely acculturated regions. If the literary customs within it are
acquired from an unthinking allegiance to its system of political
groupings, that in itself is cause for comment. Separatism, as Northrop Frye observes with regard to Canadian literature, is 'culturally
the most sterile of creeds'.[4]

In the face of such immense potential one does tend to retire into
that part of the divided territory claimed by this book — English
Southern African, which is encompassed at this time with relative
ease. But I retreat with the proviso that any comment made here
about the relationship between the English language, its literature
and black writers in Southern Africa is made in no absolute sense. I
stress the interim nature of this book for some very practical reasons:
firstly, it is by no means certain that all the documents that are necessary to seeing the early stages of such a study clearly are uncovered
and available to the researcher, and, secondly, the post-1960 works of
black English writing have been so extensively banned or otherwise
put beyond the legitimate reach of the South African reader that, at
both ends of the spectrum, he is obliged to improvise where he would
rather argue from evidence.

There is another reason why black English studies in South Africa
are embattled and fragmentary. The various controls which operate
in the making of black English literature include barely detectable
prejudices, the subtlety of which is insidious and damaging to true
assessment. Despite the fact that 'unwritten literature', as Ruth Finnegan describes it,[5] has in recent times been accorded some standing in
universities where black English studies are researched and taught, it
enjoys little status within South Africa. Black literature, one fears, is
studied in its written form; its preliterate forms remain the preserve
of the anthropologists and linguists, whose work rarely impinges
upon that of the literary historian who takes it that literature itself
begins with the printed page. The prejudice against oral literature frequently applies to both black and white critics; for white critics and
writers it is a phase which, no matter how subtle, mature or 'artistic',
remains at a remove across social and language barriers which they are

ill-equipped to bridge, and for the black critic and writer within South Africa the legacy of oral culture is often taken as a reminder of the 'primitive' past which he or she is trying to escape. Significantly, the most urgent plea for some scrutiny to be made of oral origins that has emerged in Southern African academic life recently comes from a critic resident in Botswana. It is dated 1977, a full century after a philologist like W.H.I. Bleek started collecting breakwater tales from his Bushman interviewees.[6]

Bob Leshoai's motives are as follows:

We know that long before the white man's arrival our honourable ancestors had created their own culture, their own way of life that we are proud of today. One of the most important ingredients of this culture was a rich and profound oral literature of myths, legends, folk tales, folk songs, rhymes, praise and heroic poems, proverbs, idioms and riddles.

It was through this rich oral literature that the nation of children, men and women learned about morality, religion, philosophy, wisdom, geography, history and politics and the entire spectrum of human existence in the various communities.[7]

Professor Leshoai's assumptions about the value of the study of oral culture are of real interest here: he implies that oral culture assumes value once one is proud of it, because its literary merit is not inferior to that of any written culture's. The motivation to show that this is so gives him his resourceful energy, an energy which few critics with a purely literary interest in the field appear to be able to summon to hand. One refers for inspiration to Okot p'Bitek's grassroots re-education programmes in post-independence East Africa. Leshoai's motives are themselves part of literary history; the desire to rediscover the past and to re-value standing orders of literary merit is part of the new consciousness of the black African scholar who can overcome his recent status as colonial dependent in favour of reappraising his 'honourable ancestors'. But one must note that it is also part of the literary history of Southern Africa that in the past there have been vested interests seeing to it that the job remained undone.

When Bleek undertook his pioneering researches, although his own motivation might have been a linguist's fascination for his subject and a desire that material be preserved for posterity, the whole of his project of literary recovery was financially sustained thanks to different factors. The history of the suppression of oral indigenous literature is a long, grinding and inevitable one. No early traveller inland in touch with centres of tribal oral culture could resist recording it as part of his amateur ethnography. We have already noted that Camoens himself made a poet's response to Da Gama's encounter with the chanting tribesmen of the Mossel Bay coast, but Camoens is an exception to the rule. Travellers like Le Vaillant and James Alexander (1838)[8] may be relied upon to bring back folk tales and sayings to the Western world's printing presses with as little mutilation in translation as possible. But where the traveller's motivation is more than to record a good tale as part of a disinterested illustration of the characteristics of the 'discovered tribes', we may begin to suspect that the ends of documentation might well have been twisted. With some of the missionaries, in their spearheading of the drift towards colonization inland, the literary judgements begin to go awry.

In his painstakingly collected appendix of Tswana fables, the Rev. John Campbell, for example, cannot resist delivering this stinging evaluation:

The following absurd and ridiculous fictions are presented to the notice of the reader only because they exhibit, in a striking manner, the puerile and degraded state of intellect among the natives of South Africa. Who can contemplate the ignorance and imbecility which marks this display of Bootchuana *literature* without the liveliest emotions of pity and concern? especially when it has been fully demonstrated, by many pleasing facts, that the African mind is capable by the blessing of God of entertaining the exalted views of revealed truth, and of escaping from the shackles of ignorance and the bondage of Satan.[9]

Despite Campbell's sentiments towards oral culture, his collection does stand, a document of literary archaeology in spite of itself. Campbell's collection happens to be of the same material that Leshoai is referring to, and when the linguist Daniel Jones collaborated with Sol Plaatje in London to produce the first phonetically spelled Tswana reader,[10] the same tales served their purpose well enough.

But the Campbell view of the 'imbecility' of oral literature is the one which generally prevails among white supremacists for the century following his mission to the 'Bechuanas'. His literary opinion is the necessary complement to a political and religious view that any culture without an alphabet and a system of paper documentation must perforce belong to what Matthew Arnold and a host of other empire-builders came to call their 'fosterlings',[11] the so-called child races.

In the annual address to the meeting of the subscribers of the Public Library of the Cape of Good Hope in 1868, Professor Roderick Noble commended Dr Bleek on his researches (Bleek was then custodian of the Grey Collection), on the grounds that they were a true part of the general advancement of knowledge. That advancement, one notes, included Speke and Grant's solving of the enigma of the source of the Nile and the deeds of

> our own Livingstone . . . come back to us as the living from the dead, his charmed life defiant of peril, plague, or treachery, still preserved through all his wondrous wanderings, and within a few months or weeks we may expect to have revealed by him the whole mystery of those most interesting highlands, woodlands and inland seas of South Eastern Africa.[12]

Noble's view of Livingstone's traipse through the greatest field of Southern African oral literature yet exposed to a white man is unconsciously couched in terms of a voyage into hell; both Livingstone and Noble believed not in cross-cultural fertilization, but in redemption.

When in his speech Noble refers to another collecting project, one underway in the hands of the Xhosa Rev. Tiyo Soga, the first ordained black minister in South Africa, he cannot refrain from stressing the terms on which he would find such a collection acceptable:

> [it will be] a series of most interesting legends, tales, and apologues which — endowed as he is with a keen sense of humour, as well as a power of graphic expression — he can set forth in fitting English garb in a style that would render them of the deepest interest to all of us. (pp. 17–18)

The conditions on which white critics will countenance black oral culture are clear: it must conform to British standards of English expression, appropriateness and even humour before it can be welcomed into the fold. Noble is intent to sever oral culture from its living roots for it to become worthy of consideration as literature. Soga's collection remains largely unpublished to this day.

A similar but more blatant attitude is struck by the speaker at the annual Public Library meeting of nine years later, Sir Bartle Frere, Governor of Cape Colony and High Commissioner for South Africa. We may take it that his attitude to oral literature was official:

> It is true that [the clergy's] primary function, is to preach the Gospel to the heathen, but [they] have given much time, labour, and attention, we can hardly say to the *literature* of the heathen, because they have no literature at present, but to the task of making a literature for them, to learn about their language and the affinities of their language. Just consider for a moment of how much practical money value is the work of Dr Bleek . . . to all those dealing with the languages of South Africa.[13]

Frere's 'practical money value' is not to be derived from any knowledge that may be extracted from the tribal culture of 'our honourable

ancestors' for its own interest. The Bible has to be translated into the
indigenous languages and effect a conversion of tribal thought first.
With reference to the Rev. Robert Moffat's version of the Bible in
Tswana, he remarks:

> Apart from all questions of theology and morality, that Book is the Magna Carta
> of civilization to those people and it is the business of any man who wishes to
> raise them or make them anything better than they are, to give them a translation
> of the Bible. (p. 30)

There are no half-measures in this matter of civilizing the subject
tribes; the scramble for Africa, theology and morality aside, was a
matter of violent uprootings and imposed credos, during which oral
culture was not encouraged to be sustained unless it could be shown
to serve the ends of the scramblers.

The results of such attitudes are obvious. One recollects the courage
of the artistic statement Pringle was making in rendering Xhosa songs
into English ('Makanna's Gathering' and 'The Brown Hunter's Song'
are examples): such material, he was demonstrating in somewhat
idealized terms, could also be the right and proper concern of everyone's literature. Nevertheless, the very act of transposing a song from
its own language into literary English, although performed for the
right reasons, could often lead to the wrong results; it was an act of
incipient language colonialism that would lead to the further down-
grading of tribal art. The prevalent attitude towards the wealth of
black literary material beneath the noses of Pringle's heirs on the
frontier remained the one that, if it did not exist for purposes of
convenient manipulation, it did not exist at all.

In May 1834, John Centlivres Chase summed up the common feelings of the white English settlers towards the new environment between them and the frontier:

> It is very annoying to myself, as well as to all the multitudinous chroniclers of
> modern settlements, that we are debarred the advantages of our elder brethren,
> the Historians of Antiquity, in the possession of those distant and dusky periods
> called the Fabulous Ages. Bless ye, courteous readers, if these were our birthright,
> which, alas! they are not! how we would plunge into the mists of obscurity, and
> dive into the unfathomable depths of past centuries, and bring up shapes and
> shades of all by-gone times to amuse and instruct ye! . . .
> It is not alone that we sorrow over the loss of the fertile period just glanced at,
> but we have also the other misery of remembering that we have adopted a coun-
> try discovered and inhabited so long after the second fabulous reign, the times
> emphatically denominated the *Dark Ages,* which would otherwise have given us
> food for embellishment; for have we not *materiel?* in glittering streams, fitted to

be sung by any water-bibbing poetaster or wandering minstrel; umbrageous
woods, gloomy enough to shelter any midnight murderer 'by your leaf'; caverns
calculated to cover any 'hole-and-corner-gentlemen' banditti; defiles yet to be
polluted by invading forces; crags upon which Baronial Castles ought to be
perched, and over which stupid serfs might be scragged and dangled in mid-air
— 'gallows high'; have we not all these favours of providence to make our land
illustrious like those of Europe? . . . [14]

This deep-felt need for a fabulous past, no less deeply felt for all
Chase's grotesque humour, was an expression of a desire on the part
of the English artist to have access to a local landscape of fable, romance, ballad and myth. The desire arose on account of his feeling of
deracination from his own heritage of oral culture, which could find
no new roots in the neighbouring black cultures that had for centuries
enjoyed an established sense of literary belonging, the precondition
for development within a literature. No one thought of reminding
Chase that fable first entered European literature through the mouth
of the African Aesop, and that while fable had on the one hand per-
colated down the byways of Africa right to the other side of the Cape
frontier, it had, on the other hand, managed also to become absorbed
into the very fibre of the taproots of written European literature as
well.

Bleek was not one to miss the irony. In naming his collection of
'Hottentot' fables and tales *Reynard the Fox in South Africa,* he indi-
cated that a comparison should be made between indigenous material
and the proliferation of fabulous epics featuring cunning foxes, and so
on, prevalent in the Middle Ages and available for use by writers as
diverse as Chaucer and Goethe in the creation of their written hybrids.
That similar hybridization did not occur post-Bleek in Southern Africa
is an index not of the inherent literary qualities of the possible consti-
tuent parts, but of the society that never realized that such hybridization is a natural and normal part of literary fermentation. The case of
Bain's hybridization of Kaatje Kekkelbek's song and dance culture
with the routines of imported music hall has already been noted as an
example of a successful attempt at closing some of the gap between
black and white, but *Kaatje Kekkelbek* is exceptional. That *Kaatje
Kekkelbek* could also synthesize English and Afrikaans is an indication
that the premise of there being one Southern African literature is not
far-fetched. Bain's work is situated at the intersection of all the cross-
currents.

While white English culture in all its administrative manifestations
has always been resolutely against accepting black culture as a viable

expression of human feeling, the same, at the deepest level, may not always be said of individual white artists. There have been the odd useful break-throughs in understanding which are all the more memorable in the light of the general antipathies. One remembers Thomas Baines, artist and diarist, painting an ikon for us of a moment of empathy between two of his forerunners, one from the Stone Age and the other lately of the Anti-Slavery Society in London — Thomas Pringle's signature, dated 1825, painted above and to the left of an anonymous fresco of Bushman cave paintings in the Baviaan's River Valley.[15] One remembers the anonymous master and the live romantic, both with a common art of graffito.

In Thomas Baines one can detect the desire for an art form which would convey more than realism, a form beyond mere recording and annotation, when he meditates on the limits set on the functions of art in mid-nineteenth-century colonial culture:

My art, indeed, seemed at a discount on the frontier, and was regarded as a trade preferable to wagon making only as involving manual labour. A picture was supposed to be a thing made to the order of the purchaser, and subject, when finished, to any alteration his caprice suggested; all exercise of the imagination, even in the play of light and shade so essential to the beauty of the picture, was denied me, and I was required to bring out every nicety of detail. One of my earliest patrons ordered me to paint the front, the sides, and as much as possible of the back, of his house, with 'at least' twelve bullock wagons in line across the foreground, two spans of oxen ploughing, a third drawing the harrow in his field, and, if I could possibly contrive it, the young corn just beginning to look green; and another refused his picture because, for the sake of contrast with the distant mountains I had slightly elongated a pole in the foreground, and placed upon it a hawk that did not happen to be there at the time.[16]

Baines's client who desired to have all sides of his house on one canvas with a simultaneous display of spring and autumn thought he was a realist. He probably would not have enjoyed the ironic observation that he in fact exhibited the potential to think cubistically, and that the cubist impulse would be one which African tribal sculptors would donate to Europe, like Munchausen's Wau-wau bird, for the edification of his grandchildren's generation of aesthetic theorists.

Baines himself was not insensitive to the fact that he was witnessing the origins of Southern African drama when on 13 April 1848 he spent an evening near Bushman's School in the Eastern Province:

the night was spent by the Gonah Hottentots in the performance of various native dances. Matross, the younger of the two gathering his shirt loosely about his arms in imitation of wings and tying it so as to leave his slender legs bare to their whole length, enacted what he called the Volstruys loop, apparently an *ad libitum* imitation of the motions of the ostrich; and Boozak, desiring me to bring my book that he might go to England as well as the rest, undertook the execution of a more regular Kafir dance; the wild gestures of both being shown to advantage by a brilliant fire of dry mimosa which not only lighted up the group immediately round it but cast its fitful glare even on the more prominent portions of the distant landscape. (p. 79)

A critic like Wilfrid Mellers, in formulating a theory of the origins of music, can today remark:

the African Bushmen who live in the Kalahari desert create a weird music by emulating the twitters, yawps, barks, grunts and grizzles of birds and beasts; in becoming, in sound and movement, their totemic creatures, they employ disguise and illusion as a propitiatory act, conquering fear of the unknown in making a gesture of reverence to the creatures on whom they rely for subsistence. The music they make is an aural mask that complements the visual masks they may wear; in being metamorphosed, aurally, visually and corporeally, into Nature they acquire some of the attributes of divinity.[17]

One cites Baines and interprets him through the media-conscious eyes and ears of Mellers in order to arrive at a simple statement: the barrier between oral culture and English written culture is one of terminology, of custom, of political policy, of colonialism, of racial pride, if you like; but there is no aesthetic reason why there should be any hostility between the two, and none for the white side not to understand the meaning and function of oral culture in a performance like this today. Yet the distance is there. Baines does not hear the performer's sound signals at all. He is acutely conscious of his alienation from both performance and landscape, although he does note that his subjects view *his* art as magical. If one were to go through travellers' records of experience in Southern Africa from 1600 onwards, one would find many similar examples of cultures facing one another across a barrier of misunderstanding about media — the indigenous ludic forms of sympathetic invocation as against the white representational artist, an act of natural empathy as against a scientific curiosity. Baines's drawing of the occasion, or at least the oil based on it, captures the firelight as footlights, the glowering, hostile mountains as backdrop, and he is unable to reconcile two modes of thinking about theatre. One needs a revised, broadened poetics, one which can accommodate and assess the significance to Southern African culture of both Matross as the ostrich and the performance of, say, Shakespeare in imitation of the latest London style.

One can see why the function of oral culture has not been of interest to the mass of white writers and artists using English culture as a measure of civilization between 1800 and recent times. Oral culture, with its particular notions of a direct and harmonious rapport with nature, could not be available to the white artist who viewed nature as hostile and threatening, as a force to be overcome. The conflict between oral and written culture, then, has been fought out as a battle between a mythology of belonging in nature and an alien mythology that has maintained its hostility, using strategies like map-making and the erection of fences as a means of taming it. One mode of communication has had to give way in the face of the next for the country to become controllable in political, economic and the related literary terms. The war against a myth of pastoral contentment, as embodied in the work of a poet like Arthur Shearly Cripps, the Spenser of Africa, the only white poet to have adapted his evangelism to a black view of theology, has had to proceed in the face of nature, because the Englishman's Wordsworthian assumptions deserted him the moment the Lake District was substituted for the dry wastes of the Kalahari Desert in his literary imagination.[18] 'Africa for the Africans', Cripps would reply, going native himself in opposition to the invading gods.

But the new myth of the mission to civilize beyond the frontier spread apace: watersprites gave way to dams, wood-spirits to bulldozers, the protective isolation of mountains to the passes of Andrew Geddes Bain's heavy engineering. The accompanying myths of progress and industry had to obliterate cultures which maintained that progress was an illusion and which stressed self-sufficiency. The new mythology of technological progress could not but help looking down upon the isolation of bucolic order, while it swept up victims as the labouring muscle and bone that would feed the machine. The evangelism of the missionaries in a contact situation with 'primitive' man represented merely the substitution of adequate gods for an unattainable God, one who would promise admission into the lower rooms of His mansion, the quarters reserved for those converted from Satanism, in exchange for life-long labour in homage to His main manifestation, the demonstration of His power to control the hostile universe. A similar battle, fought between the self-sufficient Boer communities, dependent on nature's bounty, and the British Raj was waged so that they, too, would acknowledge the ingenious, all-powerful deity of industrial man.

But with the current world-wide scepticism over the achievements of technology, and the shrinkage of the earth into one global village, we see that the ascendance of industry over the bucolic existence has reached a new turning-point. There are no longer moral grounds upon which the superiority of white English culture in Southern Africa can be maintained. That culture itself is now seen to be the destroyer and exhauster of a subdued nature, and South Africa's citizens, instead of flocking into the cities in retreat from nature and in search of comfort, now turn from the communication cell of the city outwards to nature again for consolation. The return to the old mystique and reverence for nature is couched in the neo-tribal rhetoric of ecology studies, and the story of migration to the cities (which occupies the attention of the major part of Southern Africa's writers) finds its ironic reversal as the children, like Mellers, of Marshall McLuhan's new 'oral society' feel the need to turn back to the roots they never knew they had.

Before demonstrating that this is the basic pattern that applies to both black and white writing in Southern Africa, it remains to show an ancillary theme in action here, one which complicates an understanding of the status of oral culture and its written derivatives. Oral society presupposed a role for the poet which included him within the society, both as its repository of historical precedent in poetry, and as its commentator and entertainer. To the white man the imbongis of tribal life might have appeared nameless, faceless functions of the society, but they were an integral part of its cohesion and continuity. A writer like Haggard could grudgingly play the role of imbongi himself, in imitation of those sterling virtues of sustaining, low-profile patriotism.

Haggard's own English culture in Southern Africa turned up its own imbongis in the form of a number of ballad writers and folk singers, all of whom flourished not in the court of Queen Victoria but in the columns of her newspapers abroad. If black tribal culture is a neglected facet of Southern African life, so is its white counterpart, the popular spoken poetry of the nineteenth-century English press which, likewise, has been systematically downgraded by those who believe that removing literature from the human voice into the textual grandeur of the written word awards it an automatic superiority. The bards of English oral culture in South Africa are there,[19] but they are mostly overlooked: Albert Brodrick and his many fellows appear in Alexander Wilmot's collection of South African verse (1887), but they are phased out by the time of Francis Carey Slater's first and revised Centenary collections (1925 and 1945), and in Guy Butler's Oxford collection. (No oral black poets, even in translation, appear in any of these anthologies.)

But what industrialization brought with it, as both the tribesman and Schreiner's Waldo were to discover, was a new battle which, as Frye observes of Canadian literature, was the 'real terror . . . when the individual feels himself becoming an individual, pulling away from the group, losing the sense of driving power the group gives him, aware of a conflict within himself far subtler than the struggle of morality against evil' (Conclusion, p. 290). The deathblow to both black tribal cohesion and the white garrison mentality was the emergence of an outsider figure whose quitting of the tribe or the garrison varies in Southern African literature from the appearance of Ntsikana Gaba, the first African convert among the Xhosas, all the way down the line to the white English exiles like Campbell and Plomer, who had no end of scorn to pour upon their earlier tribal holdings, and an Afrikaans writer like Breyten Breytenbach today. The perfect manifestation of this figure is Mphahlele, whose autobiographical novel, *Down Second Avenue* (1959), is a veritable chart of the breaking of enclosing and securing shells, from the black tribal to the urban black to the urban mixed to the African international, with all the violence and struggle that that implies.

An understanding of the emergence of black English written literature, then, is important not only to a study of any beaconed-off compartment in the literature marked 'Black Studies', but as a reflection of the processes at work integrally within the whole. Like Don Quixote and Sancho Panza, written and oral literatures are dependent on one another. The problem is the matter of what exactly is at stake when equal and opposite literary forces meet and fight it out, when John Doe takes on Jim Crow. There is no need to back sides here; one spectates in order to describe and to interpret. The case history of a manuscript like Sol T. Plaatje's *Mhudi,* it so happens, is tailor-made to illustrate this.

Mhudi is the first English novel by a black South African writer. It was first published over a century after Ntsikana (d. 1821), a convert of Rev. Johannes van der Kemp, had begun the absorption of the form of the English hymn into Xhosa and become the first individualized black African poet.[20] As we would expect, 'the story of Ntsikana [formed] a connecting link between that period of utter darkness . . . and the now dawning epoch of civilization'.[21] At around the same time (1802) the first Cape printing press was running off South Africa's first indigenous printed poem, M. Borcherds's 'De Maan'. By the 1830s, the period of action of Plaatje's novel, the Rev. Mr Archbell could record that:

[it takes] a year or two while they can repeat their catechism, when they are taken to the Parsons to be heard, and to make a confession of sins, of which they have not the most distant idea, nor of which they had never heard, having never visited a church before in their lives. They are then baptized, and they then suppose they are Christians . . . [22]

While Archbell's 'beloved heathen' were intertwining Christian ritual with tribal poetry, as were the converts of Moffat and others, Harris was galloping through his 'fabled creation'. A commentator on the white poetry that recorded intercultural contact across the moving frontier of the time remarked tendentiously that 'few poets have considered the native races sufficiently beautiful to deal with poetically'.[23] A convert like Thomas Mofolo could, in his *Moeti oa Bochabela* (1907), advocate, as Daniel P. Kunene notes, 'an "exodus" by his people, a wholesale spiritual migration from "heathenism" to Christianity',[24] from 'the black darkness, very black, in the times when the tribes were still eating each other like wild beasts. . . .'[25] The drift is irreversible.

It is against a background of a mixture of antagonistic and interacting mythologies like this that Plaatje proceeds to write. His outlet conditioned his work, for only a missionary press would publish this first 'Native venture' into prose fiction. *Mhudi* has been read and commented upon in terms of its being a missionary product; Plaatje himself was a Lutheran and a lay-preacher. The common assumption is that between the 1830s of Mr Archbell and the 1930 of the first publication of *Mhudi,* a century of confrontation and synthesis had been completed for *Mhudi* to have the final shape that it does have. Critics react with a mixture of praise and aversion — Jahn classifies *Mhudi* as a work of tutelage, situated between 'apprentice literature' and 'protest literature' — that is, where African English literature is 'hedging or half-in-half'.[26] He asserts that it bears no connection with the 'skokiaan' culture which urbanization was to breed.[27]

Only recently, with the reappearance of the original typescript of *Mhudi,* can an interpretation of the printed work against Plaatje's original intentions be undertaken. The results are illuminating, because they exemplify very precisely and in an extensive way the tensions that have to be taken into account at the juncture where oral literature is transposed into the written. One must observe at the outset that the difficulties facing Plaatje in finding a publisher, and his final settlement with the Lovedale Press to give out a bowdlerized version of his novel, form a neat example of some of the mephitic confusions which characterize the battle for literary supremacy here. The secret imbroglio waged between Plaatje and his white editors at Lovedale, one of the

few such imbroglios that can be chronicled in detail, is symbolic of
the dilemma of a considerable amount of African English literature.
There is a process of possible editorial screening that occurs when
works in African English arrive on the desks of English publishers who
face the text across a no-man's land in which mistakes, conscious or
unconscious prejudices, and potentially contradictory preconceptions
may exert a distorting influence on the final printed product. *Mhudi*
is, one hopes, an extreme example of this distortion having taken
place. At the time of *Mhudi's* first going to press the textual emenda-
tions and cuts may have appeared as 'improvements' to the work, and
there can be no doubt that without the missionary presses black writing in English in Southern Africa would not have seen the light of
day at all. But the fact that it was controlled into seeing the light of
day, in a way which was desirable to the missionary presses themselves, and which might have been quite undesirable in terms of any
purely literary criteria, is where the commentary can begin.

The publishing policy of the Lovedale Press as it affected an earlier
novella in English, R.R.R. Dhlomo's *An African Tragedy,* was clear-
cut: that forty-page text appeared 'just as it left the writer's hand',
with the exception, duly recorded, that there had been alterations of
punctuation. But the truth about *An African Tragedy* might be that
it was so calculated to be 'a contribution towards staying the decline
of Native life in large cities and towns'[28] in the face of liquor, gam-
bling, whoring and thievery, and so in line with the proselytizing
intentions of a press using its printing works for the general propaga-
tion of the Christian message, that it probably needed no more than
changes of punctuation.[29] But the very fact that this rudimentary
attempt at transforming pamphleteering into fiction has such a publisher's note demonstrates that a missionary press could not contemplate printing a manuscript unless it conformed in some way to its
general policy.

One of the ancillary themes of *Mhudi* is indeed an endorsement of
the missionary effort; within the period of history Plaatje is dealing
with in his novel, the establishment of the first Matabele Empire and
its conflict with the intruding Voortrekkers migrating inland, he makes
it clear that he feels the missionaries played an arbitrating and peace-
making role. When Chief Massouw of the Qorannas delivers judgement
in his tribal court, he cites the message of the 'white missioner Moffat'
(Quagga edition, *Mhudi,* p. 70) as a new factor to be taken into account
in the computation of legal morality, and when Chief Moroka of the
Barolong and Sarel Cilliers genteelly disagree on a point of doctrine,

they defer to Archbell himself (p. 76).

Yet a more basic theme in *Mhudi*, despite its support of missionary zeal, is a critique of the destructive action of Christianity in the respects in which it debases or suppresses the original virtues of pre-Christian tribal life. For Plaatje those days cannot be viewed as days of 'black darkness, very black'. As the opening chapter of *Mhudi* establishes, up to the end of the eighteenth century '[those] simple folk were perfectly happy without money and without silver watches' (p. 23). Plaatje's intention in writing *Mhudi* was, from a missionary point of view, perhaps a little two-faced, for he meant at the same time as extolling Christian virtue, like Ntsikana's bell, to assert that so-called pagan virtue was also wholesome and perfectly able to maintain a morally viable community life. The fact that the book is full of trial scenes stresses how law-abiding that community was. Mofolo in his *Chaka* chose to celebrate and also to abhor Zulu militarism, while Plaatje opted to admire the culture of the altogether pacific and law-abiding Barolong to whom Zulu militarism represented as great a threat as it ever did to Piet Retief. Plaatje's intention was to deny that the history of Southern Africa was one of a simple black–white confrontation; pastoral harmony, that the Barolong and the Griquas and the Boers had firmly in common, is set against the tyranny of the racial exclusivity that first manifested itself in Shaka Zulu, and was impelled across the subcontinent by Mzilikazi, whose son, Lobengula, finally met his match in the person of Rhodes. Plaatje did not believe in colour frontiers.

This facet of Plaatje's general theme is the one that has suffered in the lengthy story which is the saga of the *Mhudi* text. What happened between the original typescript, completed in 1917,[30] and its first publication in 1930 was that the parts of the text that could be thought to favour the black–white confrontation view of history were played up, and the detail which countered such a view in favour of a subtle and delicate religious and mythical syncretism was played down. Since Plaatje wrote *Mhudi* 'to interpret to the reading public one phase of "the back of the Native mind" ' (Quagga text, Preface, p. 17), we see that his task could not have been an easy one.

The original edition of *Mhudi* in boards was a 225-page text that appeared with the subtitle 'An Epic of South African Native Life a Century Ago'. The evidence of the typescript is that if Plaatje wrote *Mhudi* as an 'epic', it was not to be a mere documentary of life all that lost time ago. He was not concerned to use the inherited novel form in imitation of standard British epic-adventure models of the Haggard and

Buchan type. Nor was he using history as a source of escapist romance. For Plaatje the acceptance of the novel form was merely the acceptance of a flexible enough medium which he could use for his own ends. When Anne Tibble comments that 'Plaatje writes [more] as a traditional tale-teller might have spoken',[31] she is relying on inspired guesswork, for the Lovedale text gives precious little evidence that that was so. In fact, the corrections and revisions that the typescript shows point to an attempt having been made to screen out this 'traditional tale-teller' tone of voice. The *Mhudi* which we have from Lovedale is a fundamentally different work from the *Mhudi* reassembled from the original manuscript source for publication in the Heinemann African Writers Series. There is one slight but overwhelmingly convincing detail which reveals this. What is cut in the Lovedale edition is the fact that the whole of *Mhudi* was meant to be a narrative told by some other storyteller to the writer.

The HAWS text shows what was missing in the Lovedale edition. The Lovedale Chapter 12 ('Queen Umnandi') begins:

Here, we may be permitted to digress and describe the beauty and virtues of one of King Mzilikazi's wives — the lily of his harem, by name Umnandi, the sweet one. She was a daughter of *Umzinyati* (the Bison-city) the off-spring of a lineage of brave warriors with many deeds of valour to their credit. Such was the description of her given to the writer by a hoary octogenarian that it reminded him of a remarkable passage in the Song of Songs . . . (p. 94)

The corrected HAWS edition reads:

Half-a-Crown may be permitted to digress here and describe the beauty and virtues of one of King Mzilikazi's wives — the lily of his harem, by name Umnandi, the sweet one. . . . Such was the description of her given to Half-a-Crown, the hoary octogenarian, that it reminded him of a remarkable passage in the Song of Songs . . . (Chapter 10, 'Umnandi', p. 91)

In other words, what the Lovedale text, in deleting the appearance of 'Half-a-Crown', omitted to give evidence of was that Plaatje viewed himself not so much as a novelist but as a scribe, whose role was to record the story told him by an intermediary, this missing link between those who knew the history of the 1830s at first hand and who in his eighties was handing it on to Plaatje. After quoting Half-a-Crown's, not his own, comparison of Umnandi with the 'black but comely' passage from the Song of Songs, Plaatje remains neutral, or at least apparently so; he lets Half-a-Crown himself infer that pastoral life under King Solomon was very like that of the pre-Christian society of his parents' days.

But this is merely a leading clue in what turns out to be the illumination of several obscure passages in the Lovedale text. One feels that the missing narrator has been deleted elsewhere, and the typescript confirms that he played a crucial and consistent role in the original. In truth, this 'Half-a-Crown' character is the single narrator of all of *Mhudi*. We are dealing not with the abstract calculations of the Western historical novel, but with a document of living oral narrative. The structure of the novel suddenly leaps into meaningful focus. All of *Mhudi*, then, breaks down into passages (chapters) which are shaped according to oral formulations which Half-a-Crown has heard and recollected intact. Some passages emerge as fireside tales, which he relays verbatim. The sequence from the Lovedale p. 19: ' "How can I explain?" commenced Mhudi . . . ' through to the end of the Lovedale chapter 4 is in fact one chapter (no. 3), the 'Rays of Sunshine' of the typescript in the HAWS edition, which is one uninterrupted monologue from, in this case, the mouth of Mhudi herself.

But Plaatje the novelist stands outside this type of narration, building into it what is a critique of oral culture at the same time. In a scene of cross-culturation between the Qoranna and Mhudi and her husband, he shows how, thanks to language misunderstandings, Ra-Thaga's brave deeds compound into mythical proportions (Quagga, p. 64). Conversely, in the scene where the news of the passing of the first Voortrekkers is reported over and over again, he shows how a trespass on the part of a few unknown mermen becomes a full-scale invasion in the local imagination (Quagga, p. 80). Since the Boers on trek were also, we are reminded, mostly preliterate, Plaatje shows how overblown images of the 'kaal Kaffers' motivate them — all Plaatje's characters move in a world of giants and pygmies.

The binding power of such oral features as proverbs, for example, as rationalizers of inflated situations, is underplayed by Plaatje's editor, for several proverbs that he persuaded Plaatje to cut from the original show how this technique used at critical points served to deflate and level impulsive responses. Where the Lovedale text reads: 'Let the Boers come here and camp at the foot of the Black Mountain [said Chief Moroka]. Here Sarel and I will tarry' (Quagga, p. 99), the typescript reads: 'Here Sarel and I will parry the Matabele assegai together. Old people say the quarry of two dogs is never too strong' (HAWS text, p. 113).

The pointers throughout the work are that Half-a-Crown could quite legitimately have gathered every phrase of the work that is *Mhudi* from one or another source personally and faithfully. He is no omniscient narrative mouthpiece devised to lend verisimilitude and colour to a mixture of historical research and imaginative speculation, for he is none other than the actual son of Mhudi and Ra-Thaga. 'That's exactly how my father and mother met and became man and wife', he tells Plaatje (HAWS opening of Chapter 5, 'The Forest Home', p. 59 — cf. Lovedale's 'That is exactly how our hero and heroine met . . . ', p. 49). Born within the early chapters of the book, or soon afterwards, he is the only character on the long cast list of *Mhudi* to survive into the 1910s. His real name, since his father's name was Ra-Thaga (i.e. father of Thaga) is possibly Thaga, and he can trace his ancestry back through a male line of several centuries. His 'European' nickname, then, is the half-pejorative, half-ironic 'Half-a-Crown' that conceals his true origins and makes of him a back-door storyteller robbed of ancestry and dignity by a society which denies his oral heritage any literary status.

Once the action of *Mhudi* concludes with his parents in possession of their second-hand ox-waggon, the symbol of the new age of the wandering trader, Half-a-Crown becomes the archive of an extensive cross-section of the untold history of Southern Africa. On a sliver of paper tucked into the Cory Library typescript, heavily crossed out, Plaatje has Half-a-Crown actually account for how his parents garnered that history, including their information about the internal rituals of their enemies, the Matabele Empire, which they could not possibly have witnessed at first-hand: ' "Your trading trips have never taken you to Buluwayo [*sic*], Half-a-Crown", [says Ra-Thaga] "so possibly you don't know the Matabele, the ferocious race whose King, Mzilikasi, ruled over this country. . . ." ' The Matabele scenes in the novel are thus reconstructed with hindsight by Ra-Thaga, victim of the Matabele himself, who in later life can collect even Matabele oral history during his wanderings through a newly peaceful Southern Africa in an attempt to explain that early collision of cultures for the enlightenment of his son.

When in the 1930 preface to *Mhudi* Plaatje mentions that his second aim in 'writing' *Mhudi* was to preserve the folk tales and other literary forms of black culture, together with their content, 'which, with the spread of European ideas, are fast being forgotten' (Quagga, p. 17), we see that he meant it more earnestly than could have been supposed. *Mhudi* is itself that act of preservation.

Other details that are changed are again minute and apparently in-significant, yet they reveal the extent of the psychological war that took place between Plaatje and his editors. There is again a systematic screening of the author, when he writes about African values from an African point of view that has the effect of turning him into one who blindly conforms to the norms of white English literature. In the process of 'prettifying' *Mhudi,* Lovedale in fact emasculated it. Whoever entrusted himself with the task of getting *Mhudi* up to scratch was one bred on Wordsworth and Tennyson, one who would rather drop a well-worn British cliché than an observation about that forgotten black past. The difference is one of tone: the tone of factual authenticity rendered in English as against the tone of the Bible, Bunyan and the English hymnal.

For example, here is Ra-Thaga himself reminiscing about the lost glory of the good old days before the Matabele invasion of Barolong land:

Lovedale, p. 19: 'Kunana, where we enjoyed a peace and prosperity that were unequalled anywhere; where our cattle waxed fat along the green valleys and bred like so many wild animals; where our flocks with the jocund lambs around their dams would frolic, while the she-goats fed from two to three kids each, till we were forced to increase and extend our outposts to give them more and still more space to roam about . . . '

HAWS, p. 39: as above, with the exception of clause 3, which reads: ' . . . where our flocks increased — most of the ewes feeding two lambs each, while the she-goats fed from two to three kids each — . . . '

The tonal difference is between Ra-Thaga's original plain, factual statement of pastoral abundance — a farmer's observation about natural fecundity — and the revised and quite inappropriate description which transforms the entire paragraph into a statement of proto-Christian sentiment. The word 'flocks', a neutral enough agricultural term, takes on a new overtone as the reviser confuses statistics with an image of potential converts. A stable and prospering African community is transformed into a Biblical landscape in which woolly-headed Christians frolic in happy ignorance.

Line 13 of Ra-Thaga's blues song, 'Sweet Mhudi and I', reads, in the Lovedale edition: 'Give me the palmy days of our early felicity' (p.64), as if such a sentiment were an impossible nostalgia for days unfortunately now lost, but the typescript version of that line reads: 'Give *back* [my italics] the palmy days of our early felicity / Away from the hurly-burly of your city' (HAWS, p. 71), which has the implication that those early days were forcibly taken away from the tribesmen — by a succession of tyrants, Mzilikazi, the Voortrekkers, the British imperium — and that they should be restored to him. A legitimate grievance is altered, by the stroke of an editorial pen, into a vain and reactionary-sounding gripe.

This editorial bias, or blindness, arising out of the conflict of ideologies, particularly affects military matters within the novel. Plaatje's editor really takes sides, and his side tacitly endorses the genocidal warfare that Plaatje abhors. The editor cuts part of the following paragraph from his version of the battle of Mosega:

The devastating machines of war had spread a pall of death and desolation over the plains. [cut begins:] The new moon, expected to make all things new, had instead brought an appalling revolution, for blood and terror had taken the place of the peace of yesterday. The stillness of the woods which had enjoyed peace and tranquillity for a thousand years was suddenly broken by a new and hitherto unknown din of war. [continues correctly:] The forest shook with the awful thunder of the guns . . . (HAWS, p. 146)

Plaatje's view of nature is that it contains its own inevitable processes of change, as displayed in the reference to the excised 'moon' above, from order through eclipse to restitution. He originally entitled the Lovedale Chapter 14, 'Light and Shade of Memorable Days', 'A Sportive Dawn and Gloomy Dusk' (HAWS, Chapter 12). Even this chapter is integral to his overall theme of the process of cyclical change, as in showing how the spirit of sporting camaraderie gives way to unequal social odds it criticizes a view of history like the one expressed in Gillmore's account of Tswana sports. The original title implies the coming of a period of darkness which would be relieved only with the inevitable release from oppression and domination. *Mhudi* is written to show that the balance not only should be, but will naturally be redressed. But the view of historical change to which Plaatje's pro-British, pro-status quo editor subscribes is one which cannot see the relationship between cosmic cycles and historical movements; to him the arrival of the Fish-eaters (the British), complete with rifle and Bible, represents the culmination of a drift towards improvement and enlightenment which had to come, and which must stay. Clearly, Plaatje's editor thought of this chapter as a mere intermission in a rather long and shapeless work of fiction; he renamed it as if it were an interlude, more appropriate to a list of disconnected sketches on a variety bill than to a work of cumulative insight. Their world-views collide disastrously. If one were to unscramble these views of history with reference to another Lovedale editorial product, H.I.E. Dhlomo's play, *The Girl Who Killed to Save* (1935), one might well emerge with a similar set of observations. It is only in recent times that a play like

Fatima Dike's *The Sacrifice of Kreli* (first performed in 1976) has been allowed to handle the same themes from a black African point of view.

Plaatje's novel is structured so that the 1830s serve as a model for the 1910s. By a process of predictive logic the 1910s become a time in which the past can be used as a means of determining the future, which is about now in terms of actual history. The recurrences of Halley's Comet (1835, 1910, 1985) underscore this periodization within the novel. Happenings on one notch of the time scale parallel those of the next, and so the future can be prescribed, as is commonly done in praise-singing and, indeed, within the various trial scenes in the novel, where historical precedent is always invoked when the action of justice is in question. Thus it is no surprise that the climactic moment of *Mhudi,* the moment which explains to us why the work was written at all, has been distorted.

The passage comes in the much mutilated 'The Exodus' chapter, which should be read in the Heinemann edition against the Lovedale version for the full implications of the changes to become apparent. The brunt of the chapter, and of the whole work, however, is as follows:

[On viewing his army's decimation the crestfallen Mzilikazi was] almost delirious with disappointment. He had for years been cherishing a beautiful dream. He had dreamt of establishing a kingdom stretching east, west, north and south. He had made enormous preparations for overpowering and annexing the adjacent nations one by one and for augmenting the Matabele contingents from the fighting men of the conquered people and, having inured them with Matabele pluck, he had hoped to rule over the most terror-inspiring nation of death-defiers that ever faced an enemy. Then with his power thus magnified he had looked forward to a march upon Zululand, the crown of his ambition, recapturing the ancient dynasty with superior fighting forces and establishing an empire from the northern extremity of Bechuanaland to the sea coast of Monomotapa, embracing the Tonga, Swazi and Zululand kingdoms and extending with the sea shore as its boundary right away to the Pondoland coast. This was his dream of many years, but now he saw the Imperial structure of his super-expansionist dream shattered and blown away like so many autumn leaves at the mercy of the violent hurricane. (HAWS, pp. 170–1)

The political forecast shines through the allegorical transparency of the text. But, despite Plaatje's most canny subterfuges, the point obviously did not escape the notice of his editor. Mzilikazi's rhetoric of the 1830s bears a marked resemblance to the rhetoric of his successor, Rhodes, whose dream of super-expansionism and annexation had been codified in words like 'crown', 'ambition', 'empire' and even the inevitable 'pluck'. Plaatje was wittily parodying the language and thought of the British supremacist. As if we need irrefragable evidence of it now, it remains only to remark that the invisible Imperial censor caught him at it, and the passage was considerably diluted.

Finally, it is a commonplace to say that Mhudi, Plaatje's central character, is something of a Mother Africa figure within the novel, the first in a gallery which informs the entire sequence of black Southern African literature through Abrahams's *Wild Conquest* to the Soweto protest poetry of today. She motivates and tests the novel's characters; she is life-giving, unconquerable, firm, never to be cheated nor to be manipulated unjustly. The Lovedale editor misunderstands Plaatje's Mhudi and typecasts her as a black version of Pauline in peril: whenever Mhudi has an 'experience' he turns it into an 'alarming adventure', as if to her the wilds of Africa represent some melodramatic backdrop for thrills and spills and not what Plaatje meant the landscape to be for her, a normal and integral part of her life of fortitude and endurance.

The last words one could say about Mhudi and the birth of black written literature in Southern Africa are, in fact, the last words of the novel. Ra-Thaga, her husband, lover, follower and devotee says (in the Lovedale edition): ' . . . from henceforth . . . my ears shall be open to one call only besides the call of my Chief, namely the call of your voice – Mhudi.'

It is a consummate irony that the original version of that sentence contains only a single call. It reads as follows: 'I have had my revenge and ought to be satisfied; from henceforth I shall have no ears for the call of war or the chase; my ears shall be open to one call only – the call of your voice.'

The single pure call of Mhudi was a new one, a rallying call to the peasants of black culture who 'were content to live their monotonous lives, and thought nought of their oversea kinsmen who were making history on the plantations and harbours of Virginia and Mississippi at that time' (i.e. from 1800 onwards) (Quagga, p. 23). It was born in Southern Africa coincidentally with the rise of political consciousness of black nationalism expressed by the South African Native National Congress in the 1910s, a movement in which Plaatje and other novelists like the Zulu Rev. John L. Dube were foundation members. It is the birth of the 'Come back, Africa' theme which, as Nadine Gordimer remarks, sought 'to recreate a lost identity; and it was as if a long-stilled string were plucked that set shivering a deep reverberation through Africa . . . where that [African] identity existed still, discounted and overgrown'.[32] It is the basic theme of the Négritude poets and the writers of the Harlem Renaissance, and an aesthetic necessity in the creation of pre-independence literature throughout Africa. That the birth of black consciousness it presaged in Southern Africa has been delayed, as N.W. Visser shows in a recent article,[33] is part of the history of Southern African literature to date, for where the descendants of early writers like Plaatje have continued to encounter the literary frustrations that shape the literature, Mhudi's call has been muffled. Her name, Mhudi, means 'the harvester'. The harvest itself might not have been reaped yet, but there can be no denying that its germination is evidenced in the emergence of Black English.

In an article on the 'Nature and Variety of Tribal Drama', H.I.E. Dhlomo, whose own plays represent an extraordinary feat of synthesis between black dramatic ritual and English theatrical conventions, commented on the state of the arts in Southern Africa in 1939:

We do not claim much for the tribal dramatic poet. We do not pretend that he dealt with matters of abstract thought and metaphysics. But he certainly created works of art. And to those who hold that tribal man was incapable of intellectual work of this kind, let us say that by means of intuition and imaginative art, the Universal Mind can and does express itself actively through primitive men and humble. Even those who may be inclined to think that we have elevated tribal representation into one of the highest expressions of art, will agree that upon these tribal dramatic sources, great original African drama can be built. This is most important. To-day, in music, in poetry, in dancing, in drama, painting and architecture, men seek new forms, idioms and styles of technique to express the evergreen artistic impulse. Cannot Africa infuse new blood into the weary limbs of the older dramatic forms of Europe? Are African scholars and artists and writers incapable of creating something fresh and young from these archaic tribal artistic forms?[34]

One might contest the views of a writer like Dhlomo all the way, deplore his own myth of the youth of African literary impulses, or disagree with his view of the functions of art, but that would not matter. His central point is that the new and old bloods can and should mix, that a kind of literary cross-fertilization is desirable.

One notes how far it has taken place in Southern African literature, and one trusts that readers and critics might continue to take account of it. For, in widening the focus of the English lens through which Southern African literature may be viewed, one hopes that some of its range has been suggested, and, in narrowing the focus within that range, some of its interest.

16 Douglas Blackburn in 1906.
17 Olive Schreiner with her husband Cron.

18 Perceval Gibbon in 1910.
19 Pauline Smith.

20 Portrait by Johannes Meintjes of William Plomer.
21 Bessie Head.
22 Sol T. Plaatje in the 1930s.

Notes

APPROACHES TO A NEW LITERATURE (pages 1-14)

1. J.R. Wahl (ed.), *Thomas Pringle, Poems Illustrative of South Africa* (Cape Town, 1970), p. xxiv. See also p. 1, pp. 115-17 and pp. 165-7.
2. Galley proofs ed. S.T. Coleridge, South African Library, Cape Town.
3. Reitz means 1826; Pringle did not arrive at the Cape until 1820.
4. Deneys Reitz, *Commando: A Boer Journal of the Boer War* (London, 1929), pp. 12-13.
5. See, for example, Arthur Ravenscroft, 'South African English Literature', ed. André de Villiers, *English-speaking South Africa Today: Proceedings of the National Conference, July, 1974* (Cape Town, 1976), p. 320: 'One of the finest, most moving and yet most beautifully controlled accounts of personal experience in war that has ever been written in English is by an Afrikaner. . . .'
6. Ms. of *Commando*, Brenthurst Library, Johannesburg. Quoted by permission.
7. C. Louis Leipoldt, 'Cultural Development [of South Africa]', *The Cambridge History of the British Empire* (Cambridge, 1936), p. 386.
8. General Piet Joubert, quoted in Reginald Fenton, *Peculiar People in a Pleasant Land* (Kansas, 1905), p. vi.
9. I. Pinchuk, 'The South African Image', *The Purple Renoster*, no. 5 (Summer 1963), p. 72.
10. Manfred Nathan, *South African Literature* (Cape Town, 1925), p. v.
11. Further examples are F.D. Sinclair, 'On the Spirit of South Africa', *Trek* (May 1949); Alan Paton, 'The South African Novel in English', delivered 1956, *Knocking on the Door* (Cape Town/London, 1975); and Lewis Nkosi, 'Fiction by Black South Africans', *Home and Exile* (London, 1965).
12. Albert Gérard, 'Towards a History of South African Literature', ed. Hena Maes-Jelinek, *Commonwealth Literature and the Modern World* (Brussels, 1975), p. 80.
13. Further examples are Jack Cope, 'A Turning Point in South African English Writing', *Crux* (Oct. 1970); A.C. Partridge, 'English Literature in South Africa', ed. Eric Rosenthal, *Encyclopedia of Southern Africa* (London, 1961); and John Povey, 'South Africa', ed. Bruce King, *Literature of the English World* (London, 1974).
14. See Anthony Trollope, *South Africa* (London, 1878).
15. See J.A. Ramsaran, *New Approaches to African Literature* (Ibadan, 1965); Ulli Beier (ed.), *Introduction to African Literature* (London, 1967); and O.R. Dathorne, *African Literature in the Twentieth Century* (London, 1976).
16. See Martin Tucker, *Africa in Modern Literature* (New York, 1967); and

G.D. Killam, *The Image of Africa in English Fiction* (Ibadan, 1969).
17. George Sampson and R.C. Churchill, *The Concise Cambridge History of English Literature*, 3rd ed. (Cambridge, 1970), p. 761.
18. See Daniel J. Weinstock, 'The Two Boer Wars and the Jameson Raid: A Checklist of Novels in English', *Research in African Literatures*, vol. 3, no. 1 (Spring 1972).
19. G. Dekker, *Afrikaanse Literatuurgeskiedenis* (Cape Town, n.d.); and Rob Antonissen, *Die Afrikaanse Letterkunde van Aanvang tot Hede* (Cape Town, n.d.).
20. The title of Guy Butler's first volume of poems is *Stranger to Europe* (Cape Town, 1952).
21. A.C. Partridge (ed.), *Readings in South African English*, 6th ed. (Pretoria, 1959), p. 13.

THE WHITE MAN'S CREATION MYTH OF AFRICA (pages 15-37)

1. Ian D. Colvin, Introduction, Sidney Mendelssohn, *Mendelssohn's South African Bibliography* (London, 1910).
2. John Purves, 'Camoens and the Epic of Africa', *The State* (Nov./Dec. 1909), p. 542.
3. Luis de Camoe[n]s, 'Rounding the Cape', trans. Alexandre Quintanilha, ed. Stephen Gray, *Writers' Territory* (Cape Town, 1973), p. 2. This translation, which is of Canto V of *The Lusiads* only, is more accurate and more readily available than the most recent complete translation (see below). The common English spelling of Camoens has been adopted here.
4. W.P. Ker (ed.), *Essays of John Dryden* (Oxford, 1926), vol. 1, p. 190.
5. C.R. Boxer, *The Portuguese Seaborne Empire, 1415-1825* (Harmondsworth, 1973), p. 36.
6. Frank Brownlee, 'The Clash of Colour in South Africa', *Journal of the Royal African Society* (Apr. 1938), p. 240.
7. Luis de Camoens, *The Lusiads*, trans. William C. Atkinson (Harmondsworth, 1952), pp. 75-6.
8. E.M.W. Tillyard, *The English Epic and its Background* (Oxford, 1954), p. 381.
9. See A.M. Lewin Robinson, *None Daring to Make us Afraid: A Study of English Periodical Literature in the Cape from its Beginnings in 1824 to 1835* (Cape Town, 1962), pp. 159-61.
10. *The Cape of Good Hope Literary Gazette*, no. 4 (Sept. 1830), p. 48.
11. F.W. Reitz, 'Kaap de Goede Hoop', *Twee en Sestig Uitgesogte Afrikaanse Gedigte* (Pretoria, 1916), p. 3.
12. Rowland Smith, *Lyric and Polemic: The Literary Personality of Roy Campbell* (Montreal, 1972), p. 65.
13. Roy Campbell, *Light on a Dark Horse* (Harmondsworth, 1971), p. 183.
14. *Selected Poetry* (London, 1968), p. 34.
15. *Sons of the Mistral* (London, 1941), p. 48.
16. Heather L. Jurgens, 'The Poetry of Roy Campbell', *Lantern* (June 1965), p. 32.
17. Roy Campbell, 'Poetry and Experience', *Theoria* no. 6 (1954), p. 37.
18. 'The Literary Loss to South Africa of Writers who Gravitate Oversea',

Sunday Times (16 March 1947), p. 11.

19. D.J. Opperman, 'Roy Campbell en die Suid-Afrikaanse Poësie', Wiggelstok (Cape Town, 1959).

20. The Sea my Winding Sheet, ed. Stephen Gray, Theatre One: New South African Drama (Johannesburg, 1978). Other re-workings are numerous: see, for example, David Wright, 'A Voyage to Africa', To the Gods the Shades (Manchester, 1976); and Charles Eglington, 'The Blighter (after Fernando Pessoa)', Under the Horizon (Cape Town, 1977).

THE FRONTIER MYTH AND THE HOTTENTOT EVE (pages 38–71)

1. Jack Beeching (ed.), Hakluyt's Voyages and Discoveries (Harmondsworth, 1972), p. 187.

2. John Donne, 'The Progress of the Soul' (1601), line 307.

3. Herbert's Travels (1638 ed.), quoted in Norman H. Mackenzie, 'South African Travel Literature in the Seventeenth Century', Archives Yearbook for South African History, vol. 2 (Pretoria, 1955), p. 34.

4. R. Raven-Hart, Before van Riebeeck: Callers at South Africa from 1488 to 1652 (Cape Town, 1967).

5. Thomas Herbert, Some Yeares Travaile into Afrique and the Greater Asia (London, 1638), p. 14.

6. John Purves, 'South African Literature', Cape Times (31 May 1910), Commemorative supp., p. 21.

7. H.B. Thom (ed.), Journals of Jan van Riebeeck (Cape Town, 1952), vol. 1, p. 208.

8. I. Schapera (ed.), The Early Cape Hottentots (Cape Town, 1933), p. 126.

9. Dates given refer to first general availability in English.

10. François le Vaillant, Travels in Africa (Paris and London, 1790 and 1794), Second Voyage, vol. 3, p. 488.

11. Le Vaillant on his first voyage, quoted in Vernon S. Forbes, 'Le Vaillant's Travels in South Africa, 1781–4', François le Vaillant: Traveller in South Africa, 1781–1784 (Cape Town, 1973), p. 41.

12. Cowper Rose, Four Years in Southern Africa (London, 1829), p. 271.

13. Voyage de Monsieur le Vaillant dans L'Intérieur de L'Afrique par Le Cap de Bonne-Espérance (Paris, 1790), vol. 1, pp. 366–7. Own translation.

14. Jane Meiring, The Truth in Masquerade: The Adventures of François le Vaillant (Cape Town, n.d.).

15. Percival R. Kirby, 'The Hottentot Venus', Africana Notes and News (June 1949) and 'More about the Hottentot Venus' (Sept. 1949).

16. 'The South African Exhibition in London, as Overheard by G. Duff', Sam Sly's African Journal (12 Oct. 1848), p. 4.

17. Charles Dickens, 'The Noble Savage' (originally in Household Words), Reprinted Pieces (London, 1921), pp. 106–7. There is also Swinburne's anti-romantic remark: 'Mr Whitman's Venus is a Hottentot wench under the influence of cantharides and adulterated rum' (Whitmania, Studies in Prose and Poetry).

18. Margaret H. Lister (ed.), Journals of Andrew Geddes Bain (Cape Town, 1949).

19. Sol. T. Plaatje, Mhudi (Johannesburg, 1975), p. 21.

20. Thomas Pringle, 'The Hottentot', *Poems Illustrative of South Africa,* p. 95.

21. Stephen Black, 'How I Began to Write', *Cape Argus* (17 Oct. 1925), p. 17.

22. Stephen Black, 'Discovering South African Stage Talent', *The Outspan* (14 Sept. 1928), p. 49.

23. See George Bernard Shaw, *The Adventures of the Black Girl in her Search for God* (written in Knysna, 1932).

24. J.P.L. Snyman, *The Works of Sarah Gertrude Millin* (Johannesburg, 1955), p. 54.

25. Sarah Gertrude Millin, *God's Step-children* (London, 1924), pp. 1–2.

26. J.C. Smuts, Foreword, Sarah Gertrude Millin, *King of the Bastards* (London, 1950).

27. Athol Fugard, *Boesman and Lena* in *Three Port Elizabeth Plays* (London, 1974), p. 220.

THE IMAGINARY VOYAGE THROUGH SOUTHERN AFRICA
(pages 72–92)

1. René Wellek and Austin Warren, *Theory of Literature*, 3rd ed. (New York, 1956), p. 53.

2. Trader Horn is the three-volume invention of Johannesburg novelist, Ethelreda Lewis (1920s).

3. Carl van Doren, Introduction, *The Travels of Baron Munchausen* (New York, 1929), p. vli.

4. S. Baring Gould, 'The Original Munchausen', *The Gentleman's Magazine* (Oct. 1888), p. 342.

5. John Carswell, *The Prospector, Being the Life and Times of Rudolf Erich Raspe* (London, 1950), p. 188.

6. *The Surprising Travels and Adventures of Baron Munchausen* (London, n.d.), pp. 158–9.

7. François Rabelais, *The Histories of Gargantua and Pantagruel,* trans. J.M. Cohen (Harmondsworth, 1963), bk. 2, p. 173. See also Giacomo Meyerbeer's Opera, *L'Africaine* (1860s) for Adamastor on stage.

8. Cf. Marlowe's Faustus (I, lines 344–9):
... I'll be great emperor of the world,
And make a bridge thorough the moving air ...
I'll join the hills that bind the Afric shore,
And make that country continent to Spain,
And both contributory to my crown.

9. See Olive Schreiner, *The Story of an African Farm* (Johannesburg, 1975), pp. 52–3.

10. See Lucian, *The True History* in *Satirical Sketches,* trans. Paul Turner (Harmondsworth, 1961), pp. 249–50: '[They] wrote so-called histories of their travels describing all the huge monsters, and savage tribes, and extraordinary ways of life that they came across in foreign parts. . . . I shall be a more honest liar than my predecessors, for I am telling you frankly, here and now, that I have no intention whatsoever of telling the truth.'

11. Captain Munchausen, G.C.B.A., *Munchausen at the Pole* (London, 1819), p. 4.

12. Lady Anne Barnard, *Journal of a Tour into the Interior,* ed. A.M. Lewin Robinson, *The Letters of Lady Anne Barnard to Henry Dundas* (Cape Town, 1973), pp. 155-6.

13. *The Travels of Sylvester Tramper* (London, 1813), p. 7.

14. Le Vaillant, *New Travels,* vol. 1, p. 168.

15. M.C. Seymour (ed.), *Mandeville's Travels* (London, 1968), p. 123.

16. Jules Verne, *L'Étoile du Sud: Le Pays des Diamants* (Paris, 1884), trans. as *The Vanished Diamond: A Tale of South Africa* (London, n.d.); and as I.O. Evans (ed.), *The Southern Star Mystery* (London, 1966).

17. See Jean Chesneaux, *The Political and Social Ideas of Jules Verne* (London, 1972), p. 173.

18. Jules Verne, *Aventures de Trois Russes et de Trois Anglais dans L'Afrique Australe* (1872), in English variously as *Meridiana, Measuring a Meridian* and *The Adventures of Three Englishmen and Three Russians in South Africa.* Under the last title it appeared trans. by Ellen E. Frewer (London, 1886).

19. Michel Serres, *Jouvenances sur Jules Verne* (Paris, 1974), pp. 63-73.

20. *L'Étoile,* p. 3. Own translation.

21. 'African Adventure as Jules Verne saw it', *Rand Daily Mail* (7 Aug. 1929).

22. Eric Rosenthal, 'Jules Verne Looks at South Africa', *South African PEN Yearbook* (Johannesburg, 1955), p. 63.

23. Jean Jules-Verne, *Jules Verne: A Biography* (London, 1976), p. 150.

24. Marie A. Belloc, 'Jules Verne at Home', *Strand Magazine* (Feb. 1895), p. 207.

25. Roland Barthes, 'The *Nautilus* and the Drunken Boat', *Mythologies* (London, 1973), p. 65.

26. Jules Verne, *The Exploration of the World,* vol. 1 of *Celebrated Travels and Travellers* (London, 1879), p. 171. For more on the continuity of travel-writing, see Margaret B. Marsh, *South Africa in Literary England before 1815.*

27. Serres names his chapter on *Star of the South* 'Wonderland in Alice'.

28. Jonathan Swift, 'On Poetry: A Rhapsody' (1733), lines 157-60.

THE RISE AND FALL OF THE COLONIAL HUNTER (pages 93-132)

1. Herman Charles Bosman, 'Aspects of South African Literature', *Trek* (Sept. 1948), p. 24.

2. Dominique O. Mannoni, *Prospero and Caliban: The Psychology of Colonization,* trans. Pamela Powesland (London, 1956), p. 105.

3. W. Basil Worsfold, 'South African Literature', *South Africa: A Study in Colonial Administration and Development* (London, 1895), p. 187.

4. Francis Brett Young, 'South African Literature', *London Mercury,* vol. 19 (1929), p. 507.

5. Laurens van der Post, Introduction, William Plomer, *Turbott Wolfe* (London, 1965), pp. 28-9.

6. James Anthony Froude, *Two Lectures on South Africa* (London, 1900), p. 12.

7. Captain W. Cornwallis Harris, *Portraits of the Game and Wild Animals of Southern Africa* (Cape Town, 1969), p. 1.

8. Thomas Pringle, 'The Lion Hunt', *Poems Illustrative of South Africa,* p. 29.

9. Geoffrey Haresnape (ed.), *The Great Hunters* (Cape Town, 1974), p. xv.

10. William Charles Baldwin, *African Hunting and Adventures from Natal to the Zambezi (1852-60)*, 3rd ed. (London, 1894), p. 3.

11. Theodore Roosevelt, Foreword, F.C. Selous, *African Nature Notes and Reminiscences* (London, 1908), p. xi.

12. R. Gordon Cumming, *The Lion Hunter: Five Years' Hunting and Sporting Adventures in South Africa* (London, 1850), p. 19.

13. Dorothy Hammond and Alta Jablow, *The Africa that Never Was: Four Centuries of British Writing about Africa* (New York, 1970), p. 190.

14. Charles Darwin, *The Voyage of the Beagle* (1839) (London, 1961), p. 81.

15. F.C. Selous, Foreword, J.H. Patterson, *The Man-eaters of Tsavo* (1907) (London, 1974), p. 10.

16. *Punch's* response to the publication of Cumming's book, quoted in the *Port Elizabeth Telegraph* (on Boxing Day, 1850), is as follows:

> *The Gordon is Cumming*
> A Roar from a Wild Beast
>
> The Gordon is Cumming, oh dear, oh dear!
> The Gordon is Cumming, oh dear, oh dear!
> To slaughter us wholly; that's clear, quite clear —
> (I've a bullet of his in the rear, the rear) . . .
>
> The sea-cow he peppers, pop, pop, smash, smash!
> She flounders and rolls in her gore, splash, splash!
> At last goes a ball through her skull, crash, crash!
> What a mercy it settles her hash, her hash! . . .
>
> As he in his volume explains, explains,
> Disregarding the animal's pains, its pains. . . .

17. David Livingstone, *Travels and Researches in South Africa* (1857) (London, 1905), p. 49.

18. J.P. Fitzpatrick, *Jock of the Bushveld* (London, 1972), pp. x–xi.

19. Major General Bisset, *Sport and War, or Recollections of Fighting and Hunting in South Africa* (London, 1875), pp. 194-7.

20. E.A. Kendall, *The English Boy at the Cape: An Anglo-African Story* (London, 1835), vol. 3, pp. 9-10.

21. Captain Marryat, *The Mission, or Scenes in Africa*, intro. by Tony Harrison (London, 1970), pp. 3-4.

22. Russell J. Linnemann, *The British Literary Image of Africa in the Nineteenth and Twentieth Centuries*, Ph. D. thesis, Univ. of Michigan, 1972, p. 193.

23. Oliver Warner, *Captain Marryat: A Rediscovery* (London, 1953), p. 144.

24. E.E. Burke (ed.), *The Journals of Carl Mauch (1869-1872)* (Salisbury, 1969), p. 132.

25. See Sheila Fugard's inversion of this pattern in her portrait of Miss Fairfax, the British governess who adopts savagery above extinction (in *The Castaways*, 1972).

26. Harriet Ward, *Hardy and Hunter: A Boy's Own Story* (London, 1858), pp. v–vi.

27. Unpublished letters from Harriet Ward, 'Frontier', Grahamstown, S.A.,

Apr. 2, 1847 and Feb. 19, 1846, to Sir J. Philiphardt, *A.S. Magazine*, London; Brenthurst Library, Johannesburg. Quoted with permission.

28. R.M. Ballantyne, *Six Months at the Cape, or Letters to Periwinkle from South Africa* (London, 1879), p. 42.

29. Parker Gillmore, *The Amphibion's Voyage* (London, 1885), p. 19.

30. H. Rider Haggard, *King Solomon's Mines* (New York, 1966), dedication.

31. Morton Cohen, *Rider Haggard: His Life and Works* (London, 1960), p. 85.

32. Graham Greene, 'Rider Haggard's Secret', *Collected Essays* (Harmondsworth, 1970), p. 160.

33. H. Rider Haggard, *Allan Quatermain* (1887) (London, 1969), p. 11.

34. John Buchan, *Prester John* (London, 1957), p. 237.

SCHREINER AND THE NOVEL TRADITION (pages 133–159)

1. Ralph Waldo Emerson, 'The American Scholar', *English Traits, Representative Men and Other Essays* (London, 1908), p. 293.

2. Vera Buchanan-Gould, *Not without Honour: The Life and Writings of Olive Schreiner* (London, 1948); D.L. Hobman, *Olive Schreiner: Her Friends and Times* (London, 1955); Marion V. Friedmann, *Olive Schreiner: A Study in Latent Meanings* (Johannesburg, 1955); A.C. Partridge, 'Olive Schreiner: The Literary Aspect', Olive Schreiner Centenary Number, *South African PEN Yearbook*, Johannesburg, 1955; Uys Krige, Introduction, *Olive Schreiner: A Selection* (Cape Town, 1968); Ursula Laredo, 'Olive Schreiner', *Journal of Commonwealth Literature*, no. 8 (Dec. 1969); Richard Rive, 'An Infinite Compassion', *Contrast*, no. 29 (Oct. 1972), reprinted with minor changes as 'Olive Schreiner: The Novels', *Selected Writings* (Johannesburg, 1977), and Introduction, *The Story of an African Farm* (Johannesburg, 1975); Ridley Beeton, *Olive Schreiner: A Short Guide to her Writings* (Cape Town, 1974); and Jean Marquard, 'Hagar's Child', *Standpunte*, no. 121 (Feb. 1976).

3. D.H. Lawrence, *Studies in Classic American Literature* (1924) (Harmondsworth, 1971); James Olney, *Tell me Africa: An Approach to African Literature* (Princeton, 1973); J.M. Coetzee, 'Alex la Guma and the Responsibilities of the South African Writer', ed. Joseph Okpaku, *New African Literature and the Arts*, vol. 3 (New York, 1973); and Wole Soyinka, *Myth, Literature and the African World* (Cambridge, 1976).

4. For example, J.P.L. Snyman, *The South African Novel in English*, or Mary Morison Webster, survey of the novel, ed. Alan Lennox-Short, *English and South Africa*.

5. W.T. Stead, 'The Novel and Modern Woman', *The Review of Reviews* (July, 1894), p. 64.

6. J.C. Smuts, Introduction, *Not Without Honour*, p. 16.

7. Christopher Heywood, 'Olive Schreiner's *The Story of an African Farm*: Prototype of Lawrence's Early Novels', *English Language Notes*, vol. 14 (1976).

8. Olive Schreiner, *The Story of an African Farm* (Johannesburg, 1975), p. 242. All quotations from this edition.

9. An exception is A.E. Voss, 'A Generic Approach to the South African Novel in English', *UCT Studies in English*, no. 7 (Sept. 1977).

10. Howard Thurman (ed.), *A Track to the Water's Edge: The Olive Schreiner*

Reader (New York, 1973).

11. Raymond Sands, 'The South African Novel: Some Observations', *English Studies in Africa*, vol. 13, no. 1 (March 1970), p. 95.

12. Olive Schreiner, *Thoughts on South Africa* (London, 1923), p. 50.

13. For example, Alan Paton, 'The South African Novel in English'; Ezekiel Mphahlele, *The African Image* (London, 1962); William Plomer, Introduction, ed. Zelda Friedlander, *Until the Heart Changes: A Garland for Olive Schreiner* (Cape Town, 1967); Dan Jacobson, Introduction, *The Story of an African Farm* (Harmondsworth, 1971); and Doris Lessing, Afterword, *The Story of an African Farm*, ed. Paul Schlueter, *A Small Personal Voice* (New York, 1974).

14. S.C. Cronwright-Schreiner, Introduction, *The Story of an African Farm* (London, 1924), p. 16.

15. Michael Wade, *Peter Abrahams*, Modern African Writers Series (London, 1972), p. 49.

THE EMERGENCE OF BLACK ENGLISH (pages 160-182)

1. Peter Weiss, *Song of the Lusitanian Bogey*, trans. Lee Baxandall (New York, 1970), p. 28.

2. Sir James George Frazer, *The Golden Bough: A Study in Magic and Religion* (1922) (London, 1974), p. 348.

3. See Donald Burness, *Shaka, King of the Zulus, in African Literature* (Washington D.C., 1976), with end papers by Jordan K. Ngubane and Daniel P. Kunene. Also Wole Soyinka, *Ogun Abibiman* (London, 1976).

4. Northrop Frye, 'Conclusion to *A Literary History of Canada*', *The Stubborn Structure: Essays on Criticism and Society* (London, 1970), p. 290.

5. Ruth Finnegan, *Oral Literature in Africa* (Oxford, 1970), p. 2.

6. W.H.I. Bleek and L.C. Lloyd, *Specimens of Bushman Folklore* (London, 1911).

7. Bob Leshoai, 'The Nature and Use of Oral Literature', *New Classic*, no. 4 (1977), p. 1.

8. Sir James Edward Alexander, *Expedition of Discovery to the Interior of Africa* (London, 1838).

9. John Campbell, *Travels in South Africa at the Request of the London Missionary Society: Second Journey to the Interior* (London, 1822), vol. 2, p. 362.

10. Daniel Jones and Solomon Plaatje, *A Sechuana Reader* (London, 1916).

11. Matthew Arnold, *An Eton Boy*, in Susanne Howe, *Novels of Empire* (New York, 1949), p. 117.

12. *Proceedings of the 39th Anniversary Meeting of the Subscribers of the Public Library of the Cape of Good Hope*, 23 May 1868, p. 13.

13. *Proceedings of the 48th Anniversary Meeting of the Subscribers of the South African Public Library*, 19 May 1877, p. 30.

14. John Centlivres Chase, 'Odds and Ends from a Settler's Scrap Book: Albaniana No. 2', *The Cape of Good Hope Literary Gazette*, vol. 4, no. 5 (May 1834), pp. 68-9.

15. Thomas Baines, oil in Africana Museum, Johannesburg, dated 1849.

16. Thomas Baines, *Journal of Residence in Africa, 1842-1853*, ed. R.F. Kennedy (Cape Town, 1961), vol. 1, p. 126.

17. Wilfrid Mellers, 'Music, Europe and Communication', *The Malahat Review*,

no. 40 (Oct. 1976), p. 78.

18. Cf. Aldous Hoxley, 'Wordsworth in the Tropics', *Collected Essays* (London, 1960), p. 1: 'The Wordworthian who exports [his] pantheistic worship of Nature to the tropics is liable to have his religious convictions somewhat rudely disturbed. Nature, under a vertical sun . . . is not at all like that chaste, mild deity who presides over the *Gemütlichkeit,* the prettiness, the cozy sublimities of the Lake District.'

19. Guy Butler's view of 1959 that 'South African [English] poetry is not, and never has been, a poetry with popular roots. We have no popular songs. . . . We have no anonymous ballad literature, either, no folk songs . . . ' (*A Book of South African Verse,* p. xix) is untenable today.

20. A.C. Jordan, *Towards an African Literature: The Emergence of Literary Form in Xhosa* (Berkeley, 1973), p. 38.

21. John Knox Bokwe, *Ntsikana, the Story of an African Convert* (Lovedale, 1914), p. 4.

22. James Archbell, *Travels in the Vicinity of the Orange River* (c. 1821), photocopy of Ms. in Grey Collection, Cape Town, p. 17.

23. W.L. Speight, 'South African Poetry', *The Empire Review and Magazine,* vol. 57, no. 384 (1933), p. 41.

24. Daniel P. Kunene, *The Works of Thomas Mofolo: Summaries and Critiques* (Los Angeles, 1967), p. 8.

25. Thomas Mofolo, *The Traveller to the East,* trans. H. Ashton (London, n.d.), p. 7.

26. Janheinz Jahn, *Neo-African Literature: A History of Black Writing* (London, 1968), p. 98.

27. Janheinz Jahn, *Muntu: The New African Culture* (London, 1961), p. 17.

28. Publisher's note, R.R.R. Dhlomo, *An African Tragedy* (Lovedale, 1928), p. 3.

29. A comparison between Dhlomo's style in the twenty short stories of the same period, collected in *English in Africa,* vol. 2, no. 1 (March 1975), and *An African Tragedy* might reveal the corruption of the latter text.

30. Plaatje's typescript of *Mhudi,* Cory Library, Rhodes University, Grahamstown. Quoted by permission of the Lovedale Press. See also Tim Couzens, Introduction, *Mhudi* (Johannesburg, 1975) and revised Introduction (London, 1978). The Lovedale first edition of *Mhudi* (1930) and the Heinemann African Writers Series No. 201 text, revised from the Cory typescript, are relevant here.

31. Anne Tibble, *African-English Literature: A Survey and an Anthology* (London, 1965), p. 44.

32. Nadine Gordimer, *The Black Interpreters* (Johannesburg, 1973), p. 6.

33. N.W. Visser, 'South Africa: The Renaissance that Failed', *Journal of Commonwealth Literature,* vol. 11, no. 1 (Aug. 1976).

34. H.I.E. Dhlomo, 'Nature and Variety of Tribal Drama', *Bantu Studies,* vol. 13, no. 1 (1939), p. 48.

Notes on Some Authors

ABRAHAMS, Peter (1919–   ), novelist. His substantial opus displays the spectrum of possible themes in South African and African pre- and post-independence fiction. Like Alex la Guma's, his social realism shows the erosion of human values in a segregated society, as his autobiographical novel, *Tell Freedom* (1954), explains in substantial detail. Born in Vrededorp, Johannesburg, he was the earliest of the middle generation of black writers to adapt from protest poetry in the 1930s to journalism and fiction, making him a precursor of the black renaissance movement in the 1950s with its revival in the 1970s. See Hans Zell and Helene Silver, *A Reader's Guide to African Literature* (London: Heinemann Educational Books, 1972).

BAIN, Andrew Geddes (1797–1864), geologist & road-builder. His passes from the southern and eastern Cape littoral over the mountainous barriers that protect the central inland of Southern Africa made him the opener of the way of British settlement. Arriving in the Cape Colony in 1816, he was the first white ivory trader to penetrate over the Orange River into the Matabele Empire, and as an ensign in a British Cape Hottentot corps in the 1830s he initiated the first irrigation schemes and ploughing experiments among Xhosa chieftains, one of whom was Tiyo Soga's father. As a popular poet, many of his ballads and drinking songs remain unpublished, but these trifles are a witty commentary on the life-style and hard times of the colonial frontiersman.

BAINES, Thomas (1820–1875), prolific artist & documentor, whose encyclopedic efforts to record the opening world of the mid-nineteenth century in sketches and oils make him indispensable to visualizing the literary background of the period. Inspired by *The Wild Sports* of Harris, he traversed from Grahamstown to the Transvaal, with Livingstone up the Zambezi, and with James Chapman through South West Africa. As a professional with no training, like the primitive caricaturist, Frederick I'Ons, he celebrated the heraldic universe of exploration with clarity and wit, and frequently posed himself on canvas before his local subjects to establish the role of the artist as mediator of his historical environment.

BLACK, Stephen (1880–1931), dramatist & satirist, whose comedies subsumed local colour into genuinely South African works of popular culture. As a bread-and-butter journalist, he worked during the First World War as a Fleet Street drama critic, and by 1920 had crystallized the post-Union tensions of community life, featuring British loyalists vs. Boer 'rebels', and white exploiters vs. black underdogs, in a novel entitled *The Dorp*. As one of the first colonial-born South African writers of consequence, he returned to his roots in the mid-20s to revamp his five comedies on stage, and edit a Johannesburg-based monthly, *The Sjambok*, which started R.R.R. Dhlomo and Bosman on their careers in magazine journalism.

His silent movie scenarios (unproduced) include the first attempted feature film on the black urban bourgeoisie's search for a place in the sun.

BLACKBURN, Douglas (1857–1929), prolific novelist, whose ability to turn the news of his day into fiction remains unacknowledged. The first writer to record the founding and growth of urban industrial culture in the crucible of the Transvaal, he bridges the gap between Schreiner's rural realism and the emergence of the novelists of the '40s and '50s. A sojourner-correspondent in President Kruger's Transvaal from the early 1890s, he converted the raw material of the mining romance of novelists like J.R. Couper, and the flamboyant quest novels of Haggard, into works of parody, with vice, crime, greed, cultural dislocation and clashes of ideology as his themes. Like his half-section, Perceval Gibbon, he worked as a reporter in Natal after the war, and satirized what he viewed as the tourist writers of the war (A. Conan Doyle, Winston Churchill, Edgar Wallace and A.E.W. Mason, etc.), their failure to grasp the tragic proportions of South Africa's racial and language dilemmas, and their lack of equanimity on political themes.

BOSMAN, Herman Charles (1905–1951), novelist & journalist. He chose the short story collection as the ideal medium for anthologizing the range of Southern African experience, notably in *Mafeking Road* (1947), where his mouthpiece, Oom Schalk Lourens, succeeds Gibbon's Vrouw Grobbelaar and C.R. Prance's Tante Rebella as the backveld Boer humorist. Like Pauline Smith, he explored the rural Afrikaans character in great depth. Always an independent, he was the first white novelist to exploit the parallels between American and Southern African experience, by applying themes from the popular short story writers of the turn of the century, like Jack London and O. Henry, to Southern African situations. His last and most achieved novel, *Willemsdorp* (published posthumously in 1977), charts the rise of the Afrikaner underdog to political dominance in the white elections of 1948, and is thus the first of the novels to deal with the institutionalization of apartheid as a theme. He is the only white writer of his generation not to achieve a reputation through publishing in London, but his regionalism with its local voice shows a greater involvement with the minutiae of the Southern African world from inside. See Lionel Abrahams, Introduction, in Herman Charles Bosman, *A Cask of Jerepigo: Sketches and Essays* (Cape Town: Human and Rousseau, 1964).

CAMPBELL, Roy (1901–1957), poet & translator, whose blunt and aggressive lyricism asserted a unique personality which reacted to mass-mindedness with a series of flamboyant statements of his individuality. With William Plomer and Laurens van der Post, he edited the first three numbers of the literary review, *Voorslag*, in Natal (1926). All three writers have subsequently much publicized *Voorslag* as a unique literary revolt against the stagnant conformism of the colonial backwaters of South Africa, despite the fact that Pringle and Fairbairn had enacted the same declarations of the artist's independence a century before, and the fact that, to the present day, with the exception of some conservative magazines, virtually all literary reviews in the history of English literature in Southern Africa have regularly collided with popular taste and the institutions of officialdom. His subsequent conservative tack, as glorifier of past individual prowess and upholder of unfashionable faiths, has seen that his reputation as an innovator is in obscurity. Yet his influence on the generation of the war poets of the 1940s and '50s remains profound, both through his promotion of younger artists and because of his statement that a figure of dedicated gusto could transcend his obscure colonial origins. See Alan Paton, 'Roy Campbell: Man and Poet', *Theoria*, Pietermaritzburg, no. 9 (1957).

DHLOMO, H.I.E. (1903–1956), English-language poet & voluminous dramatist; younger brother of R.R.R. Dhlomo, editor of the Zulu–English newspaper, *Ilanga lase Natal*, on which H.I.E. was assistant editor. A vastly under-researched figure, he is a product of the 1930s, and his epic poem, *Valley of a Thousand Hills* (1941), frequently described as no more than a nature panegyric, recalls the greatness of the Zulu Empire of Shaka and his successors as an ironic commentary on the status of blacks a century later. Like Mofolo (in Sotho) and John L. Dube (in Zulu), Dhlomo used the supposedly lost African glories of the Shakan period as an indirect allegorization of the power struggle of his own time. In one of his two published plays, *The Girl Who Killed to Save: Nongquase the Liberator* (1936), he blended the ideas of European enlightenment with the virtues of pre-colonial black life to show, in chronicle fashion, the violence and horror of ideological trespasses on established patterns, and his heroine, Nongquase, emerges as a Mother Africa figure not to be placated, as she does in several subsequent black plays. See N.W. Visser (ed.), *H.I.E. Dhlomo: Literary Theory and Criticism, English in Africa*, Grahamstown, vol. 4, no. 2 (Sept. 1977).

FAIRBAIRN, John (1794–1864), editor with Pringle of the first English literary review and general magazine, *The South African Journal* (1824), which because of pressures of censorship lasted two issues only. Pringle and Fairbairn's wrangles with the Colonial administration for licence to publish free opinion are widely construed as the founding of the principle of press freedom in South Africa. As the liberal editor-proprietor of the Cape Town *Commercial Advertiser* for four decades, he championed Dr John Philip's London Missionary Society policy of equal rights on the Eastern Province frontier, and as a philanthropist enjoyed much execration from the Grahamstown settler press, notably from Robert Godlonton, editor of *The Grahamstown Journal*, with its pro-annexation of tribal lands policy. As a founder member of the short-lived South African Literary Society in 1824, he established the notion of the gentleman generalist, and coined witty maxims such as: 'The passions hate truth' and 'Politics are male scandal'. The works of Bain and Ballantyne implicitly criticize his anti-slavery views.

FITZPATRICK, James Percy (1862–1931), apologist for the British Uitlander cause and supporter of the Jameson Raid on the Transvaal, an architect of Union of the four provinces of South Africa in 1910, pamphleteer in the jingo cause and short story writer, his account of his young days (1880s) of transport riding in the early goldfields of the Barberton District, *Jock of the Bushveld* (1907), has remained a classic. His *Through Mashonaland with Pick and Pen* is probably the first book printed and published in the Transvaal (1892). See *Dictionary of South African Biography*, vol. 1 (Cape Town: Tafelberg, 1968).

LEIPOLDT, C. Louis (1880–1947), poet & novelist, cosmopolitan writer in Dutch, Afrikaans and English, was one of the founding triumvirate of Afrikaans letters with his first volume of poems, *Oom Gert Vertel* (1911), written mostly during the turn-of-the-century war. An early Afrikaans dramatist, he also conducted a versatile career in journalism, in the 1930s published an autobiography, *Bushveld Doctor*, and completed a trilogy of novels in English (unpublished), recounting the Western Cape's history over a century. He was an advocate of a multi-cultural approach to Southern African life, but the stress of language separatism has tended to subdivide the full range of his works.

MILLIN, Sarah Gertrude (1888–1968), author of some thirty novels, biographer of Cecil Rhodes and General Smuts, and in-depth surveyor of her contemporary South Africa. Her austere and driving style dominated South African letters for four decades (1920s to 1960s), during which she was a widely-read apologist for South African affairs, historian and conservative rebel. Despite the unfashionableness of her major themes — the moral lapses of miscegenation, the purity of white civilization and her disgust at cross-acculturation — she remains the great practitioner of social realism in its most comprehensive, documentary aspects, particularly as an historical novelist intent on relating the nineteenth century to her own times. Now classed as an eccentric racialist, her reputation is in eclipse — undeservedly, because as the avatar of white supremacy she symbolizes the political and social opinions of the period of South Africa in the Commonwealth. See Martin Rubin, *Sarah Gertrude Millin: A South African Life* (Johannesburg, 1977).

MPHAHLELE, Ezekiel (1919–   ), novelist & short story writer. His autobiography, *Down Second Avenue,* recorded his rural and urban-ghetto youth in Pretoria and experiences as a teacher and journalist up to 1957, the year of his exile from South Africa, and was to become the archetypal story of the black South African intellectual of the 1950s who, under restrictions and bannings, was driven abroad. His story is repeated with variations in the lives and works of many *Drum* magazine writers of the period — Can Themba, Jordan K. Ngubane, Arthur Maimane, Todd Matshikiza and William Bloke Modisane — all of whose works remain unavailable in South Africa. As a spokesman on the problems of the exiled generation and critic of emergent African English literature in the context of South Africa's white literary hegemony, his work is seminal. See Ursula A. Barnett, *Ezekiel Mphahlele* (New York: Twayne, 1977).

PLAATJE, Sol T. (1876–1932), historian, transcriber of oral literature & novelist, whose encyclopedic skill as a preserver of the historical and literary material affecting the history of black folks and whites places him at an almost unique crux in Southern African literature between the oral and the written. As a translator of Shakespeare into Setswana, and of Setswana folk tales into English, he exhibits the polymath linguistic skills required to encompass the range of all the literature. Responsive to the self-help and self-education schemes of the American negro élite, he applied the precepts of men like Booker T. Washington to the dilemma of the black man in South Africa, disenfranchised and dispossessed by the Natives Land Act of 1913, the effects of which he annotated in *Native Life in South Africa* (1916). Thereafter, as a founder of the South African Native National Congress (later the African National Congress), he advocated common rights for all blacks in Southern Africa. Essentially a transitional figure between the missionary-educated and the modern urban black, he adumbrates the African personality that was to appear in the 1940s. See Tim Couzens and Brian Willan (eds.), *Plaatje Centenary Issue, English in Africa*, Grahamstown, vol. 3, no. 2 (Sept. 1976).

PLOMER, William (1903–1973), poet, novelist & critic. His association with Campbell and Van der Post in the *Voorslag* days crystallized about the scandal of his first novel, *Turbott Wolfe* (written at the age of 19 and first published in 1926), which features the wandering trader as narrator, consists of his hallucinatory passage through inland, and advocates an all-race policy in the face of missionary racial exclusivity. Although he later claimed the novel a first in more respects than it in fact is, its effect is undeniably polemical even today, although in later poems like 'Tugela River' he clarified his stance of multiracialism and praise of innate African values more effectively. Despite his later trivializing of his African reformist mission as he became an all-round gentleman of letters, the young Plomer remains probably the finest South African lyric poet, cerebral and precise, of the period between 1920 and 1945.

PRINGLE, Thomas (1789–1834), poet & polemicist, who before emigrating to the Cape frontier as an 1820 Settler, co-edited the *Edinburgh Monthly Magazine*, which later as *Blackwood's Edinburgh Magazine* was regularly to feature writers of the colonial heyday, like Blackburn, Gibbon and Francis Carey Slater. First librarian of what is now the South African Library, and founder of one of the first English public schools in Cape Town, he joined Fairbairn as co-editor of *The South African Journal*, in which many of his South African poems, including 'Afar in the Desert', were first published. On his return to Britain in 1826, he became secretary of the Anti-Slavery Society which promoted the Abolition Act of 1834, the effects of which in South Africa, like the Boers' Great Trek away from the emancipated Cape to re-establish their feudal order in the Orange Free State and Transvaal, he was not to witness. His *African Sketches* (1834), including his poems, has been republished in four different editions, and is considered the founding artwork of South African English literature.

SCHREINER, Olive (1855–1920), novelist, feminist & polemicist. Her *The Story of an African Farm* (1883) is held to be the first indigenous novel of merit, although, as explored here, it cannot be explained as the manifestation of a spontaneous eruption of genius, as is widely supposed. The daughter of a Wesleyan missionary, her life spans the mid-Victorian drift into free-thinking and modernism in which she herself played some role; and as an upholder of liberal views she ran an independent course against aspects of imperialism, capitalism and male chauvinism, as expressed most pungently in her allegories — symbolic prose pieces using psychological dream imagery as a release from the tyranny of realism. As most of her creative work was published posthumously by her husband, Samuel Cronwright-Schreiner, the dating of her continuing relationship with Southern African literature in general is problematic, and the potency of her immediate relationship to the sociological developments of her society has been blurred; thus biographers invariably insist that her life is of greater interest than her supposedly arrested development as an artist. By maintaining her relationship with South African events, even during her many visits abroad, she defined a place for the engaged writer in society. See Richard M. Rive, *Olive Schreiner: A Bibliographical and Critical Study*, Ph. D. thesis (unpublished), Oxford, 1974.

For further biographies, see *The Penguin Companion to Literature*, though the Penguin classification of 'white' Southern African writers as part of British and Commonwealth Literature (vol. 1, 1971), and of 'black' Southern African writers as part of African Literature (vol. 4, 1969), is not acceptable here.

Select Bibliography

ON OR RELATING TO SOUTHERN AFRICAN ENGLISH LITERATURE IN GENERAL

Antonissen, Rob. *Die Afrikaanse Letterkunde van Aanvang tot Hede.* Cape Town: Nasou, n.d.

Beeton, D.R., and Helen Dorner. *A Dictionary of English Usage in South Africa.* Cape Town: Oxford University Press, 1975.

Beeton, D.R., ed. *A Pilot Bibliography of South African English Literature from the Beginnings until 1971.* Pretoria: University of South Africa, 1976.

Beier, Ulli, ed. *Introduction to African Literature.* London: Longman, 1967.

Book in South Africa, The. Catalogue. Bloemfontein: Union Festival Committee, 1960.

Bosman, Herman Charles. 'Aspects of South African Literature.' *Trek*, Johannesburg, September 1948.

Branford, Jean. *A Dictionary of South African English.* Cape Town: Oxford University Press, 1978.

Cartey, Wilfred. *Whispers from a Continent: The Literature of Contemporary Black Africa.* London: Heinemann Educational Books, 1971.

Cope, Jack. 'A Turning Point in South African English Writing'. *Crux*, Pretoria, October 1970.

Dathorne, O.R. *African Literature in the Twentieth Century.* London: Heinemann Educational Books, 1976.

Dekker, G. *Afrikaanse Literatuurgeskiedenis.* Cape Town: Nasou, n.d.

de Villiers, André, ed. *English-speaking South Africa Today: Proceedings of the National Conference, July, 1974.* Cape Town: Oxford University Press, 1976. This includes Arthur Ravenscroft, 'English South African Literature'.

Ferres, John H., and Martin Tucker, eds. *Modern Commonwealth Literature.* New York: Ungar, 1977.

Finnegan, Ruth. *Oral Literature in Africa.* Oxford: University Press, 1970.

Gérard, Albert S. *Four African Literatures.* Berkeley: University of California Press, 1971.

Gorman, G.E. *The South African Novel in English since 1950: An Information and Resource Guide.* Boston: G.K. Hall, 1978.

Herdeck, Don E. *African Authors: A Companion to Black African Writing.* Washington, D.C.: Inscape, 1974.

Heywood, Christopher, ed. *Aspects of South African Literature.* London: Heinemann Educational Books, 1976.

———. *Papers on African Literature.* Sheffield: Dept. of English, 1976. This includes Lewis Nkosi, 'Sex and Politics in Southern African Literature'.

Jahn, Janheinz. *Muntu: The New African Culture*. London: Faber, 1961.
——. *Neo-African Literature: A History of Black Writing*. London: Faber, 1968.
Jordan, A.C. *Towards an African Literature: The Emergence of Literary Form in Xhosa*. Berkeley: University of California Press, 1973.
Killam, G.D. *The Image of Africa in English Fiction*. Ibadan: University Press, 1969.
King, Bruce, ed. *Literatures of the World in English*. London: Routledge and Kegan Paul, 1974. This includes John Povey, 'South Africa'.
King, Bruce, and Kolawole Ogungbesan, eds. *A Celebration of Black and African Writing*. Ahmadu Bello: University Press / Oxford: University Press, 1975. This includes T.J. Couzens, 'Early South African Black Writing'.
Klima, Vladimir. *South African Prose Writing in English*. Prague: Oriental Institute, 1971.
Leipoldt, C. Louis. 'Cultural Development [of South Africa]'. In *The Cambridge History of the British Empire*. Cambridge: University Press, 1936.
Lennox-Short, Alan, ed. *English and South Africa*. Cape Town: Nasou, n.d.
Maes-Jelinek, Hena, ed. *Commonwealth Literature and the Modern World*. Brussels: Didier, 1975. This includes Albert Gérard, 'Towards a History of South African Literature' and Tim Couzens, 'Black South African Literature in English, 1900–1950'.
Mahood, M.M. *The Colonial Encounter: A Reading of Six Novels*. London: Collings, 1977.
McLeod, A.L., ed. *The Commonwealth Pen: An Introduction to the Literature of the British Commonwealth*. Ithaca: Cornell University Press, 1961. This includes Randolph Vigne, 'South Africa'.
Mendelssohn, Sidney. *South African Bibliography*. London: Holland Press, 1910.
Meyers, Jeffrey. *Fiction and the Colonial Experience*. Ipswich: Boydell Press, 1972.
Miller, G.M., and Howard Sergeant. *A Critical Survey of South African Poetry in English*. Cape Town: Balkema, 1957.
Mphahlele, Ezekiel. *The African Image*. London: Faber, 1962 and 1974.
Nathan, Manfred. *South African Literature*. Cape Town: Juta, 1925.
New, William H. *Among Worlds: An Introduction to Modern Commonwealth and South African Fiction*. Erin, Ontario: Press Porcepic, 1975.
Nkosi, Lewis. *Home and Exile*. London: Longman, 1965.
Olney, James. *Tell me Africa: An Approach to African Literature*. Princeton: University Press, 1973.
Pichanick, J; A.J. Chennells; and L.B. Rix. *Rhodesian Literature in English: A Bibliography (1890–1974/5)*. Gwelo: Mambo Press, 1977.
Pieterse, Cosmo, and Donald Munro, eds. *Protest and Conflict in African Literature*. London: Heinemann Educational Books, 1969.
Pinchuk, I. 'The South African Image', *The Purple Renoster*, no. 5, Johannesburg, Summer 1963.
Proceedings of a Conference of Writers, Publishers, Editors and University Teachers of English held at the University of the Witwatersrand, Johannesburg, 10–12 July 1956. Johannesburg: Witwatersrand University Press, 1957.
Purves, John. 'South African Literature', *Cape Times*, Cape Town, 31 May 1910.
Racster, Olga. *Curtain Up! : The Story of Cape Theatre*. Cape Town: Juta, 1951.
Ramsaran, J.A. *New Approaches to African Literature*. Ibadan: University Press, 1965.

Roscoe, Adrian. *Uhuru's Fire: African Literature East and South.* Cambridge: University Press, 1977.

Rubin, Martin. *Sarah Gertrude Millin: A South African Life.* Johannesburg: Donker, 1977.

Sampson, George, and R.C. Churchill. *The Concise Cambridge History of English Literature,* 3rd ed. Cambridge: University Press, 1970.

Sinclair, F.D. 'On the Spirit of South Africa', *Trek,* Johannesburg, May 1949.

Smith, Rowland. *Exile and Tradition: Studies in African and Caribbean Literature.* London: Longman / Dalhousie: University Press, 1976.

Snyman, J.P.L. *The South African Novel in English (1880–1930).* Potchefstroom: University Press, 1952.

South African Writing in English and its Place in School and University: Proceedings of the English Academy of Southern Africa Conference held at Rhodes University, Grahamstown, 7–11 July 1969, English Studies in Africa, vol. 13, no. 1. Johannesburg, March 1970.

Soyinka, Wole. *Myth, Literature and the African World.* Cambridge: University Press, 1976.

Speight, W.L. 'South African Poetry', *Empire Review and Magazine,* no. 384. London, 1933.

Tibble, Anne. *African-English Literature: A Survey and an Anthology.* London: Owen, 1965.

Tucker, Martin. *Africa in Modern Literature: A Survey of Contemporary Writing in English.* New York: Ungar, 1967.

van Wyk Smith, M. *Drummer Hodge: The Poetry of the Anglo–Boer War (1899–1902).* Oxford: Clarendon Press, 1978.

Voss, A.E. 'A Generic Approach to the South African Novel in English', *UCT Studies in English,* no. 7. Cape Town, September 1977.

Walsh, William, *Commonwealth Literature.* Oxford: University Press, 1973.

Wanjala, Chris L., ed. *Standpoints on African Literature: A Critical Anthology.* Nairobi: East African Literature Bureau, 1973.

Wästberg, Per, ed. *The Writer in Modern Africa.* Uppsala: Scandinavian Institute of African Studies, 1968.

Wauthier, Claude. *The Literature and Thought of Modern Africa: A Survey.* London: Pall Mall Press, 1966.

Wilhelm, Peter, and James Polley, eds. *Poetry South Africa: Selected Papers from Poetry '74.* Johannesburg: Donker, 1976.

Worsfold, W. Basil. *South Africa: A Study in Colonial Administration and Development.* London: Methuen, 1895.

Young, Francis Brett. 'South African Literature', *London Mercury,* London, March 1929.

ON ASPECTS OF SOUTHERN AFRICAN ENGLISH LITERATURE

Beeton, Ridley. *Olive Schreiner: A Short Guide to her Writings.* Cape Town: Timmins, 1974.

Buchanan-Gould, Vera. *Not without Honour: The Life and Writings of Olive Schreiner.* London: Hutchinson, 1948.

Burness, Donald. *Shaka, King of the Zulus, in African Literature.* Washington

D.C.: Three Continents, 1976.

Cohen, Morton. *Rider Haggard: His Life and Works.* London: Hutchinson, 1960.

Friedlander, Zelda, ed. *Until the Heart Changes: A Garland for Olive Schreiner.* Cape Town: Tafelberg, 1967.

Friedmann, Marion V. *Olive Schreiner: A Study in Latent Meanings.* Johannesburg: University of the Witwatersrand Press, 1955.

Gordimer, Nadine. *The Black Interpreters.* Johannesburg: Ravan, 1973.

Heywood, Christopher. 'Olive Schreiner's *The Story of an African Farm:* Prototype of Lawrence's Early Novels'. *English Language Notes,* Denver, September 1976.

Hobman, D.L., *Olive Schreiner: Her Friends and Times.* London: Watts, 1955.

Howarth, Patrick. *Play Up and Play the Game: The Heroes of Popular Fiction.* London: Eyre Methuen, 1973.

Jurgens, Heather L. 'The Poetry of Roy Campbell'. *Lantern,* Pretoria, June 1965.

Kirby, Percival R., 'The Hottentot Venus'. *Africana Notes and News,* Johannesburg, June 1949.

——. 'More about the Hottentot Venus'. *Africana Notes and News,* Johannesburg, September 1949.

Laredo, Ursula. 'Olive Schreiner'. *Journal of Commonwealth Literature,* Leeds, December 1969.

Leshoai, Bob. 'The Nature and Use of Oral Literature'. *New Classic,* no. 4, Johannesburg, 1977.

Lessing, Doris. *A Small Personal Voice.* Ed. Paul Schlueter. New York: Knopf, 1974.

Mackenzie, Norman H. 'South African Travel Literature in the Seventeenth Century'. *Archives Yearbook of South African History,* vol. 2. Pretoria: Government Printer, 1955.

Marquard, Jean. 'Hagar's Child'. *Standpunte,* Cape Town, February 1976.

Marsh, Margaret B. *South Africa in Literary England before 1815: A Prophetic Image.* Ph. D. thesis (unpublished), Harvard, 1958.

Meiring, Jane. *The Truth in Masquerade: The Adventures of François le Vaillant.* Cape Town: Juta, n.d.

Millin, Sarah Gertrude. 'The South Africa of Fiction'. *The State,* Cape Town, February 1912.

Opperman, D.J. *Wiggelstok.* Cape Town: Nasionale, 1959.

Partridge, A.C. 'Olive Schreiner: The Literary Aspect'. *South African PEN Yearbook.* Johannesburg, 1955.

Paton, Alan. *Knocking on the Door.* Ed. Colin Gardner. Cape Town: Philip, 1975.

Purves, John. 'Camoens and the Epic of Africa'. *The State,* Cape Town, November/December 1910.

Rive, Richard. *Selected Writings.* Johannesburg: Donker, 1977.

Robinson, A.M. Lewin. *None Daring to Make us Afraid: A Study of English Periodical Literature in the Cape from its Beginnings in 1824 to 1835.* Cape Town: Maskew Miller, 1962.

Sands, Raymond. 'The South African Novel in English: Some Observations'. *English Studies in Africa,* Johannesburg, March 1970.

Smith, Rowland. *Lyric and Polemic: The Literary Personality of Roy Campbell.* Montreal: McGill-Queen's University Press, 1972.

Snyman, J.P.L. *The Works of Sarah Gertrude Millin*. Johannesburg: Central News Agency, 1955.

Sulzer, Peter. *Schwarz und Braun in der Afrikaansliteratur*. Basle: Der Kreis, 1972.

Visser, N.W. 'South Africa: The Renaissance that Failed'. *Journal of Commonwealth Literature*, Leeds, August 1976.

Wade, Michael. *Peter Abrahams*. London: Evans, 1972.

Weinstock, Daniel J. 'The Two Boer Wars and the Jameson Raid: A Checklist of Novels in English'. *Research in African Literatures*, Austin, Spring 1972.

FACTUAL WORKS

Alexander, James Edward. *Expedition of Discovery to the Interior of Africa*. London: Colburn, 1838.

Anderson, Andrew A. *Twenty-Five Years in a Waggon: Sport and Travel in South Africa*. London: Chapman and Hall, 1888.

Archbell, James. *Travels in the Vicinity of the Orange River*, Ms., Grey Collection, South African Library, Cape Town.

Baldwin, William Charles. *African Hunting and Adventure from Natal to the Zambezi (1852–1860)*. London: Bentley, 1894.

Bisset, John. *Sport and War, or Recollections of Fighting and Hunting in South Africa*. London: Murray, 1875.

Bokwe, John Knox. *Ntsikana, the Story of an African Convert*. Lovedale: Lovedale Press, 1914.

Brownlee, Frank. 'The Clash of Colours in South Africa'. *Journal of the Royal African Society*, London, April 1938.

Bruce, James. *Travels to Discover the Source of the Nile in the Years 1768 to 1773*. London: n.p., 1790.

Burke, E.E., ed. *The Journals of Carl Mauch*. Salisbury: National Archives, 1969.

Campbell, John. *Travels in South Africa at the Request of the London Missionary Society: Second Journey to the Interior*. London: n.p., 1822.

Chase, John Centlivres. 'Odds and Ends from a Settler's Scrap Book: Albaniana No. 2'. *The Cape of Good Hope Literary Gazette*, Cape Town, May 1834.

Cumming, R. Gordon. *The Lion Hunter: Five Years' Hunting and Sporting Adventures in South Africa*. London: Simpkin Marshall, 1850.

Fenton, Reginald. *Peculiar People in a Pleasant Land*. Girard, Kansas: Pretoria Publishing, 1905.

Harris, William Cornwallis. *Portraits of the Game and Wild Animals of Southern Africa*. Cape Town: Balkema, 1969.

Herbert, Thomas. *Some Yeares Travaile into Afrique and the Greater Asia*. London: Stansby, 1638.

Herman, Louis, and Percival R. Kirby, eds. *Travels and Adventures in Eastern Africa by Nathaniel Isaacs*. Cape Town: Struik, 1970.

Kennedy, R.F., ed. *Thomas Baines' Journal of Residence in Africa (1842–1853)*. Cape Town: Van Riebeeck Society, 1961.

le Vaillant, François. *Voyage de Monsieur le Vaillant dans L'Intérieur de L'Afrique par Le Cap de Bonne-Espérance*. Paris: Leroy, 1790.

——. *Travels in Africa*. London: William Lane, 1790.

——. *New Travels.* London: William Lane, 1794.

Lister, Margaret H., ed. *Journals of Andrew Geddes Bain.* Cape Town: Van Riebeeck Society, 1949.

Livingstone, David. *Travels and Researches in South Africa.* London: Amalgamated, 1905.

Quinton, J.C., and A.M.L. Robinson, eds. *François le Vaillant: Traveller in South Africa (1781–1784).* Cape Town: Library of Parliament, 1973.

Raven-Hart, R. *Before van Riebeeck: Callers at the Cape from 1488 to 1652.* Cape Town: Struik, 1967.

Reitz, Deneys. *Commando: A Boer Journal of the Boer War.* London: Faber, 1929.

——. *Commando,* Ms., Brenthurst Library, Johannesburg.

Robinson, A.M. Lewin, ed. *Thomas Pringle's Narrative of a Residence in South Africa.* Cape Town: Struik, 1966.

——. *The Letters of Lady Anne Barnard to Henry Dundas.* Cape Town: Balkema, 1973.

Rose, Cowper. *Four Years in Southern Africa.* London: Colburn and Bentley, 1829.

Sandeman, E.F. *Eight Months in an Ox-waggon.* London: Griffith and Farran, 1880.

Selous, F.C. *African Nature Notes and Reminiscences.* London: Macmillan, 1908.

Smith, Andrew. *Report of the Expedition for Exploring Central Africa.* London: n.p., 1836.

Stuart, James, and C. McK. Malcolm, eds. *The Diary of Henry Francis Fynn.* Pietermaritzburg: Shuter and Shooter, 1967.

CREATIVE AND RELATED WORKS

Abrahams, Peter. *Mine Boy.* London: Crisp, 1946.

——. *Wild Conquest.* London: Faber, 1950.

——. *The Path of Thunder.* London: Faber, 1952.

Anon. *Makanna, or The Land of the Savage.* London: Simpkin Marshall, 1834.

——. *The Surprising Travels and Adventures of Baron Munchausen.* London: Wells, Gardner, Darton, n.d.

——. *The Travels of Baron Munchausen.* New York: Limited Editions Club, 1929.

——. *Captain Munchausen at the Pole.* London: Johnston, 1819.

——. *The Travels of Sylvester Tramper.* London: Walker, 1813.

Bain, Andrew Geddes. 'Polyglot Medley'. Ms., National English Documentation Centre, Grahamstown.

Ballantyne, R.M. *The Settler and the Savage.* London: Nisbet, 1877.

——. *Six Months at the Cape, or Letters to Periwinkle.* London: Nisbet, 1879.

Becker, Jillian. *The Keep.* London: Chatto and Windus, 1967.

Black, Stephen. 'How I Began to Write'. *Cape Argus,* Cape Town, 17 October 1925.

——. *Love and the Hyphen.* 1928. Ms., Strange Collection, Johannesburg Public Library.

——. 'Discovering South African Stage Talent'. *The Outspan,* Johannesburg, 14

September 1928.

Blackburn, Douglas. *Prinsloo of Prinsloosdorp.* London: Dunbar, 1899.

——. *A Burgher Quixote.* London: Blackwood, 1903.

——. *I Came and Saw.* London: Rivers, 1908.

——. *Leaven: A Black and White Story.* London: Rivers, 1908.

Bosman, Herman Charles. *Cold Stone Jug.* Johannesburg: A.P.B., 1947.

——. *Unto Dust.* London: Blond, 1963.

Bradbury, Ray. *The Illustrated Man.* London: Hart-Davis, 1925.

Buchan, John. *Prester John.* London: Nelson, 1957.

Butler, Guy. *Stranger to Europe.* Cape Town: Balkema, 1952.

Camoens, Luis de. *The Lusiads.* Trans. William C. Atkinson. Harmondsworth: Penguin, 1952.

Campbell, Roy. *Sons of the Mistral.* London: Faber, 1941.

——. 'The Literary Loss to South Africa of Writers who Gravitate Oversea'. *Sunday Times,* Johannesburg, 16 March 1947.

——. 'Poetry and Experience'. *Theoria,* no. 6, Pietermaritzburg, 1954.

——. *Selected Poetry.* London: Bodley Head, 1968.

——. *Light on a Dark Horse.* Harmondsworth: Penguin, 1971.

Coetzee, J.M. *Dusklands.* Johannesburg: Ravan, 1974.

Couper. J.R. *Mixed Humanity.* London: Allen, n.d.

Dhlomo, H.I.E. *The Girl Who Killed to Save.* Lovedale: Lovedale Press, 1935.

——. 'Nature and Variety of Tribal Drama'. *Bantu Studies,* no. 1. Johannesburg, 1939.

Dhlomo, R.R.R. *An African Tragedy.* Lovedale: Lovedale Press, 1928.

Edson, J.T. *Bunduki and Dawn.* London: Corgi, 1976.

Eglington, Charles. *Under the Horizon.* Cape Town: Purnell, 1977.

Fitzpatrick, J.P. *Jock of the Bushveld.* London: Longman, 1972.

Forester, Thomas. *Everard Tunstall: A Tale of the Kaffir Wars.* London: Bentley, 1851.

Fugard, Athol. *Three Port Elizabeth Plays.* London: Oxford University Press, 1974.

Fugard, Sheila. *The Castaways.* Johannesburg: Macmillan, 1972.

Gibbon, Perceval. *Souls in Bondage.* London: Blackwood, 1904.

——. *Margaret Harding.* London: Methuen, 1911.

Gillmore, Parker. *The Amphibion's Voyage.* London: Allen, 1885.

Gordimer, Nadine. *The Lying Days.* London: Gollancz, 1953.

——. *Occasion for Loving.* London: Gollancz, 1963.

——. *The Late Bourgeois World.* London: Gollancz, 1966.

——. *The Conservationist.* London: Cape, 1974.

Haggard, H. Rider. *King Solomon's Mines.* New York: Pyramid, 1966.

——. *Allan Quatermain.* London: Macdonald, 1970.

Head, Bessie. *A Question of Power.* London: Davis-Poynter, 1974.

Jacobson, Dan. *A Dance in the Sun.* London: Weidenfeld and Nicolson, 1956.

Kendall, Edward Augustus. *The English Boy at the Cape: An Anglo-African Story.* London: Whittaker, 1835.

Lessing, Doris. *The Grass is Singing.* London: Joseph, 1950.

Lewis, Ethelreda. *Trader Horn.* London: Cape, 1927.

Livingstone, Douglas. *The Sea My Winding Sheet and Other Poems.* Durban:

University of Natal, 1971.

Marryat, Captain. *The Mission, or Scenes in Africa.* London: Collings, 1970.

Millin, Sarah Gertrude. *God's Step-children.* London: Constable, 1924.

——. *King of the Bastards.* London: Heinemann, 1950.

Mofolo, Thomas. *Traveller to the East.* Trans. H. Ashton. London: S.P.C.K., n.d.

——. *Chaka.* Trans. F.H. Dutton. London: Oxford University Press, 1931.

Moorcock, Michael. *The Land Leviathan.* London: Quartet, 1974.

Mphahlele, Ezekiel. *Man Must Live and Other Stories.* Cape Town: African Bookman, 1946.

——. *Down Second Avenue.* London: Faber, 1959.

Mtshali, Oswald J. *Sounds of a Cowhide Drum.* Johannesburg: Renoster, 1971.

Paton, Alan. *Cry, the Beloved Country.* London: Cape, 1948.

Phillips, E.W. *Richard Galbraith, Mariner, or Life among the Kaffirs.* London: Barfoot, 1872.

Plaatje, Sol T. *Mhudi, An Epic of South African Native Life a Hundred Years Ago.* Lovedale: Lovedale Press, 1930.

——. *Mhudi.* Johannesburg: Quagga Press, 1975; London: Heinemann Educational Books, 1978.

Plomer, William. *I Speak of Africa.* London: Hogarth Press, 1927.

——. *Turbott Wolfe.* London: Hogarth Press, 1965.

Pringle, Thomas. 'The Bechuana Boy'. Proofs, Grey Collection, South African Library, Cape Town.

Reitz, F.W. *Twee en Sestig Uitgesogte Afrikaanse Gedigte.* Cape Town: H.A.U.M., 1916.

Rive, Richard. *Emergency.* New York: Collier, 1970.

Schreiner, Olive. *The Story of an African Farm.* London: Chapman and Hall, 1883; Harmondsworth: Penguin, 1971; Johannesburg: Donker, 1975.

——. *Stories, Dreams, Allegories.* London: Unwin, 1923.

——. *Thoughts on South Africa.* London: Unwin, 1923.

——. *Trooper Peter Halket of Mashonaland.* Johannesburg: Donker, 1974.

Small, Adam. *Kanna Hy Kô Hystoe.* Cape Town: Tafelberg, 1965.

Smith, Pauline. *The Beadle.* London: Cape, 1926.

Soyinka, Wole. *Ogun Abibiman.* London: Collings, 1976.

van der Post, Laurens. *The Face beside the Fire.* London: Hogarth Press, 1953.

——. *A Story like the Wind.* London: Hogarth Press, 1972.

Verne, Jules. *Aventures de Trois Russes et de Trois Anglais dans L'Afrique Australe.* Paris: Hetzel, 1872.

——. *The Exploration of the World.* London: Simpkin Marshall, 1879.

——. *L'Étoile du Sud.* Paris: Hetzel, 1884.

Wahl, J.R., ed. *Thomas Pringle's Poems Illustrative of South Africa.* Cape Town: Struik, 1970.

Ward, Harriet. *Jasper Lyle: A Tale of Kaffirland.* London: Routledge, 1851.

——. *Hardy and Hunter: A Boy's Own Story.* London: Routledge, 1858.

Wheatley, John. 'The Cape of Storms'. *The Cape of Good Hope Literary Gazette,* Cape Town, September 1830.

Wright, David. *To the Gods the Shades.* Manchester: Carcanet, 1976.

Young, Francis Brett. *They Seek a Country.* London: Heinemann, 1937.

ANTHOLOGIES AND COLLECTIONS

Bleek, W.H.I. *Reynard the Fox in South Africa, or Hottentot Fables and Tales.* London: Trübner, 1864.

Bleek, W.H.I. and L.C. Lloyd. *Specimens of Bushman Folklore.* London: Allen, 1911.

Butler, Guy, ed. *A Book of South African Verse.* Cape Town: Oxford University Press, 1959.

Cope, Jack, and Uys Krige, eds. *The Penguin Book of South African Verse.* Harmondsworth: Penguin, 1968.

Gray, Stephen, ed. *Writers' Territory.* Cape Town: Longman, 1973.

——, ed. *Theatre One: New South African Drama.* Johannesburg: Donker, 1978.

Haresnape, Geoffrey, ed. *The Great Hunters.* Cape Town: Purnell, 1974.

Jones, Daniel, and Solomon Plaatje. *A Sechuana Reader.* London: London University Press, 1916.

Krige, Uys, ed. *Olive Schreiner: A Selection.* Cape Town: Oxford University Press, 1968.

Partridge, A.C., ed. *Readings in South African English Prose.* Pretoria: Van Schaik, 1957.

Slater, Francis Carey, ed. *The Centenary Book of South African Verse.* London: Longman, 1925.

——, ed. *The New Centenary Book of South African Verse.* London: Longman, 1945.

Thurman, Howard, ed. *A Track to the Water's Edge: The Olive Schreiner Reader.* New York: Harper and Row, 1973.

Wilmot, Alexander, ed. *The Poetry of South Africa.* London: Sampson Low, 1887.

Index of Authors, Editors, Critics and Anonymous Works